# COUNSELLING IN
# PSYCHOLOGICAL SERVICES

# · COUNSELLING IN CONTEXT ·

*Series editors*
Moira Walker and Michael Jacobs
University of Leicester

Counselling takes place in many different contexts: in voluntary and statutory agencies; in individual private practice or in a consortium; at work, in medical settings, in churches and in different areas of education. While there may be much in common in basic counselling methods (despite theoretical differences), each setting gives rise to particular areas of concern, and often requires specialist knowledge, both of the problems likely to be brought, but also of the context in which the client is being seen. Even common counselling issues vary slightly from situation to situation in the way they are applied and understood.

This series examines eleven such areas, and applies a similar scheme to each, first looking at the history of the development of counselling in that particular context; then at the context itself, and how the counsellor fits into it. Central to each volume are chapters on common issues related to the specific setting and questions that may be peculiar to it but could be of interest and value to counsellors working elsewhere. Each book will provide useful information for anyone considering counselling, or the provision of counselling in a particular context. Relationships with others who work in the same setting whether as counsellors, managers or administrators are also examined; and each book concludes with the author's own critique of counselling as it is currently practised in that context.

## Current and forthcoming titles

# COUNSELLING IN
# PSYCHOLOGICAL SERVICES

*Dilys Davies*

OPEN UNIVERSITY PRESS
*Buckingham • Philadelphia*

*This book is dedicated to J. Richard Marshall (1945–95)
and to my father, Daniel E. Davies (1913–94). Their love
and encouragement enabled me to write this book.*

Open University Press
Celtic Court
22 Ballmoor
Buckingham
MK18 1XW

and
1900 Frost Road, Suite 101
Bristol, PA 19007, USA

First Published 1997

A catalogue record of this book is available from the British Library

ISBN 0 335 19164 9 (pbk)

*Library of Congress Cataloging-in-Publication Data*
Davies, Dilys.
Counselling in psychological services / Dilys Davies.
p. cm. — (Counselling in context)
Includes bibliographical references and index.
ISBN 0–335–19165–7. — ISBN 0–335–19164–9 (pbk.)
1. Counseling. 2. Clinical psychology. I. Title. II. Series.
BF637.C6D36 1997
158′.3—DC21 96–54224 CIP

Typeset by Graphicraft Typesetters Ltd, Hong Kong
Printed and bound in Great Britain by
Biddles Ltd, Guildford and King's Lynn

# Contents

# Series editors' preface

It may seem strange today, but for a very long time there has been deep antipathy between psychology and the dynamic and humanistic psychotherapies. Of course at one time it was mainly clinical psychologists and psychiatrists who trained as analysts; and each of us editors is aware that our own psychodynamic or integrative psychotherapy training was as a member of a group of (mainly) clinical psychologists. So perhaps the divide was never that clear, but psychologists sympathetic to counselling in Britain have, for many years, been the exception rather than the rule. Psychologists, frequently claiming an academic credibility far superior to their psychoanalytic or counselling rivals, have often espoused narrow views of behavioural therapy as the only method with any proven efficacy.

Dilys Davies makes clear how this has changed in this book through this book's historical perspective. To have psychologists training for and receiving chartered status as counselling psychologists is a remarkable step, given the antagonism of the mid-twentieth-century debates fuelled by Eysenck's crusade against Freud. To see counsellors employed within psychological services (and hopefully not just because they cost less) is also a welcome move. To know that cognitive-behavioural therapists can belong to the same United Kingdom Council for Psychotherapy as the humanistic or psychoanalytic sections is again a sign of the times, recognition that wisdom and technical expertise is not confined to any one system of psychological or psychotherapeutic thought and practice.

All this makes it appear that we as editors, coming from the tradition we do, are welcoming the academic and behavioural psychologists to our camp, which of course is far from our intention.

It is rather that the two sides have met on common ground. There always was more in common than the two sides normally allowed themselves to acknowledge: one of us remembers discussing a client seen separately by an academic psychologist with a private behavioural practice, and by the editor, at that time a somewhat proselytising psychoanalytic supporter. It is interesting to reflect now on how surprising it was to find that we had seen the same features in the client, and understood what may have caused those features in similar ways, although we had very obviously different terms, and slightly different methods, to work with the client.

One of the real strengths of this particular psychological tradition, which counselling can always learn more of, has been its ability to approach areas of concern with academic rigour. It is this same rigour which the reader will find in this book, from an author who has really researched her topic, and who has marshalled a wealth of references for further study, placing counselling psychology firmly on the map, both within psychological disciplines and in the counselling world. Divisions of course still exist – perhaps it is no accident that both the British Association for Counselling and the British Psychological Society call their different interest areas 'divisions', as if stating separateness is a constant need. But there are clear signs that each is learning from the other.

What Dilys Davies also brings to this book is a concern for the social setting in which counselling and clinical psychologists work, and for the social construction of definitions of mental illness and mental health. Is it nature or nurture, that Welsh passion of hers for social justice? It is at any rate a welcome perspective upon the subject, which means that the reader never forgets the constant need to be alert to and critical of what is asked by institutions and society of its psychologists.

*Moira Walker*
*Michael Jacobs*

# Acknowledgements

I would like to express my gratitude to the many people who by their personal and academic help and encouragement made the completion of this book possible. In particular, I would like to acknowledge the unfailing encouragement and academic contribution of J. Richard Marshall to this book. Through our many discussions together, when I first set out to write this book, his views and diligent analysis of core psychological constructs informed and influenced my understanding of the main issues involved in this book. I would like to thank the series editors Moira Walker and Michael Jacobs for their support and patience. My thanks go to Helen Jones and Elie Godsi for their assistance in proofreading earlier drafts of this book and for their helpful suggestions. Finally, I would like to acknowledge my gratitude to Dr Phillip McLean, for his personal encouragement, his help in providing relevant background sources and for his theoretical comments, and to Fiona, Ashwin, Gordon, Jane and Rachel for putting theory into practice.

·  ONE  ·

# The development of counselling in psychological services

## FACTORS INFLUENCING THE FORMATION AND DEVELOPMENT OF PSYCHOLOGICAL SERVICES

Although clinical psychology and counselling psychology are part of, respectively, a relatively new and a very new profession within the National Health Service, psychological services formed and developed within a socio-economic historical context. Before clear definitions of terms such as counselling and clinical psychology can be attempted, in Chapter Two, it is first important to outline some of the contextual factors which have led to the formation of, and influenced the later development and content of, clinical and counselling psychology as they are practised today. Many of those historical factors contribute to our understanding of the role of counselling in the context of clinical psychology.

David Pilgrim and Andy Treacher, in their book *Clinical Psychology Observed* (1992), give an excellent account of the history of clinical psychology in the United Kingdom. They describe how its formation and development can be seen to be the result of an interaction of four contextual factors. These factors are:

- first, the role of medicine regarding mental health;
- second, the impact of the First and Second World Wars;
- third, the cultural context of the British welfare state and the National Health Service;
- and fourth, the wider cultural and academic influences on clinical psychology.

## The role of medicine in mental health

The first factor involves the development and status of psychiatry as a branch of medicine specialising in mental health. This itself took place within the wider socio-economic historical context. The nineteenth century was characterised by rapid industrialisation and urbanisation as capitalism replaced feudalism. Historical perspectives (Scull 1977, 1979, 1984; Sedgwick 1982; Busfield 1985) describe how the growth of capitalism was intrinsically linked to increased state control over those who in some way deviated from, threatened or did not fit into mainstream society. The underlying reason why such people were classified as either mad, bad, infirm or sick and were then placed in institutions (according to Scull 1984) was because of reasons to do with social control, rather than because of moral or humanitarian concerns also present in Victorian philanthropic paternalism. Further, Scull (1984) emphasises that it was the growth of these centrally governed systems that led to the segregation of people who were defined as mad into institutions such as asylums, rather than any breakthrough in scientific thought, that provided the impetus for the early development of psychiatry. Previously, the mad had been contained in communities or placed in private local hospitals (Busfield 1985).

At the same time as these developments, the emphasis on madness as illness gave further impetus to the development of psychiatry as a profession. As Pilgrim and Treacher point out, by the late nineteenth century madness had been defined as a biological fault that should be managed by physicians. The legal control of the management of the mentally ill was established by the General Medical Act of 1858. There *were* some attempts in the nineteenth century to provide a psychological rather than medical understanding of madness: for example, the moral approach underlying Tuke's setting up of the charity asylum known as The York Retreat (Digby 1985). However, the medical dominance of mental health was generally established contemporaneously with the conceptualisation of mental disorder in biological medical terms. By the twentieth century, psychiatry had expanded to include not only the involuntary control of patients, but also the alleviation of mental distress in voluntary patients.

Before the First World War, people defined as mad were confined in asylums where they were admitted, managed and treated by medical doctors. As Skultans (1979) points out, there is in fact less evidence of treatment than of the seclusion of the mentally disordered poor in sparse conditions. The primary model of mental health continued to be the biological or biochemical model based on toxic theories of madness. Theories of evolutionary biology were predominant before the First World War. Skultans (1979) describes how the primary psychiatric model at the time was that of bio-determinism, where the underlying assumption was that mental disorder as well as any other form of deviance was the result of poor or degenerate stock (or bad breeding). Alongside bio-determinism there also existed other theoretical systems such as psychoanalysis, but the early psychoanalysts were only a very small group in Britain before the First World War.

### The effect of the world wars

The second contextual factor that Pilgrim and Treacher outline as influencing the form of future mental health services was that of the effect of the two world wars. There are numerous historical and first-hand accounts of the carnage of the First World War as, for example, in accounts of the Battle of the Somme – or, to be strategically accurate, the series of partial actions in Picardy which opened on 1 July and which constituted the offensive campaign of the Franco-British armies in 1916. Into it was thrown the entire British effort of the year on the Western Front in 1916 (see, for example, A.J.P. Taylor 1966; Hart 1972; Keegan 1978) The bombardment began on 24 June. The attack originally intended for 29 June was postponed until 1 July, putting an even greater strain on the assaulting troops who after being keyed up for the effort had to remain another 48 hours in cramped trenches under the exhausting noise of their own gunfire and the enemy's retaliation – conditions made worse by torrential rain flooding the trenches.

As the British soldiers advanced from their trenches, thousands fell, strewing no man's land with their bodies before the German front trench was even reached. The waves of soldiers faced an unslackening hail of lead from the German machine guns. Only as the upstanding waves were broken up by the fire did any advance become possible. Although a military failure, 1 July was recorded by historians such as Hart as an epic of heroism, and as proof of the moral quality of the new armies of Britain. All along the attacking line these recently enlisted men bore a percentage of losses such as no professional army of past wars had ever been deemed capable of suffering – without being broken as an effective instrument of war.

Militarily, the advance had achieved nothing. Most of the bodies lay on territory that had been British before the battle began. Line after line of dead men. The British sustained 60,000 casualties, 21,000 of them killed, most in the first hour of the attack, perhaps the first few minutes. This was the heaviest loss ever suffered in a single day by a British army or by any other army in the First World War. Many were left wounded and, due to difficulties in transportation, were left in agony in no man's land throughout the day. The generals from Haig down had boasted of success too much to face the thought of reconsidering their strategy. 1 July was not the end of the Battle of the Somme, as the attack was renewed several times until it officially ended on 18 November, by which time 419,654 British soldiers had become casualties and nearly 200,000 French. The exact number of German casualties has been debated ever since, the official historians seeking to show that they exceeded those of the Allies, other estimates pointining to the contrary. A.J.P. Taylor (1966: 139–40) describes how on 14 July

> came the great set piece of which all British generals dreamt: the cavalry were to go through . . . They took a long time coming, held up in the mud and craters of the battlefield. At seven in the evening, the British infantry saw a sight unique on the Western Front; cavalry riding into action through the waving corn with bugles blowing and lances glittering. The glorious vision crumbled into slaughter as the German machine guns opened fire.

After this, the battle dragged on to no purpose as the autumn rain turned the battlefield into a sea of mud to the last attack on 13 November. Then the battle, if such it can be called, came to its dismal end. There had been no breakthrough. The front had advanced here and there about five miles. Beyond this the German line was as strong as ever. Strategically the Battle of the Somme was an unredeemed defeat where it is said idealism perished. The enthusiastic volunteers were enthusiastic no longer. They had lost faith in their cause, their leaders, in everything except loyalty to their fighting comrades. The war ceased to have a purpose. The bodies of men were sacrificed to no purpose.

Accounts of the Somme produce in readers and audiences much the same range of emotions – incredulity, horror, disgust, pity and anger – and not only from pacifists but also from military historians. Indeed, anger is the response that the account of the Somme most commonly evokes among professional military observers as they question why the attack was allowed to go on, why the commanders did not do anything about it and why did they not stop one battalion following the next to join it in death. This is most profoundly articulated in Wilfred Owen's poem 'Dulce Et Decorum

Est' (Parsons 1965) which exposes the great lie inscribed on so many war memorials in towns and villages throughout Europe of 'dulce et decorum est pro patria mori'.

There is generally a difficulty in discussing the nature of events which took place in a different socio-historical period to our own. The social context of the outbreak of the First World War had led to it being greeted with a mood of optimistic exhilaration. As I will discuss in Chapter Six, accounts of events only have meaning in the social context of the time. We cannot transpose ourselves to the socio-political context that gave rise to the events of the world wars. Even in our imagination we cannot recreate the reality that would lead us to a true understanding of events which occurred in a different socio-historical context to our own. The best we can achieve is an approximation. As I will describe in Chapter Four, even when we are discussing contemporary 'facts' it is the subjective aspect of experience which gives meaning to objective 'facts'. A fuller understanding of the context of the world wars may be gained from the accounts of experiences of the poets of the First World War whose words carry a force and meaning that echo down the years. It is those realities so appalling in stark fact and so unimaginable by those who had not experienced them, that the poems, written by men with front-line experience and who had known at first hand the realities of trench warfare, endeavour to express.

These poets give us first-hand accounts of the horrors of warfare, such as the agony of waiting during a bombardment, 'Sweating, and listening for the imminent crash which meant our death' (Richard Aldington, 'Bombardment and Resentment') or 'Worried by silence, sentries whisper, curious, nervous, But nothing happens' (Wilfred Owen, 'Exposure') (both in Parsons 1965). The poems are reports of experience and articulate for us the experiences of thousands who did not live to tell their own stories. Many of them describe the plight of ordinary soldiers, insignificant pawns in the movement of armies, and the generals who controlled and conducted them from a safe distance in the First World War.

One such poet was Wilfred Owen who enlisted in October 1915, was commissioned as an officer and sailed to France where he spent the appalling winter of 1916–17 mainly in the trenches. In June he was posted home on 'sick-leave' and sent to Craiglockhart hospital in Scotland where he joined his fellow officer and poet Siegfried Sassoon, who also was being treated for shell shock. He returned to France for active service in September 1918 and a month later was awarded the Military Cross 'for conspicuous gallantry and devotion to duty'. He was killed in action on 4 November, a week before

the Armistice. In 'Dulce Et Decorum Est' (Parsons 1965), Owen describes how:

> Bent double, like old beggars under sacks,
> Knock-kneed, coughing like hags, we cursed through sludge,
> Till on the haunting flares we turned our backs
> And towards our distant rest began to trudge.
> Men marched asleep. Many had lost their boots
> But limped on, blood-shod. All went lame; all blind;
> Drunk with fatigue; deaf even to the hoots
> Of tired, outstripped Five-Nines that dropped behind.
>
> .  .  .
>
> In all my dreams, before my helpless sight,
> He plunges at me, guttering, choking, drowning.
>
> If in some smothering dreams you too could pace
> Behind the wagon that we flung him in,
> And watch the white eyes writhing in his face,
> His hanging face, like a devil's sick of sin;
> If you could hear, at every jolt, the blood
> Come gargling from the froth-corrupted lungs,
> Obscene as cancer, bitter as the cud
> Of vile, incurable sores on innocent tongues, –
> My friend, you would not tell with such high zest
> To children ardent for some desperate glory,
> The old Lie: Dulce et decorum est
> Pro patria mori.

Pilgrim and Treacher describe how during this period the psychological model gained social acceptance, as for two major reasons
the limitations of the psychiatric model became apparent. First,
asylum-based psychiatry, the role of which was to solve the problem
of madness in society by means of segregation, was not a suitable
model when trying to resolve the problem of fear in military conditions. Stone (1985) describes how, during the carnage of the First
World War, shell shock, which may be viewed as a fear reaction in
response to terrifying circumstances, became a central problem for
military morale. As Hearnshaw (1964) points out, the term 'shell
shock' was first discussed by the psychologist Myers in 1914. At the
time psychiatrists were mainly concerned with what went on inside
the mental asylums, and it was psychologists and neurologists who
became involved with the problem of shell shock. Like any other
manifestation of distress, it is difficult to represent the pattern of
breakdown in warfare in any systematic way. Not only did the men

in the First World War face the terror of impending death, but they also endured atrocious physical conditions, discomforts and disease as well as the separations and bereavements of war. Courage and cowardice are not choices that can be made, overriding any emotional stress. A person cannot just choose or be ordered to be courageous. Running away, refusing to fight, developing tremors or becoming inert were all stigmatised as displays of cowardice. As I will discuss in Chapter 6, neither fear and cowardice nor courage and bravery are choices freely available to us through some sort of concept of will power. Men whose symptoms we now view as expressions of distress or in terms of psychiatric or emotional break-down were shot for desertion during the first two years of the First World War. The fear of the death penalty yielded a multitude of what were termed 'hysterical conversion symptoms' – such as were manifested in the loss of use of limbs, speech or sight. An uncounted number, who are generally not acknowledged in histor-ical accounts or in our public memorials, took their own lives. It is the poets who bear witness to their experience, as in Sassoon's poem, 'Suicide in the Trenches' (Parsons 1965).

The army eventually reconciled itself to the inescapable fact of the breakdown of so many of its soldiers by inventing the notion of 'shell shock', which suggested for it a single physical cause and treated the soldiers so affected in what were called NYDN (Not Yet Diagnosed, Nervous) hospitals. An excellent description of the experi-ence of shell shock victims of the First World War at the Craiglockhart Hospital in Scotland is given by Pat Barker in her novel *Regeneration* (1991). Perhaps the experiences which were classified as shell shock may best be conveyed in a poem by Wilfred Owen, 'Mental Cases' (Parsons 1965):

– These are men whose minds the Dead have ravished.
Memory fingers in their hair of murders,
Multitudinous murders they once witnessed.
Wading sloughs of flesh these helpless wander,
Treading blood from lungs that had loved laughter.
Always they must see these things and hear them,
Batter of guns and shatter of flying muscles,
Carnage incomparable, and human squander
Rucked too thick for these men's extrication.

The second main reason why the limitations of the psychiatric model became apparent was that the predominant philosophy under-pinning psychiatry at the time was bio-determinism, which was based on the assumption that deviance, including mental disorder, was based on weak or degenerate stock (Skultans 1979). Although it might have been acceptable for society to label those who had been committed to the asylums or workhouses, who were mostly poor and unemployed or unemployable, as degenerates and undesirables or the Victorian equivalent of what is referred to these days as the underclass or yobs, it was unacceptable that men breaking down under stressful military conditions should be viewed in this way. A generation of young men responded to the war and had volunteered with feelings of traditional patriotism and self-sacrifice. A.J.P. Taylor in his book *The First World War* (1966: 133–4) describes how the British infantry had enthusiasm, but not much else

> These were the men who had answered Kitchener's call; hardly any were conscripts. They had received hasty and rudimentary training. They could not shoot accurately. They could not operate in scattered bodies. They had been taught only to go forward in a straight line. They had been instructed to rely mainly on the bayonet. When it came to real war, the British infantry of the Somme never saw those whom they were fighting; and the bayonet was used only to kill men who had already surrendered ... This great army of volunteers was the most rigid army of the Great War; the army, too, of harshest discipline and the most severe punishments.

The soldiers breaking down had been working men, who had, as Stone (1985) describes, not only volunteered to give their lives for their King and country but were 'England's finest blood'.

A major blow for the hereditary model of mental disorder was that officers were breaking down under stress or shell shock in proportionately greater numbers than the rank and file. A.J.P. Taylor (1966: 134) points out that

> The junior officers were also recruits, recently trained. They, too, had enthusiasm and little else. They had been taught to expose themselves recklessly – hence officer casualties were often six times greater than those of other ranks. They had also been taught to obey unquestioningly and never to show initiative.

As under these circumstances bio-determinist models could not possibly be upheld, a vacuum was left in which other models developed. These models included the psychotherapies which were all to varying degrees based on Freud's work. Although these early psychotherapy practitioners were mostly from medical backgrounds, they contributed to the expansion of the Psychological Society which had been formed in 1901 and to the formation of its first section – the Medical Section – in 1919.

Pilgrim and Treacher outline two further significant developments as a consequence of the First World War. First, psychiatry
expanded its field to include the neuroses as well as the psychoses.
This facilitated the development of medical psychotherapists, who
now coexisted with the more biologically oriented psychiatrists. Medical psychotherapists joined the Medical Section of the British Psychological Society, which was perceived by many doctors in the 1930s as
essentially a medical society. The second significant development in
psychiatry after the First World War was that the tensions between
psychoanalysis and biologically oriented psychiatry gave way to the
development of eclecticism in psychiatry. Even the psychoanalytically oriented Tavistock Clinic, founded in 1920 as an out-patient clinic
to provide psychotherapy on the basis of psychodynamic thought,
stressed a somatic component to mental disorder. A potential conflict between biological and psychological theories of mental distress
was thus avoided by incorporating somatic components into psychological models. One consequence of this was that non-medical
practitioners such as psychologists were excluded from treatment
and a conflict with psychiatrists was avoided for the time being.

For the reasons outlined above, a significant development during the inter-war period was the growing emphasis on voluntary
patients treated on an out-patient basis. The Macmillan Report
of 1926, which was based on the findings of the Royal Commission
on Lunacy, highlighted the limitations of the narrow biological
approach to mental health and formed the basis of the 1930 Mental
Treatment Act, which emphasised the importance of issues such as
community care, out-patient clinics and the treatment of voluntary
rather than involuntary patients. Furthermore, the new psychotherapeutic models were not just concerned with the control of mental
disorder but emphasised the alleviation of emotional distress.

It was the Second World War which facilitated the development of psychology as a profession. By 1939, the problems of shell
shock and low morale had been recognized, providing an opportunity
to develop and use psychological principles and methods both in
military selection and in treatment. The usefulness of psychology
and its scientific approach, with its emphasis on measurement and
objectivity, was recognised in the field of mental health generally.
The conflict between psychoanalysis and biological approaches which
took place during the First World War was replaced by the conflict
between psychoanalysis and methodological behaviourism during
the Second World War. Two main institutions became the centre for
this conflict, the Maudsley Hospital and the Tavistock Clinic. Gibson
(1981) outlines how the medical director of the Maudsley Hospital,

Aubrey Lewis, appointed Hans Eysenck as a research psychologist in 1942. The Maudsley medical school was renamed the Institute of Psychiatry in 1948 under the directorship of Aubrey Lewis, who organised it into separate autonomous departments of psychiatry, psychology, physiology, biochemistry and biometrics. The inclusion of psychology in this context became an impetus for the development of clinical psychology in Britain.

### The cultural context of the NHS and the welfare state

Psychology is shaped by the prevailing cultural context of the time. The profession developed within the particular organisational context of the National Health Service within the welfare state, which provided a setting where there were constraints and restrictions on the development of clinical psychology in Britain. The National Health Service had been established by the post-war Labour government in 1948. The philosophy underlying this new service, that health care should be financed from general taxation delivered free at the time of need, had important consequences for post-war health professions such as clinical psychology. This service itself was set within a cultural context of Britain in the 1950s, when the values emphasised were scientific rationality and egalitarianism. We have seen earlier in this chapter how in its early years clinical psychology stressed the scientific approach in establishing its professional credibility. That scientific emphasis is still evident in current definitions of clinical psychology. The egalitarian cultural climate which characterised the post-war years contributed to the antipathy of clinical psychologists towards the hierarchically organised medical dominance of mental health. Nevertheless, medical dominance prevailed in the NHS, and psychiatry was able to withstand cultural and social pressures such as anti-psychiatry movement of the late 1960s and early 1970s. This dominance had been underpinned by the 1959 Mental Health Act, which outlined psychiatry's legal responsibility in the field of mental health. However, the conflicts between psychiatry and clinical psychology increased as clinical psychologists became more numerous within the NHS. These tensions, and the various methods clinical psychologists use to try to deal with them, will be discussed in a later chapter.

### The development of clinical psychology in Britain

In 1950, Eysenck went to the United States on a six-month visit to examine the role of clinical psychology. He returned to Britain to develop his plans for his own training course for clinical psychologists. This had major implications for the structure and content of the early development of clinical psychology in Britain. In the United States, clinical psychology had been established longer: the first psychological clinic had been set up by Witmer in 1896, and by the early 1900s training courses in clinical psychology were already established at Clark, Minnesota and Washington Universities. Within the field of psychology itself, clinical psychology was also recognised earlier in the United States than in Britain. In 1919, the same year as the Medical Section of the British Psychological Society was formed, the first section formed in the American Psychological Association was the Clinical Section. However, some of the same difficulties that British clinical psychologists encountered in the development of clinical psychology were mirrored by their colleagues in the USA. For example, the conflict over therapeutic autonomy in the United States was not resolved until the 1960s. In 1954, the American Medical Association stated that psychotherapy was a medical procedure and thus should not be practised by non-medical practitioners.

In the early 1950s the predominant role of clinical psychologists in Britain revolved around the emphasis on scientific objective measurement. Psychometrics (psychological testing) was viewed by psychiatrists as a useful role for psychologists, one which did not present a challenge to psychiatry. However, clinical psychology expanded rapidly in the 1950s, particularly in relation to behaviour therapy as advocated by Eysenck, who was made a professor of psychology at the Institute of Psychiatry in 1955.

Pilgrim and Treacher, outlining the early formation and development of clinical psychology, highlight three main features in the culture of psychologists at the Institute that influenced the development of the profession. First, there was the attack led by Eysenck (1952) on the effectiveness of verbal psychotherapies, especially the efficacy of psychoanalysis, which he viewed as being unscientific. Second, psychologists at the Institute challenged the psychoanalytic and medical tradition of the Medical Section of the British Psychological Society. By the 1970s most of the members of this section had left, and joined the Psychotherapy Section of the newly formed Royal College of Psychiatry. As Pilgrim and Treacher point out, what the Maudsley group did in the 1950s was to emphasise their claim to be the main contenders for academic and clinical leadership in the field of abnormal psychology. The third main factor influencing the development of the new profession and its bid for legitimacy revolved around behaviour therapy. A paper by Eysenck

(1958) emphasised the suitability on scientific grounds of psychologists treating neurotic complaints by means of behaviour therapy. Psychiatrists at the Maudsley, encouraged by Aubrey Lewis, responded by moving into the field of behaviour therapy, for example facilitating the setting up of a medically led behaviour therapy course for nurses at the Maudsley.

From one perspective this may be seen as the response by psychiatry to Eysenck's challenge. However, from a different perspective this can also be seen as one aspect of a continuous process in which psychiatric professional expansion subsumes and takes over different aspects of psychology. However, the Maudsley group of psychologists continued to stress the scientific basis of their approach, and increasingly emphasised its professional legitimacy in terms of its therapeutic rather than its psychometric role. Thus there were two important factors in the early development of clinical psychology which were to have great influence in shaping its future structure and content. These were the role of behaviour therapy as a dominant form of scientific knowledge; and the emergence of a therapeutic role for psychologists which was itself facilitated by the development of behaviour therapy. However, in writing of the role of ideology in the sociology and psychology of scientific knowledge, Marshall cites Perry London's perspective on the role of behaviour therapy, as a vehicle for the professional rather than theoretical development of clinical psychology: 'it never was theory, anyhow, but ideology for professional purposes, and mostly metaphor for clinical purposes' (1992: 7).

The historical context at the time influencing the formative years of clinical psychology in Britain included the issues of medical dominance and the establishment and expansion of psychiatry. This context was crucial in determining the form and content of clinical psychology as it was developed by Eysenck and the Maudsley group of psychologists in the 1950s as a profession based on scientific objectivity. Clinical psychology developed in a context of powerful theoretical as well as professional opposition and was faced with a lengthy conflict with the well-established dominant profession of psychiatry.


DEVELOPMENTS IN THE VERBAL PSYCHOTHERAPIES

Alongside the new developments in behaviour therapy, the psychoanalytic movement continued to survive and develop in post-war Britain. In the post-war years a major centre for the psychoanalytic movement was the Tavistock Clinic. Originally set up to provide systematic psychotherapy on the basis of psychodynamic thought, this orientation has continued to influence all aspects of the Tavistock's work to the present day. Under its psychoanalytically oriented medical leaders, Henry Dicks (1970) points out that after the Second World War the clinic was intended to be a model upon which more out-patient psychodynamic psychotherapy facilities inside the NHS would be based. As Miller and Rose (1988) describe, the Tavistock, with its formation between the two world wars, became a crucial force in emphasising the importance of psychological perspectives in a context where biological psychiatry was the major model. Many of the Tavistock staff had been involved with shell shock casualties during the First World War, and by the time the Second World War began they had established credibility in the use of psychotherapeutic approaches.

The Tavistock operated from a multi-disciplinary basis from its formation and included psychoanalysts, psychiatrists, psychologists and social workers amongst its staff. These were recruited for the war effort in the Second World War, where they pioneered the psychological approach to the selection, training, morale, treatment and rehabilitation of the forces (Morris 1949). Many of the staff themselves served in the forces and returned to the Clinic with the aim of developing and expanding its work on the basis of their wartime experience. This led to a wider and deeper emphasis on group and social processes and the development of psychoanalytically oriented applied psychology. The staff thus expanded their field of interest from mainly dealing with children to focusing more on adult and group work; work that continued after the war, when the Tavistock staff were at the forefront of developments in the application of psychology to psychiatric treatment, especially with NHS out-patients, and to new areas such as industrial relations. They generated both theoretical developments such as the reformulation of psychoanalytic theory as object relations theory; they integrated social psychology and object relations theory; and based on such developments they generated new approaches in a range of areas, such as group therapy (Foulkes and Anthony 1957) and therapeutic communities (Jones 1952).

## CULTURAL AND ACADEMIC INFLUENCES ON THE DEVELOPMENT OF PSYCHOLOGY

A fourth major contextual factor, described by Pilgrim and Treacher, which influenced the development of clinical psychology in Britain

concerns the wider cultural and academic influences on the development of psychology generally, of which clinical psychology was a
part. When we consider the academic traditions which shaped the
development of clinical psychology in Britain, there is one major
tradition that was handed down by Victorian psychologists. This
revolved around theories based on evolutionary biology, which was a
major academic component in Victorian philosophy generally. This
bio-determinist tradition may be seen, for example, in the work of
Sir Francis Galton (1857–1911), whose theories were influential in
the development of British psychology. Galton wrote *Hereditary Genius*
in 1869, and in 1907 he founded the Eugenics Society. This society
expressed concern about the dangers of the British stock being
weakened by the procreation of the feeble minded. According to
this bio-determinist theory, people were vulnerable to mental disorder because of some inherited weakness, or because of bad genes
rather than because of any environmental or experiential influence.

Hearnshaw (1964) outlines how British psychology was formalised as a separate discipline at University College London on 24
October 1901, when the first meeting of the Psychological Society
was held. Philosophy, not medicine, was seen as its origin. Thus,
the context within which British psychology was formalised was
that of British philosophy with its emphases on positivism and
empiricism. This was to be the underlying ideology of all the later
sections of psychology including clinical psychology, and influenced
a particular mode of conducting psychological studies. Psychology,
as the *British Journal of Psychology* emphasised, was a positivist science concerned with facts.

Pilgrim and Treacher outline the origins of psychology as a formal
discipline and the emergence of clinical psychology within that context. One major influence was the development by Galton (1857) and
Karl Pearson (1857–1936) of statistical and psychometric methodology and terminology which gave credibility to the new applied
profession both in Britain and in the United States, and emphasised
the positivist ideology of psychology. The first 50 years of formalised psychology focused around the study of individual differences.
Psychology's expansion was largely due to the practical applications
of psychometric methods with their emphasis on methodological
rigour. Both in clinical and educational fields psychometric testing
proved to be a useful tool for the classification of individuals into
categories which could be used to segregate people. For example,
children and races could be classified by measuring their IQ (e.g.
Burt 1927) and mental disorder could be classified into psychiatric
categories. Compulsory education was established in 1876 and soon

afterwards the problem of less able pupils addressed. The Royal Commission on the Care and Control of the Feeble Minded reported in 1906 that there were about 150,000 'defectives' in Britain and recommended that these be monitored, diagnosed and detained by each local authority. They further recommended a medical classification differentiating between 'idiots', 'imbeciles', 'the feeble minded' and 'moral imbeciles'. This classification system was incorporated into the 1913 Mental Deficiency Act whose governing principles remained in force until the 1959 Mental Health Act.

In order to comply with the 1913 Act, the London County Council appointed a psychologist – Cyril Burt. This meant that the employment of applied psychologists working with children for local authorities – the beginning of educational psychology – was established outside of medical control. Burt's work was largely focused on classifying children according to psychometric tests. His influence is significant, since he was Professor of Psychology at University College London from 1932 until 1951, where the school of differential psychology was to be of central importance in maintaining the Galtonian tradition in future developments of psychology.

The ascendancy of the Galtonian tradition, with its emphasis on hereditary rather than environmental factors influencing human behaviour, fitted well into the social context of the time, with its emphasis on regulating and classifying certain sections of the population. This tradition was incorporated into the first professional practice of clinical psychology, when in the 1950s Eysenck, himself a former student of Burt, emphasised intelligence- and personality-testing as a part of the role of clinical psychology. The profession of clinical psychology was thus influenced in its formative years by eugenic assumptions and by a positivist–empiricist philosophy with its emphasis on objectivity, methodological rigour and statistical procedures together with a central focus on the study of individual differences. Behaviour therapy, with its emphasis on being a scientific approach, was ideally suited to be the vehicle whereby clinical psychology changed its focus from psychometrics in the 1950s to the practice of therapy.

As I have already mentioned, the other major intellectual influence on psychology in post-war Britain was that of psychoanalysis, which was given impetus in Britain by the arrival of many of its proponents from central Europe, seeking refuge from Nazism. England became the centre for different factions within the psychoanalytic movement, with Melanie Klein arriving in 1926 and Freud and his family, including Anna Freud, in 1938. Part of this tradition – which was often in conflict with the school of differential psychology at University College London in its approach to mental disorder, child development and industrial relations – was the medically controlled psychoanalytic approach of the Institute of Human Relations associated with the Tavistock Clinic. Physicians had already incorporated psychoanalysis, and this medical protection together with its international intellectual reputation, protected psychoanalysis from many of the attacks made on it by the Maudsley group in their attempts to undermine both its theory (as pre-scientific) and its practice (as ineffective).

## ROLE OF THE VERBAL PSYCHOTHERAPIES WITHIN CLINICAL PSYCHOLOGY

Richards (1983), in his description of the development of the profession of clinical psychology, outlines three main phases, with psychometrics characterising the 1950s, behaviour therapy the 1960s, and eclecticism the 1970s. Pilgrim and Treacher suggest that this third phase has now been subsumed by a fourth phase characterised by managerialism. Other than at the Tavistock Clinic, it was only in the third phase of eclecticism that psychodynamic psychotherapy was generally recognised and practised within clinical psychology. Although the Maudsley group had nearly been successful, they did not manage to exclude this type of psychotherapy from the discipline of clinical psychology. However, for the most part dynamic psychotherapy remained in the province of the medical profession, and it was psychiatrists who directed and managed the development of the emerging NHS psychotherapy services in the 1970s. The immediate effect of this for psychology within the NHS was to leave psychotherapeutically oriented clinical psychologists isolated. As Nitsun et al. (1989) point out, by the late 1980s clinical psychologists recognised too late the consequences of the medical dominance of psychotherapy.

There are several reasons why psychoanalytic psychotherapy did not disappear completely from the realm of clinical psychology. One reason was that in addition to there being such a focus within the Tavistock itself, it was also supported by a few provincial psychology departments. Additionally, some psychology departments, even if not specifically supportive of psychoanalytic psychotherapy, were nevertheless supportive of the verbal psychotherapies generally. There was also some interdisciplinary support for psychodynamically oriented psychologists from other colleagues within the NHS. They were further supported by an absent peer group, such as the example of the work of clinical psychologists in the USA. There had not been in that country such an attack on psychoanalytic therapy from within clinical psychology. Psychoanalytic concepts had remained alongside other theoretical models such as behaviourism in the mainstream of American clinical psychology. This was reflected in American writings read by their colleagues in Britain, as well as there being more direct contact in the international academic world by the 1970s.

Although in the long term the Maudsley tradition has not continued to be a major feature in clinical psychology, it was certainly a significant force in the development of the profession of clinical psychology up to the 1970s. The Maudsley tradition dominated the training of new practitioners, because not only were the newly developing clinical courses of the 1960s and 1970s run by Maudsley-trained staff, but psychometrics and behaviour therapy were core elements of the course syllabuses. One major exception to this was the clinical psychology course run by the Tavistock Clinic where the theoretical basis of the course was psychoanalytic. It was the clinical psychologists at the Tavistock who mostly ensured that psychoanalytic psychotherapy did not disappear from the realm of clinical psychology. Many such as Herbert Phillipson and John Boreham had worked alongside their Tavistock colleagues in the war effort and returned to take part in the new developments in psychodynamic theory and practice in individual, group and organisational work in the post-war years.

The Tavistock clinical psychology course was led until the mid-1970s by Herbert Phillipson. The Tavistock psychologists, just as their mainstream clinical psychology colleagues, focused on their role in diagnostic testing and research skills, albeit in the context of object relations theory. However, instead of psychometrics the Tavistock course substituted projective testing as part of the role of clinical psychologists. Herbert Phillipson himself developed the Object Relations Test, a projective method of personality assessment derived from psychodynamic theories which links interpersonal and perceptual approaches in understanding personality. It is interesting to note that although aiming at a deeper level of understanding within the object relations theoretical framework, one of the main aims of the work was to try to develop a precise method of personality measurement, which reflected the aims of the wider clinical psychology context. This technique was designed not only for clinical work but also for industrial and social applications.

Since they were to a large extent apart from their mainstream clinical psychology colleagues at that time, clinical psychologists at the Tavistock tended to feel more in common with their colleagues in other disciplines within the Tavistock. This atmosphere contrasted with the tensions between psychologists and psychiatrists within the Maudsley. One major reason for this common feeling was that many of the Tavistock psychologists, such as John Boreham and H. Gill, were themselves trained as psychoanalysts. It tended to a large extent to be the psychoanalytic rather than the medical hierarchy that determined the pecking order at the Tavistock. Furthermore, within the Tavistock the need to defend and preserve their psychodynamic stance from what they perceived as attack from the larger mental health culture led to a group dynamic whereby the Tavistock staff came together in the face of a common enemy. Within the Tavistock, conflicts were more apparent between the various psychoanalytic factions; staff tended to align themselves according to these different factions rather than with their professional groupings. Thus there was greater collaboration between clinical psychologists and professionals of other disciplines. For example, the head of the clinical psychology department, Herbert Phillipson, collaborated with his colleagues R.D. Laing and A.R. Lee in writing *Interpersonal Perception* (Laing *et al.* 1966), which outlined a theory and method of research into interpersonal perception.

Like many of their psychoanalytically oriented colleagues in other professions, the Tavistock psychologists felt themselves to be isolated and marginalised in the wider mental health field. This was particularly true during the era when professional expansion was facilitated by the development of behaviour therapy. The Tavistock course became so out of line with other clinical courses that it terminated at the end of the 1970s, although psychologists have remained on the staff and have taken an active role in practice and training in psychotherapy.

Although the Tavistock was the main institution in which psychodynamically oriented psychologists were based, other provincial psychology departments did not follow the Maudsley-led behavioural developments, and instead maintained the practice of verbal psychotherapies within the discipline of clinical psychology. Some of these departments were either led by or were populated by clinicians who had themselves been trained at the Tavistock and had left that relatively sheltered sanctuary to attempt to use psychodynamic concepts in the wider world of the NHS. For example, the head of the clinical psychology department of Shenley Hospital, Hertfordshire was the Tavistock-trained Gareth Jones. Another source of opposition to the increasingly powerful development of behaviourism in the late 1950s and early 1960s as the definitive paradigm for clinical psychology came from clinical psychologists who were increasingly interested in the more humanistic approaches such as George Kelly's *Psychology of Personal Constructs* (1995), for example, Dorothy Rowe (1971a, 1971b) and David Smail (Caine and Smail 1967; 1970). Some of this opposition came from within the Maudsley itself, where some of its clinical psychology trainees reacted against the prevailing model. Notable examples include Don Bannister, Fay Fransella and Phil Salmon (see Bannister 1960, 1965; Bannister and Fransella 1965; Bannister and Salmon 1966; Salmon 1969; Fransella 1977a, 1977b), who wrote about and developed George Kelly's *Psychology of Personal Constructs* (1955).

## THE INFLUENCE OF CARL ROGERS IN THE CONTEXT OF CLINICAL PSYCHOLOGY

One of the most important international figures, whose work contributed to the maintenance of the verbal psychotherapies within the realm of clinical psychology, was Carl Rogers (1902–87), a professor of psychology in the United States, whom many view as the father of contemporary counselling. In their books on Carl Rogers, Kirschenbaum (1979) and Thorne (1992) outline his career and professional development. He was born in 1902 in the midwest of the USA. He trained both as an educational and clinical psychologist in the 1920s, at a time when psychology in the USA was heavily influenced by Watsonian behaviourism. As was later reflected in the development of clinical psychology in Britain, this approach was characterised by its adherents emphasising the scientific aspects of the behavioural approach together with the use of statistical methodology. The main academic context of Rogers' own training was that of behaviourism together with psychometrics. His own doctoral research involved testing the personality adjustment of children. His first professional job as a psychologist in 1928 involved working with children.

In his lifetime Rogers wrote 16 books and more than 200 articles and research studies. He began formulating his own ideas from his work with people seeking help. The first of his many books and articles, *The Clinical Treatment of the Problem Child*, was published in 1939. In this book he first presented his view that all psychological theories rested on the therapist's attitude and outlined four basic attitudes necessary for effective therapy. These were first, empathy – by which he meant a capacity for sympathy; second, respect for the individual; third, an understanding of the self; and fourth, the importance of the therapist having psychological knowledge – by which Rogers meant that therapists should have 'a thorough basis of knowledge of human behavior and of its physical, social and psychological determinants' (Rogers 1939: 279–84). These basic attitudes he later developed into the concepts of empathy, unconditional positive regard and congruence or genuineness, which were to underline his contribution to the understanding of helping relationships.

Rogers was appointed professor of psychology first at Ohio State University (1940–5) and then at the University of Chicago (1945–57). Rogers himself later dated the birth of client-centred therapy as December 1940, when he gave a lecture titled 'Newer Concepts in Psychotherapy' before an invited audience at the University of Minnesota. He stressed that his approach was to facilitate individuals to grow and develop, with the experience of the therapeutic relationship itself being the major determinant in the growth of the client. In 1945 Rogers took up the post of professor of psychology at the University of Chicago, where he was asked to set up a counselling centre. Here he continued his research and clinical work, publishing *Client-Centered Therapy* in 1951. His achievements were recognised by mainstream American psychology in 1956, when the American Psychological Association awarded him the Distinguished Scientific Contribution Award. In his next post at the University of Wisconsin Rogers further developed his work into the conditions necessary for therapeutic change and published his fifth and perhaps most influential book, *On Becoming a Person* (1961). It was also during this period that he explored the impact of his client-centred approach in research with hospitalised schizophrenics. From 1963 to 1968, Rogers worked at the newly established Western Behavioral Sciences Institute in California, where he became involved with humanistically oriented work and the encounter group movement. In 1968 he formed the Center for Studies of the Person, where he remained until his death 20 years later. It was in the mid-1970s that Rogers first coined the term 'person-centered' and during this period extended his work from individuals to groups and to the larger world context.

When we examine Rogers' work in the context of clinical psychology, certain processes may be highlighted. Although clinical psychology in the United States was established earlier than in Britain, and many themes evident in Rogers' work can be contextualised within the development of clinical psychology in the USA, some of these are reflected in similar processes in the development of British clinical psychology. Rogers' training and early work in clinical psychology was in many ways similar to that of his counterparts in Britain: for example, the emphasis on psychometrics such as personality testing as a central concern for clinical psychology. As in the early development of clinical psychology in Britain, the prevailing academic models in Rogers' training were those of psychoanalysis and behaviour therapy, with the emphasis on a scientific approach through statistical methodology. Rogers' client-centred therapy was a departure from both psychoanalytic and behaviour therapy. Client-centred therapy emphasised the capacity in clients to find their own answers, once the necessary psychological conditions had been established. Rogers pointed out the dangers of both interpretation and behavioural manipulation. He was sceptical about the use of psychometric tests if their main purpose was to diagnose and label either problems or people.

### The development of the humanistic movement

A similar creative reaction to both the prevailing behavioural and psychoanalytic models developed later in Britain, probably reflecting the later development of clinical psychology here: for example, through the followers of Kelly's personal construct theory, as is described later in this chapter. Nevertheless, throughout his career Rogers remained committed to the research emphasis of the clinical psychology role in which he was trained. Similarly in developments in Britain: the definition and form of research was to be elaborated to encompass both the observer's and the observed's subjective reality, as in the work of the personal construct theorists and in the New Paradigm research, seen, for example, in the work of Peter Reason and John Rowan (1981). One issue which influenced Rogers' work, and was apparent, as we have seen, in the development of clinical psychology in both the USA and in Britain, was that of medical dominance. Later in his career, like his British counterparts, he allied himself with what was to be termed humanistic psychology. Vitz (1977) describes Rogers as being the acknowledged leader of humanistic psychology in the USA. Likewise in Britain in the 1970s and early 1980s, reflecting wider social and egalitarian concerns, there was a trend to make psychology more accessible to other professions in order to enable a wider distribution of psychological knowledge to the general public. Perhaps, more than any other psychologist in the USA, Rogers made human psychology more accessible to ordinary members of the public. He also made a significant contribution to the demystification of psychotherapy. Believing that the personal qualities of the therapist were all-important, he encouraged and supported many people from different professional backgrounds who may not otherwise have pursued careers as psychotherapists. Thorne describes how Rogers' work has had a similar influence in Britain, attributing to Rogers' influence the evolution of a counselling profession where practitioners are drawn

222222

22222222

from a wide variety of disciplines, and which is dominated neither by medicine nor by psychology.

Thorne (1992) points out that Rogers' early experience of the main theoretical models of behaviourism and psychoanalysis in US psychology led to his reaction against both in the development of his own theoretical formulations. This may be seen in his emphasis on the importance of the therapeutic perspective being from the client's own subjective reality, and on the core therapeutic conditions which facilitate change. The parallel in Britain is a group of trainees at the Maudsley in the late 1950s and early 1960s, who also reacted against both of the prevailing models in British clinical psychology, to develop the work of George Kelly and his personal construct psychology. Like Rogers, Kelly was born in the midwest of the USA. He too became a professor of psychology at Ohio State University, in 1946. Kelly's main theory is outlined in the two-volume work *The Psychology of Personal Constructs* (1955). In these volumes, like Rogers, Kelly emphasises the importance of research, although Kelly integrated research more through his development of the repertory grid technique. Both Rogers and Kelly underline the client's subjective understanding of reality, and the importance of the therapist trying to enter into and understand this world for therapeutic change to occur. Although there are important differences in their approaches, there seem to be some important similarities in the shared historical and academic culture that fostered their development. Don Bannister, one of the main proponents of personal construct psychology, trained in the late 1950s at the Maudsley. He has described his resistance to psychoanalysis and to learning theory based behaviourism in an article describing personal construct psychology, 'A new theory of personality' (1966). In this article Bannister states:

> All psychological theories seem to imply some sort of model man, some notion of what man essentially is. Thus psycho-analytic theories suggest that man is essentially a battlefield, he is a dark cellar in which a maiden aunt and a sex-crazed monkey are locked in mortal combat, the affair being refereed by a rather nervous bank clerk. Alternatively, learning theory and stimulus–response psychology generally seem to suggest that man is essentially a ping-pong ball with a memory.
>
> (Bannister 1966: 363)

It is interesting to note that both the creative work of the personal construct theory psychologists in Britain and the formulation of the theory and practice of client-centred therapy by Carl Rogers in the

USA were fostered outside the prevailing ethos of clinical psychology of the time. Both were developed in spite of, or perhaps in resistance to, the dominant ideologies that influenced the mainstream academic culture of clinical psychology during different periods in each of the two countries.

A second major theme in the work of Carl Rogers, that has parallels in the development of British clinical psychology, was his fight to establish greater recognition for clinical psychologists, especially in the context of medical dominance. Rogers struggled to gain greater recognition for the contribution of clinical psychologists in their own right, as distinct from psychiatrists, in order that they should be able to practise psychotherapy and to have administrative responsibilities over their mental health work. When he was awarded the Distinguished Professional Contribution Award by the American Psychological Association, Rogers gave an address summarising the most important struggles and achievements of his career (Rogers 1974). He outlined his struggles with the psychiatric profession, many of whom had tried to prevent psychologists from practising psychotherapy at all. Thorne describes Rogers' response to opposition from the medical profession: 'About such matters he was implacable, and he confessed that his behaviour in what he often believed to be an all-out war was deeply surprising and even shocking to those who were more accustomed to see his thoughtful and gentle side' (1992: 59–60). Indeed the term 'counseling' itself was originally used by Rogers as a means to circumvent the objections of psychiatrists to psychologists practising psychotherapy. By changing the name of the activity psychologists were able to continue practising psychotherapy, without any other change necessary in the psychotherapeutic situation or setting.

A third main theme in Rogers' work is his emphasis on the importance of scientific enquiry and research. Kirschenbaum (1979) highlights Rogers' commitment to scientific research and his insistence that it was the psychologist's duty to anchor therapy firmly in the domain of scientific enquiry. Nevertheless, he was ambivalent about the ultimate efficacy of traditional scientific methods, and later in his career he explored alternative scientific models. Towards the end of his career, he wrote an article in the *Journal of Humanistic Psychology* (1985) in which he rejects the empirical tradition and logical positivism and advocates a 'New Science', in which research is not constrained by what he describes as the 'straitjacket of logical empiricism'. In this article he refers to studies using new methodologies and new research paradigms and cites British New Paradigm work such as that developed by Peter Reason and John Rowan (1981). In some

ways it seemed that the wheel had turned full circle, at least in the
area of psychological research methodology, with developments in
the field of British clinical psychology being a significant influence
in the further development of Rogers' own work. However, Rogers
never doubted his research commitment, and from his earlier work
using the methodology of logical positivism to his later interests in
the developments in the philosophy of science which emphasised
phenomenologically based methodology, he remained convinced that
psychotherapy needed research in order to develop its effectiveness.


## ECLECTICISM IN CLINICAL PSYCHOLOGY

Although the dominant tradition handed down to clinical psychology in the 1970s was that of behaviourism and psychometrics,
it was nevertheless superseded by an eclecticism which was able
to incorporate the verbal psychotherapies. Pilgrim and Treacher point
out that probably the most significant reason why the direction of
mainstream clinical psychology moved away from the narrow confines of the Maudsley–University College psychometrics–behaviourist
tradition was related to the wider cultural context of the late 1960s
and early 1970s. During this era of growing political and social
awareness many traditional orthodoxies were challenged, including those associated with mental health. This period saw the growth
of the anti-psychiatry movement, fermented by the writings of psychiatrists such as Laing (1968) and Cooper (1967), while within
psychology itself there was increasing unease with the political
implications of psychometric labelling and the social manipulation
of behaviour therapy. Although the predominant model was the
scientist–practitioner model with an emphasis on behaviourism and
psychometrics, by the early 1970s, as Dabbs (1972) points out, there
was an increased interest amongst clinical psychologists in the verbal psychotherapies. For example, in 1973, a significant group of
clinical psychologists emphasised the inextricable link between psychotherapy and academic psychology in the setting up of the Psychology and Psychotherapy Association (PPA). Predominant in this group
were those psychologists with an affinity with personal construct psychology such as Don Bannister (1966), Miller Mair (1970), Dorothy
Rowe (1971a, 1971b), Phil Salmon (1969) and David Smail (1970).
The attitudes and interests of new trainees entering clinical courses
was reflected to some extent in the training courses in clinical psychology. A study by Claridge and Brooks (1973) points out that the
emphasis on the psychotherapeutic aspects of the role of the clinical

psychologist in the Glasgow MSc training course in clinical psychology was mirrored by the preference of the majority of applicants for the therapeutic rather than the research element of their future role.

Psychotherapy did not replace the existing content of clinical psychology but rather was incorporated into it through an eclectic approach, or by what Richards (1983) terms a compromise of 'scientific humanism'. Pilgrim and Treacher outline three main ways in which the scientific humanism of the 1970s and 1980s was expressed. First, individual clinical psychologists were becoming more eclectic in their practice. Second, the profession generally became pluralistic, in that different sub-groups of practitioners practised different models and coexisted without the antipathy which had characterised the Maudsley–Tavistock conflict. Third, efforts were made to integrate different theoretical models, for example in cognitive-behavioural therapy. By the 1980s the new integration was reflected at both undergraduate level and in post-graduate clinical psychology courses.

By the 1990s political changes instigated by successive Conservative governments in Britain had brought about the ethos of the free market economy and managerialism in the NHS including clinical psychology services. Clinical psychology courses reflected this change by including management components in their syllabuses.

Historically, counselling psychology developed later than clinical psychology both in the USA, where clinical psychology was first formalised as a profession, and in Britain. Earlier in this chapter, I outlined how counselling was a term initially developed in the context of psychology in the USA by one of the founders of the humanistic movement in psychology, the clinical psychologist Carl Rogers. By 1952, the Division of Counseling and Guidance of the American Psychological Association had made its first attempts to define the professional goal of counselling psychology as being the fostering of the psychological development of individuals at all points of the adjustment continuum. However, it was not until 1982 that counselling psychology was first recognised within the British Psychological Society with the establishment of the Counselling Psychology Section. The rapid growth in membership led to the Section becoming a Special Group in 1989 and finally a Division of the BPS in 1994. In its Guidelines for the Professional Practice of Counselling Psychology, the Division of Counselling Psychology (DCoP) notes that historically, counselling psychology has developed as a branch of professional psychological practice strongly influenced by humanistic clinical practice and research as well as the psychodynamic and cognitive-behavioural psychotherapeutic traditions. The Guidelines point out that counselling psychology in Britain has not always had an easy relationship with mainstream academic psychology, because counselling psychology has drawn upon and developed models of practice and enquiry which have often been at odds with the dominant conceptions of scientific psychology. These issues will be explored further in Chapter Three. Counselling psychology has tried to establish relationships with other counselling and psychotherapeutic practices which have developed outside the framework of academic psychology while still continuing its connections with mainstream professional psychological practice. In terms of its current development, the membership of the Division in 1996 stood at 1,121. The report of the DCoP in the Annual Report of the BPS (1995–6) points out that proposals are currently being put forward to consider a change of title of DCoP to the Division of Psychotherapeutic and Counselling Psychology in order to reflect more accurately the wide spectrum in the practice of counselling psychologists.

This chapter has outlined the historical cultural and academic context that influenced the structure and content of contemporary clinical psychology and the place of the verbal psychotherapies within that context. Some of the issues raised will be discussed more fully in later chapters in relation to the present context of the verbal psychotherapies such as counselling in the practice of clinical psychology. However, before we go on to explore these issues, I describe in the next chapter the wider contemporary context of the psychological professions, of which clinical psychology and counselling psychology are both a part.

## · TWO ·

# Counselling in psychological services

### CONFUSION OF ROLES

Terms referring to psychologically based helping professions, such as psychologist, psychotherapist, clinical psychologist, counsellor, and counselling psychologist as well as psychiatrist and psychoanalyst, are often a source of confusion. This confusion was compounded in the 1970s and 1980s with a huge expansion of people calling themselves either psychologists, counsellors or psychotherapists. Although many were properly trained, some had no or little training, but nevertheless offered their services to the general public.

The lack of clarity of roles is also frequently reflected within the psychology-related professions themselves – about who does what, how, where and with whom. The majority of the public in Britain access psychologically based therapies through the National Health Service. Two main factors contribute to the current lack of clarity of roles there. First, during the 1970s, as I showed in Chapter One, the value of psychologically based therapy was increasingly recognised in professions other than clinical psychology, such as psychiatry and psychiatric nursing, and was incorporated into their practice. This does not however mean that clinicians belonging to these professions necessarily practise psychological therapies. Further, the extent of theoretical and practical knowledge of the psychological therapies necessary for professional accreditation in these professions at both qualification and at post-qualification level is still highly variable. However, the expansion of psychological practice has continued within the NHS with the support of clinical psychologists. Clinical psychologists are relatively few in number compared to other health care professions, and they have encouraged the understanding

of psychological principles and the use of methods based on psychological theory by other professions in order that more patients have
access to the benefits of a psychological approach.

A second factor contributing to the lack of clarity of roles, perhaps in some opposition to the first, derives from government policies. The National Health Service has undergone many changes
and reorganisations since its formation within the welfare state with
the National Health Services Act (1948). However, over the last 17
years or so government policies have brought about unparalleled
changes affecting its structure and organisation. This period of constant change and instability, as government policies based on the
philosophy of free market economics have been imposed upon the
NHS, has been reflected in uncertainties and insecurities amongst
NHS professionals generally. One of the consequences of this has
been increased competition amongst professionals, each claiming
expertise and knowledge in sometimes similar fields, in their efforts
to demonstrate that it is they who are being cost-effective and provide value for money. For example, while many professionals of many
disciplines provide good counselling or psychotherapy, the claim to
be practising psychotherapy is sometimes 'a triumph of rhetoric over
content' (Prior, T., personal communication 1994). Further, many
would argue that a consequence of the government policy of closure of the large psychiatric hospitals and promotion of community-
based multi-disciplinary mental health teams as the main provider of
mental health care is the mediocratisation of services. These teams
usually include professionals such as psychiatrists, clinical psychologists, community psychiatric nurses, social workers and occupational
therapists. Often there is a perceived lack of differentiation in the roles
of team members as the teams face increasing demands to provide
psychological help for clients in the community. The emphases on
what everyone in the team can do, regardless of profession, has led
to the dilution and mediocratisation of psychological services provided to the general public.

Professional clinicians who practise the psychological therapies,
including counselling within the NHS, face increasing pressures in
their work context, emanating from the direct organisational changes
which have affected the NHS generally (including the organisational
structures within which they work), and indirectly through changes
in the form and content of mental health provision. With mental
health policies directed towards community care and the increasing
closure of the large mental health institutions, the demand on mental
health teams to provide a comprehensive service to the community
has not only resulted in an increased number of referrals, but also

in more referrals of people with complex or longstanding psychological and psychiatric difficulties together with associated social and economic problems. Government initiatives, such as the emphasis on reducing waiting lists and on prompt response to referrals, make it a necessity that the structure or content of treatment interventions will have to be altered in some way, if more people are to be seen at a time when resources such as staffing levels remain the same or are reduced. This can be done by reducing the time allowed for sessions, by reducing the overall length of treatment or by using different forms of intervention that result in less intensive and less direct patient contact. Consequently, increasing numbers of people are offered briefer treatment interventions. However, this often compounds the problem of inadequate resources, since more complex problems generally demand more prolonged interventions. There are thus conflicts that arise from the pressure of contract-seeking and budget-balancing health care providers through the line management structures to mental health professionals for a quick response and rapid turnover marketplace approach to mental health. There is an inherent danger that the context in which counselling is placed in the NHS may be that of a briefer, cheaper intervention strategy.


PROFESSIONAL DEFINITIONS


Given the blurred distinctions between professions which provide psychological therapies, some basic definitions would be helpful at this point.

*Psychiatry* is the oldest of the mental health professions. It is a speciality of medicine which focuses on the study and treatment of mental and emotional disorders. Psychiatrists have a medical training before specialising in psychiatry. Although psychiatry draws on a knowledge of psychology, it is essentially a branch of medicine concerned with the diagnoses and treatment of psychological problems and mental illness using drugs and physical techniques. Psychiatry and allied professions such as psychiatric nursing basically work within a medical framework, conceptualising problems as biological disorders, although they may use psychological therapies as adjuncts to medication.

*Psychoanalysis* is practised by some psychiatrists, who have also trained in that discipline, but in Britain some analysts are not necessarily medically trained, and may be clinical psychologists. Psychoanalysis is a term that simultaneously describes a theoretical system,

a form of psychotherapy, a method of clinical observation and a profession. It originated in the work of Sigmund Freud, who himself
felt that psychoanalytic training and practice need not be limited to
physicians. Many of his early students, including his daughter Anna
Freud, were not medically trained.

Definitions of *psychology* include the scientific study of perception,
thought, emotion, learning and behaviour. Fundamentally, psychology is the study of people – how we think, feel, react and inter-
act with each other. Psychology is concerned with all aspects of
behaviour and the thoughts, feelings and motivation underlying
behaviour. The study of people is as long as the history of people,
in that observers throughout the ages have based their analysis and
understanding of human nature on everyday experience. However,
modern formalised psychology stresses that it is the science of human
behaviour and experience. Thus, the study of psychology, as defined
by the British Psychological Society, involves scientific methods including observation, measurement, hypothesis-testing, experimentation
and logical inference and the use of statistics to test the significance
of research results.

The British Psychological Society (BPS) is the scientific society
and professional body for psychologists, incorporated by Royal
Charter. Currently anyone can call themselves a psychologist, but
in 1987 the Society instigated the setting up of a Register of Chartered
Psychologists, which has strict entry requirements. The BPS also
maintains a professional code of conduct for all members. The Society has around 25,000 members, including many different sorts of
psychologists and many specialisms. The Society has six Divisions,
five Special Groups and 11 Scientific Sections.

The Directory of Chartered Psychologists summarises the various professional groupings who are eligible to be called *chartered
psychologists*.

The Division of Clinical Psychology of the British Psychological
Society offers a definition of *clinical psychology* in the document
Clinical Psychology, Core Purpose and Philosophy (1991a). As part
of that definition, the document states:

> Clinical psychology is the application of psychology to health
> and community care. Its central focus is the value it places on
> the experience of individuals and their attempts to understand
> that experience. It draws on a broad range of theories and
> approaches which reflect the multidimensional nature of per-
> sonal experience and the influences upon it. For example, these
> may include psychological knowledge of the way biological

factors, relationships, groups, organisations and society can inter-
act and cause distress or enhance personal fulfilment.

(1991a: 2)

The Directory describes how clinical psychologists work in a range
of specialities, from adult mental health acute services to educational and social service settings. In these various specialities, the
Directory states that,

> Clinical psychologists are problem solvers, formulating problems
> and questions in psychological terms and drawing creatively
> on a wealth of psychological theories and techniques from the
> discipline of psychology to support the finding of ways for-
> ward. Clinical psychologists work directly with complex prob-
> lems involving individuals, couples, families, groups and service
> systems. Consultancy and training is provided to carers and
> health-care professionals in order to maximise the use of their
> psychological skills.

(1994a: 3)

The Directory further points out that organisational consultancy
is carried out by clinical psychologists with provider and purchaser
organisations with respect to the psychological aspects of health and
community care.

## DEFINITIONS OF COUNSELLING

There are many and varied definitions of the term *counselling*.
For example, Hilton Davis, in a British Association for Counselling
Information Sheet (1991), defines counselling broadly as 'the range
of activities from the use of basic counselling skills to specialist
psychosocial interventions'. The British Association for Counselling
itself offers the following definition:

> Counselling is the skilled and principled use of relationship to
> facilitate self-knowledge, emotional acceptance and growth, and
> the optimal development of personal resources. The overall
> aim is to provide an opportunity to work towards living more
> satisfyingly and resourcefully. Counselling relationships will vary
> according to need but may be concerned with developmental
> issues, addressing and resolving specific problems, making deci-
> sions, coping with crisis, developing personal insights and know-
> ledge, working through feelings of inner conflict or improving
> relationship with others. The counsellor's role is to facilitate the

client's work in ways that respect the client's values, personal
resources and capacity for self determination.

(1992: 1)

In attempting to clarify the term, Richard Nelson-Jones, in his book
*The Theory and Practice of Counselling Psychology* (1982), outlines how
the term counselling is used in three main ways. It can be used to
describe a special kind of helping relationship, or a set of activities,
or as defining a specific area of service.

First, counselling as a helping relationship has often been defined
by focusing on the counsellor's qualities in the relationship with
clients. As described in Chapter One, as early as 1939 Carl Rogers outlined the importance of therapist qualities, which he later expanded
and defined as the core conditions of empathy, acceptance or unconditional positive regard, and congruence or genuineness. These qualities he viewed as necessary and sufficient conditions to promote
therapeutic change (Rogers 1957). The emphasis here is not just on
skills and techniques such as the reflection of feelings, but on the basic
attitude of the counsellor. Adherents of this view of counselling are
frequently termed client-centred or person-centred counsellors.

Second, counselling may be seen as a set of activities. Many
counsellors, although upholding the view that the core conditions
in the counsellor–client relationship are necessary, do not believe
that they are necessarily *sufficient* conditions in themselves to promote therapeutic change. They often include in their work with
clients a range of additional theoretical perspectives and methods
derived, for example, from psychoanalytic, gestalt, behavioural and
cognitive theoretical theories and practices. However, there is also
some dispute within the client-centred therapy school of thought.
Some client-centred counsellors such as Tausch (1990) advocate
that when pure client-centred therapy does not work other strategies may be added. Other client-centred therapists such as Bozarth
(1990) disagree with attempts to add other therapeutic models to
Rogers' original model.

The third way that counselling has been defined is by viewing
it as a special area for providing services. Generally counsellors,
unlike other mental health professionals working with people
suffering emotional distress, are more likely to be found working
in non-medical settings as well as in traditional health care settings.
For example, counsellors may be found in school, college or university counselling services. Counsellors were at one time also thought
more likely to be seeing a less distressed client population. But
Nelson-Jones (1982) points out that different client groups may

present differently to different agencies. For example, counsellors may be presented with more difficulties revolving around occupational choice or with examination worries or with study problems than other mental health professionals practising the psychological therapies. The experience of many counsellors is that with cuts in mental health budgets, counselling services are being used by clients with much more distressing problems than might have been the case 10 or 20 years ago. Counselling services sometimes are the only places left to go for anything like ongoing and regular help.

### Counselling psychology

Whereas counselling has been defined in terms of it being a helping relationship or as a set of activities or as delineating a specific area of services, the term 'counselling psychologist' means something else. The first attempts to define counselling psychology come from the USA. In 1952, the Committee on Counselor Training of the American Psychological Association's Division of Counseling and Guidance stated that the professional goal of the counselling psychologist was to foster the psychological development of the individual; which includes all people on the adjustment continuum. It is interesting to note that this definition included a wider category of individuals than those suffering from the more severe psychological disturbances. In 1956, a Committee on Definition of the American Psychological Association's Division of Counseling Psychology defined a counselling psychologist as a psychologist who used varying combinations of exploratory experiences, psychometric techniques and therapeutic interviewing to assist people to grow and develop. Further, Ivey (1979) in the USA describes counselling psychology as being the most broadly based of the applied psychology specialities, and states that 'its practitioners may be working in community settings, schools, hospitals and industry. They may be conducting psychotherapy or counseling, involved in education or program development or managing community change activities' (p. 3). Counselling psychology as a specialist area within the field of applied psychology developed later in Britain than in the United States, as I describe later in this chapter.

In Britain, the Directory of Chartered Psychologists (BPS 1994d) describes a counselling psychologist as working with individuals and groups in order to help them improve their sense of well-being and alleviate their distress. Counselling psychologists are concerned with helping people to cope better with normal life cycle developments. The British Psychological Society in its Regulations for the

Diploma in Counselling Psychology provides the following definition of counselling psychology:

> Counselling Psychology is a branch of applied psychology con-
> cerned with the interplay between psychological principles and
> the counselling process and is developed by substantial reflec-
> tion on practice and research. Its understanding derives from
> formal psychological enquiry and from the interpersonal rela-
> tionships between practitioners and their clients. In counselling
> psychology, there is an emphasis on the systematic application
> of distinctively psychological understandings of the client and
> the counselling process to the practice of counselling.
>
> (1994c: 1)

This document describes Counselling Psychology as further concerned with:

- the competent and imaginative practice of counselling;
- understanding and knowledge of what contributes to effective
  counselling;
- continuing personal exploration of the issues involved;
- a philosophy of enquiry which recognises the distinctive practices of the counselling relationship;
- methods which contribute qualitatively to the psychological sense
  we make of human experience and conduct;
- the use of psychological knowledge gained from other areas of
  psychological enquiry.

All this is undertaken in a spirit of service, seeking to reduce unnecessary suffering and to contribute to human well-being (1994c: 1).

## THE RELATIONSHIP BETWEEN CLINICAL PSYCHOLOGY AND COUNSELLING PSYCHOLOGY

From these definitions we can see there is much overlap between
the definitions of counselling psychology and other areas of applied
psychology such as clinical psychology. In the USA Super (1977)
suggests that the essential difference between the two specialities is
that whereas clinical psychologists tend to look for what is wrong
and how to treat it, counselling psychologists tend to look for what
is right and how to use it. Similarly in Britain, Nelson-Jones (1982)
distinguishes counselling psychology from other fields such as clinical
psychology or educational psychology or psychiatry by its emphasis on

well-being and self-actualisation rather than on sickness and mal-adjustment. He defines counselling psychology as follows:

> Counselling psychology is an applied area of psychology which has the objective of helping people to live more effective and fulfilled lives. Its clientele tend to be not very seriously disturbed people in non-medical settings. Its concerns are those of the whole person in all areas of human psychological functioning, such as feeling and thinking, personal, marital and sexual relations, and work and recreational activity. Its methods include counselling relationships, and activities, psychological education and consultancy, and self-help. People using the methods of counselling psychology include professional psychologists, paid and voluntary counsellors, and social workers. The settings for provision of counselling psychology services include education, medicine, industry and numerous community and voluntary agencies.
>
> (1982: 5)

Nelson-Jones describes counselling psychology as encompassing a broader field than counselling. Although the core conditions of the counselling relationship are essential in order that clients feel respected and understood and have their worth validated, Nelson-Jones's view is that the core conditions, although necessary, are insufficient to maximise client outcomes beyond empathic understanding. In his view counselling psychologists need to possess a range of psychological knowledge and skills to help as many clients as possible.

It needs to be emphasised that most psychologists in other applied fields of psychology to some extent use the core elements of the counselling relationship together with counselling activities and skills as part of their work. This is because counselling is a psychological process and thus there is an inextricable link between psychology and counselling. Nelson-Jones (1982) highlights three main reasons for this link. First, the aims of counselling are of a psychological nature: the objective is to work with clients to enable them to cope more effectively with their lives. Second, the underlying theories on which counselling is based and from which counselling activities are derived are psychological theories. Indeed the majority of leading counselling theorists, such as Carl Rogers, have been psychologists. Third, the process of counselling is a psychological process. Nelson-Jones describes this process as being 'a continuing interaction between two or more persons engaging in various kinds of behaviour' (1982: 2).

Psychological research has contributed both to the generation of counselling theories and to the evaluation of counselling processes and outcomes. For example, in research designed to describe and identify the elements that contribute to counsellor effectiveness, different psychological concepts are used, whether concepts such as 'empathy', 'respect' and 'congruence' for the client-centred counsellor, or 'reinforcement' and 'modelling' for the behavioural counsellor. Likewise the client's thoughts, behaviour and feelings during the counselling process may be described in psychological terms, such as self-exploration. Further, the tests and measures used in research to attempt to identify the process and outcome of counselling are frequently psychological measures assessing psychological constructs.

## PSYCHOTHERAPY, COUNSELLING AND THE PSYCHOLOGICAL THERAPIES

There is at present much confusion and misunderstanding over the relationship of the terms 'psychotherapy', 'counselling' and 'psychological therapies'. These terms are often used interchangeably to describe therapies that are based on psychological theories and that use psychological methods. In the literature, the words 'psychotherapy' and 'psychological treatments' or 'psychological therapies' tend to be synonymous. For example, in discussing definitions of counselling and psychotherapy Nelson-Jones uses the phrase 'counselling and what are better termed the "psychological" therapies' (1982: 3). Similarly, the British Psychological Society in its Regulations for the Diploma in Counselling Psychology (1994c) states: 'Throughout this document the terms counselling and psychological therapy are interchangeable. This reflects the historical and current situation in which there is considerable overlapping' (1994c: 10). Additionally, as the BPS (1990) points out, the term 'psychotherapy' is sometimes used to refer to the specific model of psychoanalytic or psychodynamic psychotherapy. The BPS stresses the necessity, when referring to psychological treatment or psychotherapy, of being clear about what is being referred to. It suggests that references to psychological treatments or psychological therapies or psychotherapy may be clarified in two ways. First, by specifying the model of therapy as defined by the theory underpinning its practice; for example, by specifying whether the underlying model is psychodynamic, behavioural or humanistic, etc. Second, the various terms may be clarified by specifying the mode or modality of therapy. The mode or modality is defined by its participant structure, for example, whether it is individual, marital, group or family therapy. Additionally the BPS suggests three methods that may be useful in defining therapies. It may be appropriate to identify the aim of therapy; for example, whether the aim is supportive or exploratory. It may be helpful to specify the proposed duration of therapy – short, medium or long. Finally, it may help clarification to specify the intensity of therapy; for example, by referring to how frequently it occurs.

Attempts to provide clear definitions that differentiate counselling and psychotherapy and psychological therapies have historically been a source of major difficulty. A major reason for this is that Carl Rogers, recognised as the originator of contemporary counselling theory and practice, originally used the word counselling as a strategy to silence psychiatrists who objected to psychologists practising psychotherapy. As we have seen, by changing the label of the activity he enabled practitioners to continue with their practice. Differentiations between counselling and psychotherapy tend either to conclude that there are few definite distinctions between the two terms; or they point out that distinctions (where they exist) rest on the different emphasis between the two activities; or sometimes conclude that there is no essential difference between the two activities. For example, Tyler attempts to distinguish the two, stating that 'the aim of therapy is generally considered to be a personality change of some sort. Let us use counselling to refer to a helping process, the aim of which is not to change the person but to enable him to utilise the resources he now has for coping with life' (1961: 12). However, enabling a person to use coping resources can be considered to be a personality change in some people.

Many writers, such as Truax and Carkhuff (1967), use the terms 'counselling' and 'psychotherapy' interchangeably, while Patterson (1974) concludes that there is no consensus on the essential difference between the two activities. The Division of Clinical Psychology of the BPS states in its report on the Working Party on the Psychological Therapies (1979) that both counselling and psychotherapy make use of a variety of theoretical models, and that both 'stress the need to value the client as a person, to listen sympathetically and to hear what is communicated, and to foster the capacity of self-help and self-responsibility' (1979: 6). Nelson-Jones (1982) concludes that 'it seems probable that no really valid distinction can be made between counselling and the psychological therapies in terms of the activities involved in the counselling or therapeutic process' (1982: 3). The only difference between definitions of counselling and psychotherapy according to the perspectives of writers such as Nelson-Jones is essentially one of emphasis rather than there being any definitive or absolute differences in the definitions. Differences in emphasis may be seen in the nature of the relationship, in the theoretical orientation of the activity, in the setting in which the activity takes place and in the different client populations.

However, even this distinction appears relative rather than absolute. Consider the point about the settings in which counselling or psychotherapy take place: definitions of counselling tend to point out that counselling is more likely to take place in non-medical rather than medical settings. In terms of client populations definitions of counselling tend to indicate that counselling focuses on less distressed clients, whereas the psychological therapies focus on moderately to severely disturbed clients. However, it should be emphasised that any such distinctions are relative rather than forming mutually exclusive categories. Carl Rogers himself worked with clients who had been diagnosed as schizophrenic, while many of the therapies which come under the term psychological therapy, such as the cognitive and behaviour therapies, are viewed frequently as the therapy of choice for less distressed clients. Further, counsellors are increasingly being employed to work in such medical settings as general practice or in health centres, as well as in clinical psychology departments and in psychotherapy departments within the NHS. Generally, it may still be the case that counsellors in these settings tend to be referred less chronically disturbed clients.

## THE CONTEXT IN WHICH THE PSYCHOLOGICAL SERVICES FUNCTION

With the question of definitions discussed although – because of the imprecise nature of some of the terms – not completely resolved, I now examine the context in which the psychological services function. Both clinical and counselling psychology are located within the wider context of professional psychology, which similarly influences the way they work and the nature of services they provide. The wider context of professional psychology includes the implications of psychologists acquiring chartered status. Also there is an overlap between the two disciplines of counselling psychology and clinical psychology in the areas in which psychologists generally offer their services. This is the context in which I consider the particular role that counselling plays.

As I have already mentioned, there has been difficulty in the psychology profession with self-styled practitioners who have called themselves psychologists and presented their varied services to the general public. But since the consumer has had no means of check-ing the credentials of psychologists, the British Psychological Society sought chartered status for its members. In 1987 the BPS was author-ised by the Privy Council to administer and maintain a Register of Chartered Psychologists, with the aim of protecting the public from those who are untrained or insufficiently trained. The Register is non-statutory, but is restricted to members of the BPS who have the required qualifications and have been accepted for registration.

The criteria for acceptance are outlined in the introduction to the Directory of Chartered Psychologists (1994d). First, the applicant has to have successfully completed a first qualification in psychology. Second, it is necessary for the applicant to have undergone a further course of supervised training in a specific area of psychology, such as educational or clinical or counselling psychology. The third criterion is that the person has to be judged fit to practise psychology without supervision. As well as the above criteria that refer to training and qualifications, applicants for chartering status have also to agree to abide by the Society's Code of Conduct. This Code is backed up by a disciplinary system, with the final decision resting with a panel consisting of a majority of non-psychologists, again to give greater protection to the public.

### The context of chartered psychologists

Psychologists, although probably best known for their work in the health and education services, work in a wide range of contexts and the Directory of Chartered Psychologists (1994d) outlines nine broad areas in which chartered psychologists offer their services. Only a brief description of these areas is given here, in order to place both counselling and clinical psychology within the context of the services provided by chartered psychologists generally. Fuller descriptions of the nature of the work of clinical and counselling psychologists are given later in this chapter. Taking the list in alphabetical order, after Clinical Psychology Services the Directory outlines the area of Clinical Neuropsychology Services: these are concerned with the changes which can occur following damage to, or disease of, the nerv-ous system. Practitioners are involved in the measurement of changes, such as in personality, intelligence, memory and other aspects of behaviour. Neurological conditions may be therefore more accurately detected, diagnosed and treated. These psychologists play a crucial role in the assessment and management of disorders and in the planning and management of treatment and rehabilitation programmes.

Following next in order is Counselling Psychology. The Directory then lists Educational Psychology Services. Educational psychologists are applied psychologists concerned with children's learning and development, and they work in the school system and in the community. They use a range of psychological and educational assessment techniques and methods to help children and young people who are experiencing difficulties in learning or social adjustment. They are involved in preventative work, and also have a central role in the assessment of children's difficulties from an early stage. They have a statutory role in multi-professional assessment under the 1981 Education Act. They have a role in improving the learning of all children, working mostly with people from birth to 19 years of age, in ordinary and in special schools. Some work with students in further education. Included in their role is liaison with parents, teachers and other professionals, as well as with institutions and organisations to whom they offer consultancy and research, including staff training, systems analysis and evaluation.

Another broad area in which chartered psychologists function is that of Criminological and Legal Services. Psychologists may focus on issues to do with individuals prior to and after sentencing; and, for example, they examine the behaviour of people within the legal system, including offending behaviour and its detection, as well as issues associated with the administration of justice. They are often called upon to be expert witnesses in the judicial process in which they will draw on their wider psychological background. Those with special forensic interests can work in settings such as prisons, special hospitals, secure psychiatric units, probation and social services departments (see the companion volume in this series by Williams (1996)).

Many psychologists are employed in Occupational Psychology Services. Occupational psychologists are concerned with people in relation to work in the widest sense of the word, including paid employment and other constructive and cooperative activities. They are concerned with the way work tasks and conditions of work affect people, and with how people and their personal characteristics determine what and how work is done. They can be involved in selection, training and personal development of employees, to ensure effectiveness and with issues to do with work procedures, organisational structures and equipment design. Additionally their interest includes facilitating participation in the work situation for greater effectiveness and satisfaction.

There are two other broad areas where psychologists offer their services, although (unlike the categories already listed) not as a distinct professional group. One area where psychologists offer a wide range of services is in social services departments (SSDs), in matters involving child care and child health, people with long-term mental illness, and the care of the elderly and those with learning disabilities. Because the clientele is similar, SSDs have traditionally used the services either of clinical psychologists employed by NHS provider units, or of educational psychologists employed by a local education authority. Although SSDs have not traditionally employed psychologists directly, the changing nature of their responsibilities for social work under government legislation, for example in directing many community services away from health to social services control, has led to the need for more interventions of a psychological nature. The second major area where there is not a distinct professional grouping is in education: teaching psychologists are concerned with the psychological aspects of teaching and learning. In order to make both teaching and learning more effective, they examine all aspects of the relevant context such as the social psychology of the classroom, skills relevant for educational achievement, and different teaching methods. They are usually based in higher education institutions rather than in schools, and may be concerned with vocational training or with teaching psychology themselves.

No classification system can accurately cover all the services offered by psychologists where their particular knowledge is of benefit. However, there are other areas of service, which either originate directly in developing areas of applied research such as health psychology and sports psychology, or which are research areas in themselves. Health psychology uses psychological principles to promote changes in people's attitudes, behaviour and thinking about health. Health psychologists are mainly concerned with the relationship between psychological factors and physical health issues, such as health-related behaviours such as smoking and exercise, health promotion issues, and the effect of health care systems on patients' well-being. Applied health psychologists are primarily involved with the implementation and evaluation of treatment interventions, and the development of health care services. They are involved in all aspects of research, and work in a variety of settings including universities, health promotion, medical wards and public health departments. They work either directly with individuals and community projects, or in a consultative role with other health professionals.

Sports psychologists may be involved in scientific research, or in applied work into psychological aspects of sport, exercise, motor skill and human performance. They offer their services to a whole range of activities, including educational and research services to teachers, coaches, and to individual and group participants. Psychologists also work in market, social and consumer research, where they are employed by market and social research agencies, and by manufacturing and service companies, as well as by government departments. Their work includes the provision of advice and consultancy on psychological research, and in attitudes and behaviours of consumers and users of goods and services. In both the public and private sector they are involved with psychometric surveys appropriate to the specific needs of the organisation, and with qualitative research on factors influencing people's response to marketing and promotional activities.

The ninth and final broad area defined by the Directory concerns psychological research. Although all applications of psychology are based in fundamental scientific research and almost all psychologists take part in some aspect of research, there are specific psychologists who offer services of applied research and consultancy as their primary role, usually within their own particular area of expertise. They may offer their services either to private industries or to government departments (for example, a government department or the aircraft industry may commission research into the effects of noise levels on the population in a given locality).

It is interesting to note that in the Directory of Chartered Psychologists, 'counselling' is referred to as one specific area of psychological services, as a specialism within the area of clinical psychology, and as an activity carried out by nearly all the other broad areas of services where chartered psychologists are employed. For example, educational psychologists' main aim is to deal with the problems faced by young people in education and this may involve learning difficulties and social or emotional problems, or the interrelationship of all of these. In, for example, addressing children's emotional needs and providing help and advice in both their academic and emotional needs counselling would form part of their role.

The term 'psychotherapy' is not used to delineate either a broad area of service, or as a specialism within any service in the Directory of Chartered Psychologists. The Directory explains why it does not list this as a separate category: 'psychotherapy represents an area in which Chartered Psychologists who have qualified in a variety of other areas offer a range of psychological and therapeutic services, which are also offered by members of other professions (e.g. psychiatry)' (1994d: 6).

The BPS views psychotherapy as a term covering the treatment of a wide range of mental and physical problems by a number of different methods, each developed in terms of its own theoretical framework. The Society's opinion is that psychotherapy, and also the use of hypnosis with psychotherapy, should be regarded as a post-qualification specialisation for members of one of the primary professional groups, for example, medical practitioners, applied psychologists or social workers. One of the reasons for this is that such professionals, in the Society's view, are more likely to have a sufficient range of professional experience and skills to evaluate when a potential client might be more appropriately helped by other methods.

## THE ROLE AND PURPOSE OF CLINICAL PSYCHOLOGISTS

The context in which the majority of clinical psychologists work is the NHS, whose structure and function to a large extent determine the administrative organisation, form and content of the services that clinical psychologists provide. Clinical psychologists work in various hospital and community settings with people with health problems and with learning difficulties. Clinical psychologists also bring with them to their work context a specific training and background, which in turn influences the nature of the services that they offer to the NHS and other organisations.

In 1992, a committee of the Division of Clinical Psychology (DCP) prepared a statement of their views on the role and purpose of clinical psychologists, both those working within the NHS (where the majority are employed) and those employed in other settings and organisations. The Division stated:

Clinical psychology incorporates a body of knowledge and methodologies that are constantly developing through innovation and research using systematic inquiry to test and evaluate new ideas. In this way new knowledge is firmly grounded in evidence.

Clinical psychologists also apply their knowledge and experience to the creation and management of health care systems. They do this by helping organisations identify and clarify the issues which affect the psychological well-being of people they serve. For example, they may advise Purchasers about identifying the psychological needs of local populations and Providers about how to take account of psychological factors in designing care delivery.

Similarly, at an individual level, the first stage is to clarify the issues that need to be tackled. Whether the health issues and concerns are those of individuals, families or institutions, clinical psychologists use their scientific understanding of behaviour, thoughts, experience and emotions to help people find a way out of their difficulties.

They use their core skills to formulate problems and questions in psychological terms and draw creatively on theories and techniques from the discipline of psychology to support the finding of ways forward. At its best this approach solves the immediate problem, enables the person or organisation to be more competent and self-directed when confronted with a similar problem in the future and also creates new knowledge and methods which can be used by other people facing similar difficulties. A psychologist may put a proposed solution into practice in person, face-to-face with the patient, or through supporting the activities of other people such as the patient's family or the other professionals involved.

(Committee of the Division of Clinical Psychology 1992)

Although psychological techniques and interventions are used by an increasing number of different professions and practitioners within those professions, the Committee of the Division of Clinical Psychology (1992) emphasises that clinical psychologists would be expected to have a greater depth of understanding of psychological problems. As such, part of their role includes providing support and consultancy to other professions. The DCP outlines aspects of the range of work that is encompassed in the work of clinical psychologists, including the following main aspects:

1 Clinical psychologists are expected to undertake more complex clinical duties where the problems require a clinical psychologist's understanding of the psychological processes involved.
2 They are expected to undertake the planning of clinical programmes concerned with psychological aspects in any area of health care concerned with patient care.
3 Clinical psychologists also have an intervention role. This includes the promotion and support of early intervention programmes for patients whose psychological problems have either been presented as physical ill health or whose physical ill health is complicated by or made worse by psychological problems.
4 Clinical psychologists are also involved with offering alternative and complementary treatments to help aid medical recovery. By

increasing treatment effectiveness and efficiency this facilitates providing more services to a greater number of clients.

5 Clinical psychologists have a consultancy role. Part of their role is to provide consultancy, support and advice to other staff concerning psychological aspects of care. The purpose of this is to enhance the work of other staff by enabling them to apply psychological principles in appropriate and relevant ways. Due to the in-depth knowledge of clinical psychologists of psychological principles they offer a consultancy role to staff who also make use of psychological principles and techniques in their work with clients. Clinical psychologists also provide a consultancy role to management.

6 Another major aspect of a clinical psychologist's role is the training and supervision of other staff. The aim is to help and support other staff to develop their psychological knowledge and skills, through direct training and supervision, and also by undertaking joint case work. It is partly due to the scarcity of clinical psychologists that it is necessary to train others in psychological principles and interventions.

7 Clinical psychologists take an active role in the setting, measuring and monitoring of standards in relation to psychological aspects of care.

8 The role of the clinical psychologist also includes developing new systems, procedures and techniques in response to service requirements. This aspect of the clinical psychologist's role is relevant to both the purchasers and providers of health care. For example a clinical psychologist may be requested to develop new methods of need assessment in relation to community care.

The Directory of Chartered Psychologists (1994d) points out that the aspects of the clinical psychologist's role outlined above apply to all clinical psychologists working in a range of health care systems, including the NHS where the majority are still employed. The NHS has had to operate within the wider social and political context of successive Conservative governments, who have applied an economic model based on a market force ideology to health care systems and organisations. All macro-economic models include implicit if not explicit assumptions about human behaviour. These are not based solely on notions of 'economic man' but on the recognition that psychological factors are crucial in determining the predictive validity of economic theories. Economic models not only carry with them psychological assumptions but they also have psychological consequences. The current economic model applied to health care has led to psychological consequences for the workforce to whom it has been applied.

There are similarities and differences in the psychological consequences for different sections and different tiers of the workforce of the NHS, as will be discussed later. The NHS went through a massive reorganisation in the late 1980s and early 1990s, directed by government policies set out in various White Papers, the most relevant aspects of which will be outlined later in this book. The cumulative effect of these changes is that all professionals working in the NHS have faced massive changes in the structure and content of almost every aspect of their professional duties; and in their working relationships both with other professionals as well as with their clients or patients. In this work setting, which has been one of continual instability and uncertainty, it is difficult to predict how the structure and function of roles of different professionals including clinical psychologists in the NHS will eventually be defined. However the new organisation of the Heath Service is characterised by many different features, each of which has its own effect which, once in place, gathers its own momentum as well as interacting with other features in a cumulative fashion. (In economic terminology these would be known as the accelerator and multiplier effects.)

The most relevant of these aspects for mental health include the introduction of the marketplace philosophy with its consequent emphasis on financial limitations; the creation of health care trusts; a non-clinical management structure which is economically based and hierarchically organised; the encouragement and establishment of GP budget holders; emphasis on community care with implications for the definition of health and social care; and emphasis on the separation between the purchasing and providing functions of health care systems. All this has given rise to a culture of continual redefinition as each profession seeks to survive the consequences of the changes, by avoiding constrictions and restrictions to its structure and function and by seeking to create opportunities to develop and expand its professional role.

### Relationship of clinical psychologists to the new systems of health care

In terms of the changing role of clinical psychologists within the new system of health care, they have a role in relation to both the purchaser and provider functions of health care. The Directory of Chartered Psychologists points out that the organisations purchasing health and community care need to consider the psychological needs of their client population generally, and also the psychological aspects of care across a wide range of services. Clinical psychologists can be of use in helping purchasers to identify psychological needs and in clarifying issues which have effects on the psychological well-being of the local population. Such issues will encompass problems and difficulties which occur throughout the life span and will be concerned with prevention, treatment, rehabilitation and continuing care in relation to both psychological and physical health. In their provision of psychological care clinical psychologists work directly with a wide range of individuals throughout the life span, who require different levels of intervention. As we have seen, clinical psychologists also provide support and consultancy to other staff working with this patient group. In addition, clinical psychologists have a role in relation to the organisations involved with providing psychological care. For example, clinical psychologists give health and community care organisations psychological advice on aspects such as service evaluation, quality assurance, and management development programmes. The Directory emphasises that the importance of the setting and maintenance of quality standards with reference to psychological aspects of care applies not just to clinical psychology services directly, but to all aspects of psychological care in health and community service.

Quality assurance is viewed by clinical psychologists not just as eliminating poor practice but as helping to construct services, using psychological principles so that good practice is built in to the system. This involves the process of continuous monitoring and the setting up of feedback systems throughout the organisation which will facilitate the continuous improvement of services to clients. The Directory suggests that clinical psychologists can make a fundamental contribution to identifying and understanding the requirements of service users. They view this as a core requirement in creating a high quality service. The role of the clinical psychologist working at the task of quality assurance ranges from the individual to the organisational system as a whole. For example, in working at an individual level with patients and staff, psychologists can aim to improve communications between them. An example of clinical psychologists' work in quality assurance is their involvement in service evaluation. Here they draw on their research background in setting up the methodological designs, to ensure valid and reliable findings. This entails a knowledge of research methodology, for example, in selecting appropriate measurement instruments, by either using established measures or devising new measures such as survey methods, questionnaires, patient satisfaction rating scales, and attitude scales. Due to their training in research methodology, clinical psychologists would know how to design the project in order for it to meet adequate scientific standards, and how to analyse the findings statistically. Clinical psychologists have often been the main project organisers in areas such as rehabilitation and the care of people with long-term service needs. For example, under the policy of closure of the large mental hospitals in recent years, and the emphasis on moving patients on the long-stay wards back to community settings, clinical psychologists were often given the task of setting up and carrying out projects to assess the needs, and level of coping and self-care, of patients while still in the hospitals, in order that they should be moved to settings in the community which best met their needs according to the resources of the health authority or NHS trust involved. This often entailed selecting and designing appropriate assessment measurements to be given directly to patients, or used for assessment of them by the direct care staff involved. Many standardised rating scales such as the Rehab Rating Scale (Hall and Baker 1983) were designed and developed by clinical psychologists in order to meet such organisational and patient needs. Such projects involved monitoring and measuring quantitative and qualitative aspects of patients' lives as well as the measurement of change as patients began their new life in the community. To carry out such projects entails a knowledge of research methodology in both its quantitative and qualitative aspects, as well as the appropriateness of the research design to the hospital and community setting and to the sample group – in this case patients, hospital staff, social service, voluntary groups, housing project groups and other carers. Another area where clinical psychologists have become increasingly involved is the user movement in psychiatry, where they help to facilitate the growing demand of patients themselves to have more rights in their health care. This may be seen, for example, in the work of authors like Turner and Newnes (1993), Trinder *et al.* (1994) and Williams *et al.* (1994), who consider in-patient views of the services they receive as a crucial component in an accurate evaluation of services. Clinical psychologists have been involved in developing means of assessing what patients' past, present and preferred treatment would be as opposed to treatment imposed upon them. A frequent finding of such projects is that patients, especially those with long-term mental health problems, have experienced no or very little counselling, their treatment often being almost exclusively physical and pharmaceutical. However, the patients themselves express a wish for counselling as part of their treatment. In such ways clinical psychologists work to improve the quality of services, delineate patients' needs and facilitate the means to meet those needs, for example by trying to provide the services themselves, or by trying to convince the provider units to facilitate the setting up of appropriate services.

Clinical psychologists can also work with relevant staff and service users in order to facilitate the setting up of processes whereby service users can influence the nature of the services they receive. In this way, clinical psychologists can contribute to the delivery of services, using psychological principles that will facilitate the meeting of service users' needs in all aspects of health care. For a high quality service it is important to carry out this role in relation to service users while simultaneously recognising the needs of the staff. Therefore it is important that systems are designed and developed, for example, to enable staff to use their own initiatives and resources in the systems within which they work so that they are participants in the process involved in forming and improving the services.

In the perhaps idealised vision of health care outlined by the Directory of Chartered Psychologists, both staff and patient needs are valued and acknowledged, so that the psychological needs of both staff and patients are balanced and taken into consideration at all stages of service delivery. The Directory views clinical psychologists as being well placed to facilitate this process: 'They are able to blend a knowledge and experience of treatment theory and practice and a broader understanding of the way organisations work and change. This is done within a framework constructed from the psychological principles underpinning people's behaviour' (Committee of the Division of Clinical Psychology 1992: 35). However, as I point out in a later chapter, the attitudes of recent government administrations to professionals generally, and to organised work groups in particular, has in many ways been reflected in the attitude of the health care systems to their staff. This is at variance with the avowed aim of quality assurance, where there should be better communication between different tiers of the organisation, ensuring that staff feel that their views are being heard and where there should be facilitative systems that encourage the ability and effectiveness of staff in shaping the form and content of the services with which they work. Clinical psychologists are participants within this process and as such are inextricably involved in the system. As will be discussed later this raises interesting questions for their subjective experience in the desired role of objective scientist engaged in objective observation, and for the processes involved with scientific enquiry.

For clinical psychologists to fulfill their role in promoting quality assurance in health care systems that the Directory of Chartered Psychologists outlines, clinical psychologists need to ensure that the elements that facilitate the establishment and maintenance of a quality service are in place. For example, they have to ensure that there is an appropriate supply of suitably trained staff, that psychological needs are fully addressed in assessment by the health authorities or NHS trusts of health care needs, and that appropriate systems are in place for effective service delivery. The Directory recommends that clinical psychologists should assist those responsible for planning, purchasing and providing health and community care, to ensure that the full range of needs is met.

### Staffing requirements of a clinical psychology service

In order for clinical psychologists to address the needs specified above, the Directory outlines a summary of required services. It bases this on the 1989–90 data for England presented by the National Professional Manpower Initiative (or NPAS). In collating this data the NPAS listed the specialities outlined below in order, to reflect as far as possible the staffing situation of clinical psychologists at the time:

1 Adult mental health acute services, including a range of psychotherapy services
2 Adult mental health rehabilitation and resettlement services
3 Child health care (including paediatric and child and family mental health services)
4 Services for people with learning difficulties
5 Care of elderly people (including geriatric and psychogeriatric services)
6 Primary care services
7 Management (including advising purchasers and consultancy on health care systems)
8 General hospital acute services (including acute medical and surgical specialities)
9 Neuropsychology (including neurological and neurosurgical services and neuropsychological rehabilitation)
10 Services concerned with substance abuse (including those for people with alcohol and drugs problems)
11 Forensic services
12 Services for people with physical and sensory disabilities (including young disabled people and those described as 'the chronic sick')
13 HIV/AIDS services.

The Directory of Chartered Psychologists (1994d) elaborates upon these specialist services, describing them as follows:

1 Adult mental health – general. Clinical psychologists working in this speciality provide services to clients and to staff working with adult clients across a broad spectrum. Within any particular locality, the exact boundary of this speciality will be defined by the availability of other specialities. Within any clinical psychology department or other health care unit, there generally tend to be more clinical psychologists working in this speciality, which tends to be broadly defined. Staff working in any particular health care system will find themselves covering a wide range of activities, according to the appointment of clinical psychologists covering other specialist services. This speciality includes a range of psychological therapy services. Typical presenting difficulties of patients include anxiety, depression, phobias, obsessive-compulsive disorders, disorders of habit (such as eating disorders and alcohol and substance abuse), as well as marital, sexual and other relationship problems. Clinical psychologists working in the adult mental health speciality may also deal with more complex and longstanding difficulties, and with the psychological elements associated with what are defined as the psychoses. This speciality, the Directory points out, may be designed as primary care service and/or as a secondary referral service.

2 The second specialist service refers to adult mental health rehabilitation and resettlement services. The main concerns of this speciality are difficulties classified as severe or chronic mental illness and the psychological and social consequences of these. Psychological assistance is offered directly to patients, and support is provided for both clients and their carers. In this specialism clinical psychologists also work with staff in helping them to formulate and carry out care treatment plans. Psychologists are involved with staff training, in direct teaching, supervision and advice; and indirectly, by joint work with other staff. Increasingly with the policy of closure of the large mental hospitals and the emphasis on community care, psychologists working in this speciality have a consultative and staff training role, as well as being directly involved with formulation, design and implementation of plans with reference to the resettlement of patients from mental hospitals and the development of community services.

3 A third specialist service is that of child health care. This service includes paediatric as well as child and family mental health services. Clinical psychologists working in this speciality offer

specialist consultation, assessment, management and treatment for individuals, families and groups. They also provide training for professional staff and organisations responsible for the care and welfare of young people. This is an increasing aspect of their role, necessitated by the consequences of government directives and by health care and social service policies regarding the recommended procedure for child protection. Due to the generic nature of their clinical training, clinical psychologists have training with adult clients as well as with children, and therefore are in a position to meet a wide range of needs. Psychological intervention can be instigated at a number of different levels, ranging from individual behaviour management of a child, or marital therapy with the parents, to giving advice to social services. In this speciality, clinical psychologists work in a range of settings including health, social services, education and the voluntary sector.

4 Services for people with learning difficulties constitute another specialist service. In this speciality, clinical psychologists can help both clients and carers by identifying the strengths and needs of clients and their situation and formulate individual programme plans. Their role includes the planning, implementation and evaluation of training programmes in order to facilitate the development of skills and to reduce behaviour problems. As well as alleviating individual difficulties, clinical psychologists in this speciality are involved with issues revolving around the resettlement of people with learning difficulties from hospital, and with the development of community services. These services are increasingly important, because of the closure of the large hospitals where many people with learning difficulties have been residing. Clinical psychologists also offer support to carers, including families and staff in various settings associated with helping those with learning difficulties, including the NHS, social services and voluntary agencies. Additionally, they are involved with staff training and consultancy work.

5 Clinical psychologists also work in a speciality involving the care of older adults. This speciality also includes geriatric and psychogeriatric services. One of the major roles of clinical psychologists working in this speciality is the assessment and management of changes in a person's psychological functioning. Such changes may arise from memory problems, confusion or dementia. They will also be involved with psychological aspects of care associated with physical disabilities and illnesses related to aging, such as strokes. Problems consequent upon losses of all kinds are

frequently a focus for psychologists working with older clients. As well as providing support for families and other carers, clinical psychologists are involved in staff training and assisting staff with the psychological care of patients as well as carrying out other consultancy work.

6  Management and planning is another service offered by clinical psychologists. This includes advising purchasers and providing consultancy on health care systems generally. Clinical psychologists can make useful contributions to all aspects of service planning in which psychological processes are a feature. For example, they can be involved in devising community care programmes for different client groups; setting up, putting into practice and evaluating the effects of the transfer of resources; researching and reporting on the most appropriate forms of need assessment and audit; and devising effective and efficient business plans.

7  The speciality of health psychology covers general hospital acute services which includes acute medical and surgical specialities. Clinical psychologists in this context are concerned with psychological reactions to physical illnesses. They also work in developing improvements to medical and surgical procedures, which involves taking into consideration psychological factors. For example, they may facilitate better care by encouraging the provision of or providing increased levels of information to patients, or by providing counselling and reassurance to patients, relatives and other carers, or by improving treatment compliance through psychological means. Working with the psychological aspects of terminal care falls within this speciality, including work directly with patients and with relatives and carers.

8  Although neuropsychology has traditionally been part of a clinical psychology department (and the majority of clinical psychologists working in the area of neuropsychology are still linked to such departments), the Directory of Chartered Psychologists lists neuropsychology as a separate area of service. This area of work is concerned with the changes that occur following damage to or disease of the nervous system. Clinical psychologists play a central role in the assessment, managing and monitoring of consequent changes.

9  The speciality concerned with addictive behaviours involves clinical psychologists working in services concerned with substance abuse including services for people with alcohol and drugs problems. As well as providing a range of therapies to clients, they also work with families, carers and other relevant organisations. Work may involve formulating, implementing and evaluating

programmes to reduce, manage or eliminate substance abuse and programmes for rehabilitation. They may also be involved in educational and other preventative work, involving a variety of services in the statutory and voluntary sectors.

10 Forensic services is another speciality offered by clinical psychologists. Although forensic psychology is listed in the Directory under a separate field of criminological and legal services, forensic psychologists have nevertheless traditionally been clinical psychologists and form part of clinical psychology departments. Their work covers the assessment of offenders, and the management of them prior to and following sentencing. They also work on a whole range of policy issues including Home Office affairs, legislation, and issues involving Mental Health Act policies. They are often involved with socio-legal work including working with solicitors in preparing court reports, and in working with the police in a variety of ways such as criminal personality profiling.

11 Clinical psychologists work in the specialism defined as services for people with sensory and physical difficulties. This covers services for young disabled people and those described as the chronic sick. Clinical psychologists in this speciality will be involved in the assessment of sensory and physical disabilities and the psychological implications of these. They plan, implement and evaluate training and rehabilitation programmes with families, carers and other staff. In addition to providing a consultancy service to staff they are involved in providing counselling support to individuals and their carers.

12 HIV/AIDS is another specialism of clinical psychology although psychologists working in this area sometimes work under the specialism of health psychology, or sometimes in drugs and substance abuse services. Psychologists working in this field are engaged in the psychological aspects of terminal care, working with the affected individuals as well as with their families and carers. They offer support, and guidance, and are involved with planning and managing the rehabilitation of clients. In addition, psychologists are involved with health promotion including the giving of advice regarding risk behaviours.

The Directory of Chartered Psychologists delineates two further broad areas of teaching and research in which clinical psychologists specialise:

13 With regards to teaching the Directory states: 'One of the major strengths of the science of psychology is that there are a large

number of theoretical frameworks which can be brought to bear on a range of problems or situations. Clinical psychologists are uniquely equipped to teach psychological principles and practices' (1994d: 9). The Directory refers to carers, members of other caring professions, and staff working with any of the client groups with whom clinical psychologists are involved.

14 In terms of research, all clinical psychologists have training in psychological research. This includes the processes involved in the design of studies, the execution of the study, data analysis and report writing, all of which their training in research methodology and statistical procedures has equipped them to carry out. The range of research topics varies widely, over, for example, individual process and outcome evaluation of treatment; exploring and developing new forms of psychological intervention and therapeutic procedures; treatment research; studies on the effects of interventions on different client groups; large-scale longitudinal studies; research into the effects of institutionalisation; and research based on measuring attitudes in various defined population groups, from individual clients to organisational and community groups. The Directory points out that although all this research is based on theoretical knowledge, typically most research that is carried out by clinical psychologists is of an applied nature, with directly applicable implications for the treatment and management of psychological problems.

## THE ROLE AND PURPOSE OF COUNSELLING PSYCHOLOGISTS

In terms of the current development of the psychological services in Britain, the Register of Chartered Psychologists numbered a total of 8,062 in December 1995. A breakdown of statistics in terms of the membership of the professional divisions of the BPS indicates that at that date membership of different divisions was as follows: Division of Educational and Child Psychology 1,102; Scottish Division of Educational and Child Psychology 140; Division of Occupational Psychology 956; Division of Criminological and Legal Psychology 1,154; Division of Clinical Psychology 2,988; Division of Counselling Psychology 1,154. It is important to stress that counselling takes place professionally in all these psychological services. The issues generally concerned with the development and practice of counselling in psychological services apply to all these divisions of the BPS, although this book focuses primarily on two divisions, Clinical

Psychology and Counselling Psychology. It is also important to note that the nine Sections (for example, the Psychotherapy Section and the Psychology of Women Section) and the three Special Groups of the BPS (Clinical Neuropsychology, Health Psychology and Psychologists in Social Services) also have an interest in varying degrees in both the theory and practice of counselling. In terms of the development of both clinical and counselling psychology, the expansion of the two professions has taken place rapidly in recent years. From a membership of just 362 in 1970, the DCP has grown in membership to 2,988 in 1995. In 1982 the Counselling Psychology Section, which merged with the Special Group in Counselling Psychology formed in 1989, numbered 225. This Special Group later became the Division of Counselling Psychology in 1994 and by 1995 had a membership of 1,154.

The general goal of counselling psychologists is to help individuals, couples, families and groups by applying psychological theories, research and techniques to improve their well-being and deal with the inevitable difficulties of life.

The Directory of Chartered Psychologists (1994d) specifies Counselling Psychology Services as one of the nine broad areas in which chartered psychologists offer services. The Directory defines counselling psychologists as follows:

> Counselling psychologists work with individuals and groups helping them to improve their sense of well-being, alleviate their distress, resolve their crises and increase their ability to solve problems and make decisions. Counselling psychologists are concerned to help people to cope more effectively with normal life cycle developmental issues, such as relationship breakdown, career change, redundancy, loss and bereavement, and illness.
>
> Counselling psychologists apply systematic research-based approaches to help themselves and others to understand problems and to develop potential solutions to them. Counselling psychologists use a range of approaches and skills including humanistic, psycho-dynamic and cognitive-behavioural, and may also employ skills of assessment and testing.
>
> Counselling psychologists work in a range of settings including Health Centres, GP Practices, industry and commerce, student counselling services and private practice.
>
> (1994d: 3–4)

The Directory elaborates on eight main service areas applicable to counselling services. The first four refer to specific client groups. First, work with adults, where counselling psychologists offer a combination of counselling and formal research-based knowledge. Their work is focused on alleviating the psychological distress associated with life transitions, and experiences such as parenting, relationship breakdown and mid-life changes. In individual sessions, 'clients are encouraged to confront and clarify the realities of their lives, including the painful aspects, and to express feelings and concerns, so as to move towards living more resourcefully' (1994d: 11). The second client group is that of students and young people, whose concerns and difficulties are assisted by counselling and career evaluation, psychometric assessment and educational guidance. Regarding services to the third group, families and couples, counselling psychologists offer to those meeting difficulties an understanding of the dynamics involved in human relationships and family systems. To this end they recommend alternative strategies of communication and human interaction. Work with the elderly, the fourth client group, includes issues to do with retirement, bereavement, chronic illness, and loss. Here they emphasise increased self-empowerment and the creative use of available resources for their clients.

A fifth service provided concerns health and medical work. Through their employment in GP surgeries, where they work alongside other NHS colleagues or in their work in specialist agencies, counselling psychologists aim to assist those suffering from life-threatening diseases such as cancer and AIDS, or other disabling conditions. They also counsel those undergoing various kinds of medical intervention. Group work is the sixth service, and is provided to meet needs in situations where life issues and needs may be more effectively explored in a group setting. Organisational or workplace counselling, the seventh, focuses on such issues as redundancy, management, job satisfaction, organisational stress and creativity. The eighth service area provided by counselling psychologists is that dealing with community and social issues. This includes services to people challenged with aspects of social diversity, such as ethnicity, gender, disability and sexual orientation. Clients in this group are supported and encouraged by counselling psychologists to explore self-empowerment, as well as community relations, through both individual and group experience.

## OVERLAPPING OF PROFESSIONAL COUNSELLING ROLES

Although an attempt has been made to define terms and roles relating to theories and practice of professions involved in providing psychological services, this chapter has shown that it is not just in the terminology referring to psychologically based helping professions that distinctions are blurred, but in the overlapping of roles within the professions themselves. This is particularly true when trying to define matters to do with counselling. Earlier on in this chapter definitions of the academic discipline and professional roles of counselling psychologists and clinical psychologist were outlined. Even though there is an inevitable overlap, due to their common background and similarity of function, nevertheless distinctions and differences may be seen between the two professions. Clinical psychologists have to be prepared to offer a generic service, covering a wide range of specialisms – for example, work with those with long-term mental health problems, neuropsychological services, primary care and work with the elderly. This means that in their training as clinical psychologists they would be expected to learn both theoretical knowledge and practical experience under supervision in order that they should be .equipped for their later role. This does not mean that when qualified and employed as a clinical psychologist, each psychologist is an expert in all these specialisms. It is usually after qualification that further specialisation takes place. However, the interests and range of experience of clinical psychologists in a particular service must reflect these very varied specialisms.

It could be argued that it is not required that counselling psychologists should encompass such a wide generic training. This is partly due to differences in the settings in which clinical and counselling psychologists work. As I have already mentioned the great majority of clinical psychologists are concentrated in the NHS, where a generic service is essential, whereas counselling psychologists are employed in more dispersed settings, such as private practice and student counselling where they can focus on a particular client group.

Further, within the role of clinical psychology the psychologist would be expected to undertake a far wider range of functions than in counselling psychology. For example, work in primary care would entail such tasks as psychological assessment, the ability to offer a range of therapies, psychometric testing, research and project work as well as counselling. Counselling would be one of a great variety of tasks undertaken by a clinical psychologist in any given specialism. Counselling may be chosen as the treatment of choice by a clinical psychologist for a particular client or task, or it may be used in relation to other aspects of clinical psychology such as an adjunct to the main task in psychometric testing. Indeed on some more psychotherapeutically oriented training courses in clinical psychology, such as those at the Tavistock Clinic, the whole psychometric testing situation was viewed not as an arid, objective scientific task but rather as a therapeutic exercise in which one could explore, for example, how, in a person's responses to the clinician and to the task in hand, emotional factors were interfering with performance. Even in the most practical psychometric testing situations, counselling is frequently used as a means of establishing rapport and a working alliance with a client to set him or her at their ease before performing the tasks, and also for debriefing after completion. Being required to undergo psychometric testing can be experienced as a very upsetting situation, for example in neuropsychological assessments, or in assessments for dementia with the elderly where the person may become acutely aware during assessment that they have lost some of their previous capabilities. In these situations counselling is frequently used with the client as part of the assessment process.

Counselling psychologists focus on counselling. This means that in their training they would be expected to have a greater depth of knowledge about the theory and practice of counselling than their contemporaries in clinical psychology. Of special importance, as we shall see in the next chapter, is that they are more in line with other professions who undertake psychotherapy and counselling in the requirement for counselling psychologists to undertake their own personal counselling during training. Another difference between counselling and clinical psychologists is not just the greater range of people with psychological difficulties with whom the clinical psychologist would be expected to work, but also the severity of the problems. Clinical psychologists, especially since the closure of psychiatric hospitals, would be expected to see people with moderate to severe psychological difficulties, where counselling may or may not be appropriate.

Another factor which can lead to a blurring of distinctions between counselling and clinical psychologists is that some clinical psychologists undertake post-qualification training in order to specialise in psychotherapeutic work with clients. Training can vary from relatively short courses for clinical psychologists desiring further knowledge in order to facilitate their practice, to extensive training which indeed fits the accreditation requirements of counselling psychologists. It is interesting to note that many such clinical psychologists were accepted under the 'grandfather' clause of eligibility for the BPS chartered counselling psychology accreditation, which ended in January 1997. The reason for this clause was to enable those with sufficient knowledge and experience in the field to qualify for membership for accreditation as a chartered counselling psychologist by the BPS. Even if such a clause did exist for accreditation as a chartered clinical psychologist, the range and experience of counselling psychologists would not make counselling psychologists eligible for membership.

Earlier on in this chapter, I outlined the roles of the different psychology professions in the BPS. Each one of these would use counselling in varying degrees in the course of their work. Take, for example, educational psychologists and occupational psychologists. Counselling psychologists are also employed in educational and occupational settings but their role would not encompass the range of activities undertaken by these other professional psychologists.

An additional reason for the blurring of roles regarding counselling is that counsellors are increasingly being employed within or managed by clinical psychology departments. These counsellors are not usually counselling psychologists but come from a wide variety of backgrounds, with a highly variable range of expertise and knowledge regarding counselling. However, with the increasing demand for clinical psychologists in other aspects of their role – notably working with people with longer-term and more severe psychological difficulties – more people with less severe problems in living are being offered a counselling service through the use of counsellors in community settings under the supervision or management of clinical psychologists. The next chapter will examine the actual practice of counselling in the psychological services, but before we can adequately describe the current situation it will first be necessary to outline the main historical and philosophical issues which underpin and have led to the development of the current theory and practice of counselling and clinical psychology.

·  THREE  ·

# The practice of counselling in psychological services

Counselling within the psychological services has developed within a context, and that context is inextricably linked in Britain with the formation and development of clinical psychology. We saw in Chapter One that clinical psychology itself developed within a context which was the formation and development of the NHS. Clinical psychology was from the inception of the NHS the main provider of psychological services and clinical psychologists remain the majority of psychologists employed within the NHS. One consequence of the reorganisation of the NHS along free market economy lines, as we shall see later, has been the greater flexibility in employing people other than those belonging to the traditional professions of the NHS. This, together with the shortage of clinical psychologists compared with demand for psychological services, has led to the increasing employment of people other than clinical psychologists to provide psychological services in the new NHS trusts. Some of these include BPS-recognised psychologists who have undertaken post-graduate training on various psychotherapy and counselling courses and are often employed, for example, as adult or child psychotherapists or counsellors either within clinical psychology services or within other services of the NHS such as psychotherapy services. Health psychologists are also making a contribution to health care. Others include members of Divisions of the BPS such as occupational psychologists, or the more recently formed Division of Counselling Psychology. However, these still make up a very small number of psychologists in total compared to the overwhelming majority who are clinical psychologists providing psychological services in the NHS. Another group of people who are increasingly employed as counsellors in the NHS are those who do not have recognised psychology backgrounds but have usually taken a course in counselling. These courses are diverse, varying enormously in quality and duration, as do the qualifications and experience of the practitioners. Yet another group of people who practise counselling in the NHS are those from various professions such as psychiatric nursing whose training and experience in counselling again vary greatly. There is also a trend in some trusts, as part of cost-cutting exercises, to employ people with no particular professional background and no formal training in or experience of counselling to undertake 'counselling' in what Prior (personal communication 1994) terms the new 'mum's army' in the NHS. The relationship of clinical psychologists to various practitioners offering counselling in the NHS will be explored in Chapter Five.

Understanding the development and role of counselling within psychology services entails looking at some of the main issues which influenced the development of mainstream academic psychology, from which present-day psychology-related services such as counselling psychology and clinical psychology are derived. The discipline of psychology emphasises its scientific basis. However, the traditional concept of science as it has been applied to the study of people and their concerns itself poses problems for the psychology-related professions. The accepted definitions of science influenced the formation and development of clinical psychology, and shaped its present-day content and practice. This may be seen in the scientist–practitioner model as the predominant model in the early years of clinical psychology training. Counselling psychology is a relatively new profession and has developed within a different historical and political context from clinical psychology. Nevertheless, as it also claims a basis in academic psychology some of the issues of mainstream academic psychology also influence the theory and practice of counselling psychology. In many ways the development of counselling psychology mirrors the status and development of the verbal therapies within clinical psychology. The emphasis in academic psychology on its scientific basis, emphasising objectivity in its definition of reality, has implications for both the theory and practice of clinical and counselling psychology, as is seen in the issues of reflexivity, subjectivity and personal training.

## THE SCIENTIST–PRACTITIONER MODEL IN
## CLINICAL PSYCHOLOGY

From its formation and in its development as a profession, the scientist–practitioner model has been a central concern in clinical psychology's definition of itself. This model emphasises the principle that practitioners should draw upon or contribute to research in the course of their clinical work. This was true both in the earlier formation of clinical psychology as a profession in the USA and in its later development, heavily influenced by the views of Hans Eysenck, in the UK. The origin of the scientist–researcher professional model for clinical psychology has its roots in the USA in 1949 in an American Psychological Association (APA) conference at Boulder, Colorado. The main conclusions of this conference, as reports such as that of Raimy (1950) point out, were crucial in developing the structure and content of clinical psychology in the USA. These conclusions emphasised an academic training, which included both psychotherapy and scientific research as core elements in that training for clinical psychology. They also highlighted professional issues such as licensing and certification. Although the US model differed from the view of Eysenck, in that psychotherapy was included as a core element of clinical psychology in the USA, the research and scientist emphasis was still to shape the structure and content of clinical psychology development in the UK.

The scientist–practitioner model remained the ideal-type model of clinical psychology throughout its development. Sturmey (1991) outlined the main reasons why clinical psychologists are encouraged to carry out research, particularly applied research, stating:

> It is good for the profession: we will be seen as an objective group of applied scientists who have a unique set of skills relevant to the new evaluative health service. It is good for the psychologists: they will gain valuable feedback concerning their work and services. It is good for the clients: they will receive services which are more carefully evaluated and empirically developed.
>
> (1991: 18)

### Difficulties in the practice of the scientist–practitioner model

There has been much discussion as to whether even after 40 years of being the dominant model of professional practice in clinical psychology, the model remains more of an ideal than a reality in the daily practice of the majority of clinical psychologists. In the USA, Barlow (1981) points to the discrepancy between the ideal held by clinical psychologists and their practice, pointing to findings that behaviourally oriented clinicians do not integrate research into their work any more than their non-behavioural colleagues; this is interesting, as the research basis of behaviour therapy is particularly cited by its adherents. Further, in an article titled 'The scientist–practitioner in practice', Milne *et al.* (1990) point out that surveys of clinical psychologists typically conclude that although most subscribe to the model, only a few actually accomplish it (e.g. Martin 1987). Results of surveys carried out on the publications of clinical psychologists point out that the modal frequency of publications is zero (e.g. Martin 1987; Barrom *et al.* 1988). Surveying the productivity of clinical psychologists in terms of published papers, O'Sullivan and Dryden (1990) found that 4.4 per cent did not spend any time on research activities, 49.9 per cent had no publications and 23.5 per cent had published three or more papers. Other studies indicate that clinicians are generally dissatisfied with what they perceive to be largely irrelevant research literature (Barlow *et al.* 1984; Allen 1985), which Milne *et al.* suggest may reflect a negative attitude to research by clinicians. Studies also point to the difficulties experienced by clinicians attempting to engage in the process or actually carrying out research work. For example, research is ranked lower than service commitments, which are felt to be more pressing (Allen 1985). A survey by O'Sullivan and Dryden (1990) on the time spent by clinical psychologists on various activities revealed that therapy took up 40 per cent, assessment 6.9 per cent and research 5.8 per cent of their time in a working week. As research tends to be an inconspicuous activity and its results often not directly applicable to the immediate clinical situation, the clinician engaging in research receives little support or encouragement from either colleagues or managers (Watts 1984) as well as being frequently frustrated by organisational constraints (Salkovskis 1984). Milne *et al.* (1990) summarise that there have been difficulties in the production, consumption and utilisation of research by clinicians. The reasons given for these difficulties range from particular characteristics of psychologists, such as the extent of their particular research training, to environmental factors, such as the amount of work time allowed for research (see, for example, Head and Harmon 1990).

However, to conclude that the scientist–practitioner role is not relevant to the majority of clinical psychologists would be incorrect. There have been many studies exploring the wider context of research which point to the continued adherence of clinical psychologists to the research model. Milne *et al.* (1990) point out that conclusions that research is largely irrelevant to the practice of clinical psychologists may be misleading and may rather reflect the narrow definitions of research used in most of the studies. For example, many of the surveys on the research work of practitioners select as evaluation criteria variables such as the publication of scientific papers. When research is more broadly defined to include research processes involved, for example, in the preparation of accounts of service evaluation for local service use, and publishing in non-refereed journals, studies are more encouraging in their findings regarding the research activities of practitioners (Martin 1987; Barron *et al.* 1988; Milne *et al.* 1990). Milne *et al.*'s survey, based on the self-reports of clinical psychologists and using a wider definition of research processes and activities, found that as a group the sample supported and adhered to the scientist–practitioner model of professional practice. In terms of the production of research this survey found that 55 per cent had presented research findings at meetings and 41 per cent had published in academic journals. Regarding the consumption of research, 20 per cent reported reading an academic article weekly, 45 per cent monthly and 25 per cent quarterly. In response to questions on how much research influenced their practice, as a measure of research utilisation, the result of Milne *et al.*'s survey revealed that 16 per cent of clinical psychologists replied 'a lot', 14 per cent 'moderately', 34 per cent 'to some extent' and 9 per cent 'a little' or 'not at all'. Commenting on their findings that showed that clinical psychologists produced, consumed and used research to a greater extent than suggested by previous surveys, Milne *et al.* state that 'the scientist–practitioner may after all be an appropriate model of good and realistic practice, particularly given a more flexible and work-centred definition of research' (1990: 30). They suggest that rather than reach erroneous conclusions about the status of research training and practice of clinical psychology, better descriptions and analyses of the implementation of the scientist–practitioner model in clinical practice are needed.

Sturmey (1991), recognising the discrepancy between the verbal endorsement of research and the undertaking and publishing of research by clinical psychologists, suggests that more appropriate paradigms for research in clinical practice should be used. He points out difficulties in attempting to carry out traditional research work in practice due, for example, to such issues as the increasing emphasis on the idea that research should not just be on applied topics but should be on clinical services, and the difficult and time-consuming nature of traditional group designs. Sturmey outlines a variety of strategies which may broaden the options open to clinicians carrying out research. These include, first, individual case studies which, although demanding a good working knowledge of the relevant research literature, nevertheless are not time-consuming and can put to advantage the clinician's experience of a wide range of varied referrals who rarely fit into precise diagnostic categories; and second, assessment which as well as including the more traditional psycho-metric research could also include such examples of the scientist–practitioner model as the individually tailored assessment procedure, or the adaptation of materials or procedures to an individual case. A third area of research concerns case studies. As the clinician has ready access to a series of consecutively referred subjects this allows the evaluation of interventions in an applied context. Also, this data, if systematically collected, can be used over time for further research. Fourth, Sturmey notes that group design can remain a useful paradigm for applied research and one which lends itself well to the clinical practice of clinical psychology. A further area Sturmey points out as being a good example of applied research is that of service evaluation.

### Current applications of the scientist–practitioner model

It is interesting to note that after a decade or so in which the majority of clinical psychologists readily adapted to what they per-ceived to be the service needs of the NHS, and perhaps their own clinical preference by focusing on developing their role as proving psy-chological therapies to meet service needs of ever-growing waiting lists, recent changes in the organisation of the NHS have resulted in a refocusing of the role of research in the practice of clinical psychology. The area in which clinical psychologists are currently encouraged to use their research skills is that of service evaluation, which, as Sturmey notes, is a good example of applied research. The NHS has always been cost-conscious. However, the emphasis on more bureaucratic bookkeeping in NHS trusts, emphasising eco-nomic skills and cost-consciousness, encourages all groups to evalu-ate their services. Further, such service evaluation-oriented research can be used, for example, to develop better client participation and more sensitive staff practices.

In a paper summarising the findings of a workshop on the applica-tion of applied psychological research to service evaluation within the NHS, Turpin (1994) notes that a sea-change has occurred in the nature of applied research, and that the growing demand for evalu-ative research might require the profession to reappraise its general approach to research. He outlines some of the influences that have brought about a change of focus, from the more traditional forms of applied research to service evaluation. These include NHS reforms which have targeted accountability, effectiveness and evaluation.

The practice of counselling in psychological services 67

There has also been a growth of service evaluation projects, commissioned both nationally and locally to respond to the requirements of the new 'Evaluative NHS'. Another influence is national research policy which emphasises greater service applicability and research questions consistent with policy developments, and greater accountability and 'value for money' as opposed to 'curiosity-led' or basic research within the NHS. Further, Turpin notes the influence of a greater diversity of research methods used by clinical psychologists; quantitative vs. qualitative, basic vs. applied, action vs. evaluative research, etc.

In Turpin's paper it is interesting to note that most of the contributors to the workshop frame their suggestions within the market force terminology. Glenys Parry outlines the range of processes by which NHS evaluations are commissioned which include 'NHS Trusts; services and "product development", quality improvements, response to complaint, feedback to management' (p. 16). Although Pauline Slade considers the ethical implications of service evaluation projects, for example the ability of staff to refuse to participate, and the possibility that the values of the psychologist may differ from those of the organisation, the rest of the contributors of the workshop focus on the practicalities and skills required by psychologists in service evaluation. For example, Tony Lavender outlines key ingredients for a psychologist to be able to carry out service evaluation. These include organisational and political knowledge and skills; knowledge of sources and ability to secure additional funds; as well as having proved to be of value to the service, both clinically and organisationally, in order to gain credibility to begin service evaluation. David Shapiro presents four issues concerning what evaluators need to do to maximise their impact on service design and provision. First, he states: 'Organisational change theory suggests that it is vital to design projects whose content, context and process are consistent with one another and congruent with those of the services upon which impact is sought . . . This provides the basis for the necessary "selling" of evaluation as integral to service provision' (in Turpin 1994: 18). Second: 'To ensure generalisability to service settings, an exploratory, naturalistic approach should predominate over the confirmatory approach emphasised in research training' (p. 18). Third: 'It is essential to develop links with a broad range of relevant political and policy-making processes'; 'Evaluators should publish their work in varied outlets to reach academic, practitioner and policy-oriented readerships' (p. 18).

Turpin reports that at the end of this workshop the contributors produced a series of handy hints which included the need to be proactive, to keep an appropriate focus, to identify the audience or 'all the relevant stakeholders within the organisation', as well as considering ethical implications and the viability of the project. In addition to needing to remember their clinical skills and developing their own research knowledge and skills, evaluators are encouraged to foster a team approach as applied service-oriented research is an organisational intervention. Turpin quotes Georgiades and Phillimore (1975) in describing that the lone innovator/researcher 'can get eaten for breakfast', to which he adds 'or lunch for that matter' (Turpin 1994: 19). So much for reflexivity and the quest for knowledge and truth for their own sake.

This situation is made even more difficult given the current occupational pressures within the NHS, mitigating in various ways against a culture which fosters research. For example, with the pressure for more direct client involvement and the issues of accountability of time, the justification for research has direct service relevance. But the NHS as it has now evolved does not currently provide a structure or culture which encourages research processes. This is particularly true of research which may not have a direct relevance.

A disturbing trend is the financing of research from commercial sources, which, if it is to follow the pattern of medical research funded by pharmaceutical companies, will result in a distortion of the process of research from the selection of topics to the interpretation of findings. This is not to say that commercially funded research is deliberately distorted, but rather the whole scientific process is compromised, albeit often unwittingly, at many different levels. The result will certainly look 'professional' and 'scientific' in streamlined presentations, but will frequently be worthless in content and lead to erroneous or even dangerous interpretation (see, for example, Marshall's critique (1996) of the findings of a WHO mental health study). As the scientific process entails that research findings which establish 'facts' are built up over time, the danger is that bodies of scientific knowledge supposedly based on such 'facts', turn out to be mythological edifices.

Controversy thus exists as to the status of the scientist–practitioner model in clinical psychology. While studies such as Milne *et al.* point to the adherence by clinical psychologists to the scientist–practitioner model, others, for example Head and Harmon (1990), take a more pessimistic view. They question Milne *et al.*'s wider definition of research and although they do not question the value of clinicians engaging in these activities, they nevertheless question if such a broad definition of research justifies a view of being 'true' scientist–practitioners. For example, Pilgrim and Treacher (1992) suggest that for clinical psychologists, interest in research is largely a careerist pursuit as research publications are highly significant in achieving regrading and better appointments, if not significant in actually influencing clinical practice. However, this view does not do justice to the adherents and practitioners of research, who continue to consume, publish and use research in their clinical practice even during the present era of increased organisational constraints and the implicit if not explicit discouragement of the present economic-management ethos of the NHS.

## THE SCIENTIST–PRACTITIONER MODEL IN CLINICAL PSYCHOLOGY TRAINING

Concerning the training of clinical psychologists in the scientist–practitioner model Head and Harmon (1990) and Berger *et al.* (1988) point out that research skills are part of the clinical competence of clinical psychologists, and this message is one frequently stressed at the training level. Head and Harmon (1990) point to the discrepancy between the emphasis on the importance of research at the training level, and the actual research activities of practitioners. However, regarding the models of training presented to new recruits, Pilgrim and Treacher (1992) examined the description of clinical psychology courses for 1989 and 1990. They found no clear consensus between training courses, with different courses presenting different versions of clinical psychology, ranging from descriptions of the complexity of the clinical psychologist's role to restatements of the rigid Maudsley position of the empirical scientist–practitioner model of 30 years ago. The latter also tend to be more behavioural in content, illustrating the view that it was behaviour therapy which expanded the scientist–practitioner role into the realm of therapy. Although, to be accredited by the Training Committee of the British Psychological Society, courses have to conform to certain criteria, courses present a wide range of models with no clear agreement between courses in terms of goals or philosophy. Currently, most courses tend to describe themselves as eclectic, while many hitherto cognitive-behavioural courses include other models for trainees to experience. Pilgrim and Treacher suggest that courses can be described along two dimensions, based on the extent to which courses emphasise the scientist–practitioner model, and the amount of emphasis placed on behavioural compared to eclectic approaches. Powell and Adams (1993) stress that clinical psychology training courses aim to integrate clinical skills and practice with research skills and research thinking so as to deliver a better service to clients and employing authorities, and to ensure that the profession develops its own potential and its unique contribution to health care. They urge a broader definition of research than the time-consuming process necessary for traditional research in its aim of achieving academic excellence and of providing highly reliable findings of a theoretical nature generalisable to a wide variety of settings. This process entails the lengthy process of an extensive literature search, a detailed proposal subjected to exhaustive peer review, major financial and personal resourcing, a write-up suitable for a peer-reviewed journal and a further wait until the article appears in print. Powell and Adams point out that research can be best taught on placement. Research skills, compared to research thinking, are not as easy to integrate with clinical practice, and are better taught explicitly. They are best taught in a clinical or service setting while the trainee is on placement. In clinical settings research of the kind done on placement will often be of a practical or pragmatic nature and often related to a single highly specific context. Further, it will often focus on service changes that are actually happening and will often provide service information or service evaluation; be carried out with the intention that it should immediately change practice; will often relate to the work of single individuals or units; be an extension of work being done; use single-case methodology; often use survey methods; use qualitative methods of data collection; and will be completed within clearly defined, usually minimal, financial and time constraints. Although the scale and goals of a placement research project will of necessity be limited, this need not imply that the thinking behind it is limited: 'research on placement is not the search for the Holy Grail – just good practice' (1993: 16).

## THE CHANGING ROLE OF CLINICAL PSYCHOLOGY

### The eclectic model in clinical psychology

The predominant role of clinical psychologists has changed from that of psychometrician–diagnostician–researcher to that of therapist. Clinical psychologists have been increasingly involved with psychotherapy and also with more complex clients. However, in terms of its development, the basic model of clinical psychology espoused by the majority of training courses has been that of the scientist–practitioner model. To accommodate this, training courses have responded by becoming increasingly eclectic.

During the 1980s and 1990s many of the clinical psychology training courses espoused an eclectic approach. In a study of all clinical psychologists practising in the South East Thames Regional Health Authority who had participated in 20 different training courses, O'Sullivan and Dryden (1990) found that the theoretical orientation of their training courses could be categorised under eight main headings. Psychologists labelled the main orientation of their training course as: behavioural/learning 22.2 per cent, cognitive 13.5 per cent, psychodynamic 21.0 per cent, eclectic 31.6 per cent, systems 6.2 per cent, person-centred 2.4 per cent, existential 0.0 per cent and other 3.7 per cent. Although it may be argued that this variability is the profession's strength, others such as David Smail point to the difficulties of the eclectic model. In his paper 'Clinical psychology – homogenized and sterilized' (1982), Smail comments on the danger of shelving philosophical debate on intellectual, epistemological and moral issues while psychologists focus on practical issues of service delivery to an increasingly wide range of client groups. Smail argues that this position constitutes a danger to both the profession of clinical psychology and the client group it serves, for philosophical and moral issues nevertheless implicitly influence our perspective and practices. Pilgrim and Treacher (1992) point to other intellectual dilemmas inherent in the model of eclecticism. For example, although behaviourism may be incorporated into the scientist–practitioner model, because it may be argued that behaviourism has a scientific, that is, research basis, it is more difficult to see how the psychoanalytic model can be integrated with the empiricism of the scientist–practitioner model.

The role of clinical psychologists has developed and evolved within a context. That role has changed from psychometrician–diagnostician with an emphasis on the objective empirical scientist role to that of a therapist involved with the subjective worlds of clients. Two main factors in the wider context, that of developments in the field of psychotherapy generally and in the role of psychiatry, facilitated the changing role of clinical psychology. Within the field of psychotherapy generally over the last 40 years, there have been new developments within psychoanalysis; the development of more client-centred approaches, such as the humanistic school of Carl Rogers; and – especially relevant to the changing role of clinical psychologists – the development of behaviour therapy. The original role of psychometrician–diagnostician was basically a paramedical role in which psychology, alongside other professional groups, was viewed a profession auxiliary to medicine. The role of these professional groups was to use their expertise to provide information to be used by medicine. This context created a climate which encour-aged the objective-scientist role of psychologists, which in turn influenced the development of training courses which emphasised scientific objectivity. As we saw in Chapter One, psychiatric dom-inance began to be challenged from both outside and within the profession. Although this had implications for the changing role of clinical psychology, in particular in relation to the practice of psy-chotherapy, the basic scientific–practitioner model of the training courses did not change. Thus, although theoretical understanding and skills in different psychotherapeutic approaches have been added on to training courses, there nevertheless remains an ethos of the scientist applying scientific principles to clinical practice rather than a consideration of self-knowledge and understanding with personal training as an essential element of the courses.

## THE ROLE OF PSYCHOTHERAPY IN THE DEVELOPMENT OF CLINICAL PSYCHOLOGY

### Eysenck's objections to psychotherapy

Pilgrim and Treacher (1992) document the smoother transition in clinical psychology in the USA than in Britain from the role of psychometrician–diagnostician–researcher to that of therapist. This, they suggest, may have been due to such factors as the original even stronger adherence to the scientific model by British compared to American clinical psychologists and the strongly empiricist British intellectual climate generally, as well as the tenacity with which the model has been held onto given the vulnerability of the role of British clinical psychologists within the NHS.

As we saw in Chapter One, the development of clinical psycho-logy training in Britain was strongly influenced in its early years by the views of H.J. Eysenck. He disagreed strongly with the perspect-ive of the American Psychological Association (APA) on appropri-ate training for clinical psychologists outlined in the findings of its Committee on Training in Clinical Psychology in 1947 and in the Josiah Macey Jr Foundation Conference on Training in Clinical Psychology in 1947. The APA's view was that training for clinical psychologists should consist of a combination of applied and theor-etical knowledge in the three main areas of diagnosis, therapy and research. Eysenck outlined his objections to this model in his paper 'Training in clinical psychology: An English point of view' (1949). In this paper, he argued that research and diagnosis should be part of the clinical psychologist's training but that therapy was not part of the clinical psychologist's role and that a separate discipline of psychotherapy should be built up alongside clinical psychology. Although the later development of clinical psychology revolved around clinical psychologists establishing themselves in the role of therapists responsive to patients needs, some of the issues Eysenck raised, such as the scientific role of clinical psychology, highlight tensions relevant to the role of clinical psychology today.

In his paper, Eysenck (1949) argued strongly against the APA's stance that psychotherapy should be included in the role of clinical psychologists. One of the main arguments put forward by the APA was that in the wake of the Second World War there was a great social need for more therapists, and clinical psychologists could help meet this need. This view was underlined by the important conference on the training of clinical psychologists in the USA at Boulder, Colorado in 1949, which stressed the need for more and better trained clinical psychologists to meet the needs of the mentally and emotionally distressed after the Second World War. However, Eysenck strongly disagreed with the view of clinical psychology as a discipline whose aim was to fulfil social needs, as this might interfere with the scientific requirements of the discipline. The second main issue raised by the APA with which Eysenck strongly disagreed was the APA's emphasis on the need for psychotherapeutic experience and its view that for clinical psychologists to carry out diagnosis and research without such a background would be a disadvantage. Eysenck cites the 1947 APA report of the Committee on Training in Clinical Psychology, which states: 'Our strong conviction about the need for therapeutic experience grows out of the recognition that the therapeutic contact with patients provides an experience which cannot be duplicated by any other type of relationship for the intensity and the detail with which it reveals motivational complexities' (pp. 173–4). However, this strongly conflicted with Eysenck's positivist position and he criticised this view as not being congruent with the values of science. He states:

> It is traditionally conceded that the value of scientific research is judged in terms of its methodology, the importance, within the general framework of scientific knowledge, of the results achieved, and the possibilities that other scientists can duplicate the experiment with similar results. We wish to protest against the background training of the scientist. To say that research . . . into the process and effects of therapy . . . cannot be carried out at all by persons who are not themselves therapists appears

to us to take the concept of research in this field out of the
realm of science into the mystical regions of intuition, idiographic
'understanding', and unrepeatable personal experience.

(Eysenck 1949: 174)

Although the APA firmly included therapy within the psychologist's role, Eysenck firmly opposed it and in his paper (1949) he
listed six further reasons for excluding therapy from the role of
clinical psychologists. The first reason he gave was concerned with
the division of labour within the field of mental illness. Eysenck
advocated a team of professionals to deal with mental health problems, with psychiatrists carrying out therapy; psychologists helping with diagnosis and specialising in research design; and social
workers investigating social conditions affecting the case. Second,
in his acceptance of psychotherapy firmly within the psychiatrist's
role, Eysenck stressed the importance of the illness model and the
usefulness of medical knowledge in understanding the underlying
causes of many emotional disturbances. However, the expansion of
behaviour therapy over the next 10 years, in which process Eysenck
himself was to have a major role, brought a complete revision of
Eysenck's view to one of therapy being part of the role of clinical
psychology. Behaviour therapy became a means of expanding the
therapeutic role of clinical psychologists. Claiming to be based on
the scientific principles of learning theory, behaviour therapy could
be readily accepted by psychologists adhering to Eysenck's positivist
scientific stance, and thus could be added on to the role definition
of clinical psychology. Further, the question of personal therapy in
training could be ignored, as a behaviour therapist is essentially an
applied scientist who objectively devises training programmes based
on scientific principles. The roles of therapist and scientist are inseparable in behaviour therapy, and, according to this point of view,
as the methodology is objective so the subjectivity of the therapist
can be ignored. Eysenck was vehemently opposed to the requirement of personal therapy for clinical psychologists advocated by the
APA, as he thought that personal therapy would undermine the
psychologist's ability to be scientifically detached. After the Second
World War the most significant school of psychotherapy was that of
psychoanalysis, which Eysenck criticised, for example, in his paper
on the efficacy of psychoanalysis (1952) and so he was completely
at variance with the APA's Committee on Training in Clinical Psychology recommendation (1947) that clinical psychologists should
have personal therapy and preferably psychoanalysis. Commenting
on the APA report, Eysenck states:

In other words, it is proposed that the young and relatively defenceless student be imbued with the 'premature' crystallizations of spurious 'orthodoxy' which constitute Freudianism through the transferences and counter-transferences developing during his training. Here indeed we have a fine soil on which to plant the seeds of objective, methodologically sound, impartial and scientifically acceptable research!

(Eysenck 1949: 175)

The issue of personal therapy in clinical psychology training, as will be discussed in Chapter Four, is still a matter of debate today. Pilgrim and Treacher (1992) point out that the majority of courses do not require personal therapy of their trainees, which reflects the Eysenckian tradition and the influence of behaviour therapy.

Eysenck's fourth objection to clinical psychologists being therapists was that he considered that training in research and diagnostic testing was itself a full-time task and the addition of a third type of training would result in a lower level of skill and training in all three. The fifth objection concerned trainee selection. Eysenck claimed that those interested in therapy would not be interested in the scientific nature of research training, and thus clinical psychology training should focus on training in diagnosis and research. The sixth objection was to do with the personality characteristics deemed appropriate for a clinical psychologist. In a comprehensive list of necessary characteristics to be a clinical psychologist the APA had included such characteristics as a therapeutic attitude in relating to people, while Eysenck stressed that a scientific attitude in order to understand people was necessary for psychology as a science.

Eysenck had a major role in shaping the development of clinical psychology in Britain and his stance against clinical psychologists being therapists is important. However, Eysenck himself had a major role in the development of behaviour therapy in the mid-1950s, when behaviour therapy began to challenge psychoanalysis as the major form of therapy. Eysenck did not only view psychoanalysis as ineffective but he also opposed its premise of the importance of personal reflection by the therapist. Behaviour therapy does not theoretically demand such personal commitment and conceptually combines therapy and research in the scientist–practitioner model. Furthermore, behaviour therapy could just be added on to the prevailing scientist–diagnostician model of clinical psychology. It was this theoretical perspective, which we shall see later in this book, which was to influence the early training courses in clinical psychology in this country particularly at the Maudsley, where, as

Yates (1970) describes, the Psychology Department was divided into a research station headed by Eysenck, and a clinical–teaching section headed by Shapiro, who emphasised the experimental aspects of the clinical psychologist's role. Shapiro's approach emphasised the application of experimental psychology to clinical case material. The importance of the approaches of Eysenck and Shapiro at the Maudsley was that not only was this approach emphasised on the Maudsley clinical psychology course itself, but students from the course went on to head and teach on other newly formed clinical psychology courses and thus influenced the content of clinical psychology training generally.

Behaviour therapy did not essentially conflict with the Maudsley approach and was soon assimilated into it. Yates discusses how the development of behaviour therapy fitted well with Shapiro's view of developing clinical psychology as an applied science based on scientific principles. As I will discuss in Chapter Five, the medical model of mental health and psychiatry in particular had a crucial role in shaping the development of clinical psychology. The scientist–diagnostician model had fitted well into the existing psychiatric model as a helpful adjunct to psychiatry in assisting diagnosis and providing a shared scientific language in which to conduct research activities. It was the development of behaviour therapy in Britain which secured the establishment of clinical psychology as an independent profession within the mental health services. This development helped psychology to expand its role into the realm of therapy as well as enabling it to separate from its dependence on psychiatry.

Another major reason why clinical psychology expanded its role to encompass therapy was the practical necessities of working in the rapidly developing NHS. Mental health services needed skilled therapists, not pure researchers, and clinical psychologists adapted to meet these service needs. The formation of the NHS was a major reason why Eysenck's early attempt to prevent clinical psychology from developing as a therapy-providing profession failed. The change of emphasis from clinical psychology being narrowly defined as a scientific discipline, whose practitioners focused on research in the 1950s and early 1960s, to the inclusion of therapy (although largely restricted to behaviour therapy in the mid-1960s) was reflected in clinical psychology training courses, in which behaviour therapy became one of the main topics in the majority of courses. In time, clinical psychologists' involvement with therapy expanded from behaviour therapy to a more broadly based flexible discipline which included the research and practice of a range of therapies, and this was reflected in the content of the training courses in clinical psychology, as will be discussed in Chapter Four.

We saw in Chapter One how British academic psychology, which was the basis for clinical psychology, was itself influenced in its development by the academic traditions of the time. The empirical positivist legacy of British academic psychology was reflected in the development of clinical psychology, both in its theory and its practice. Clinical psychology aimed to be an 'objective' applied science with its detached 'objective' scientists applying the laws of human behaviour to their human subjects. In theory, this was reflected in its adherence to traditional scientific models of science generally and in psychological thought in particular. Thus theories and models which did not fit into this rigid scientific view of the world, such as psychoanalysis and most of the verbal therapies, were rejected as unscientific, and evidence of woolly thinking. On the wider political scale the scientific emphasis fitted well into the political climate of Britain in the 1960s and 1970s, with the technological revolution advocated during the years of Harold Wilson's premiership (1964–9). The content of psychology's science, namely behaviourism, was more acceptable to many socialist supporters. Behaviourism stresses the environment as a prime force in determining behaviour, which was in line with both Keynesian and Marxist views that economic change would lead to social change, and ultimately a change in individual consciousness. This was very different from the main psychotherapeutic approaches of the time which were mainly based on the psychoanalytic position, which stressed that it was only through the individual confronting intrapsychic conflicts that change could come about.

Counselling psychology is a relatively new discipline and hence does not carry the historical legacy of clinical psychology. Counselling psychology has in a way developed as a hybrid. On the one hand, it draws on the knowledge and practice of other psychotherapeutic models which embrace concepts of subjectivity and the world of feelings of both client and practitioner. On the other hand, it also claims its basis as being that of traditional academic psychology with its empirical emphasis on scientific research.

In practice, clinical psychologists were supposed to be 'objective applied scientists' whose subjective realities were of no concern to their task of changing behaviour. Neither the subjective worlds of clinician or patient were seen of relevance in this endeavour. Feelings simply were of no relevance. When 'experimenter effects' appeared in studies they were at best viewed as nuisance or extraneous interfering variables to be controlled and, if possible, completely avoided. The empirical stance has led to difficulties for academic psychology generally, in its pursuit of understanding human concerns and for the related psychological professions, at both the theoretical and practical level. This can be seen in the issues revolving around the concept of science and the related issues of objectivity, subjectivity and reflexivity in relation to the study of psychology. In the fields of applied psychology these issues are reflected specifically around the issue of personal therapy in clinical practice, and considerations of reflexivity and subjectivity in research methodology in clinical psychology and counselling psychology.

Challenges to the narrow definitions of science have come from both within the social sciences and from developments in the physical sciences. I shall outline some of these developments in so far as they are of significance for the theory and practice of psychology.

## THE TRADITIONAL VIEW OF SCIENCE

Husserl, in *The Crisis of European Sciences and Transcendental Phenomenology* (1970), analyses the historical evolution of the events which led to the dominance of objectivism in contemporary thought. This he dates to the seventeenth century and the work of Galileo and Descartes, although they could not have foreseen the long-term implications of their work. According to Husserl, the work of Galileo, stressing the achievement of objective knowledge of the world through mathematical abstraction, precipitated the reign of objectivism and its mechanical-scientific objectivity. Descartes did not view issues of subjectivity as a concern for philosophy. Just as Galileo had done, Descartes left whole areas of reality, including affectivity, subjectivity, sensory impressions, perspectival reality and an adequate psychology and all the realities that make up our world unexplored, unknown and derided.

The traditional objective paradigm of science, or the 'old physics', as Gary Zukav (1979) terms it, is the physics of another seventeenth-century scientist, Isaac Newton. Newton's first great contributions to science were the laws of motion, which defied the accepted authority of the day. Newton's premise that he made no hypotheses (*Hypotheses non fingo*) meant that he based his laws upon sound experimental evidence and nothing else. His criteria for the validity of everything that he wrote was that anyone should be able to reproduce his experiments and find the same results. Only if something could be verified experimentally could it be accorded the status of truth. This really upset the authority of the day, which was the church, as it had been stating things for 1,500 years that were not subject to experimental verification. Like Galileo before him, Newtonian physics was perceived as a direct challenge to the power of the church. Galileo had been forced by the Inquisition to recant the view that the earth revolves around the sun (and to recant the unacceptable theological implications he drew from that view), on penalty of imprisonment or worse. The argument of the church was not with the empirical method but with the theological conclusions that were being derived from Newton's ideas. The power of the church influenced many scientists including Descartes, who may be seen as another founder of modern science. Descartes and later scientists until the beginning of this century saw the universe as a great machine. They worked on developing a science specifically to discover how this great machine worked.

The lesson of Newtonian physics is that the universe is governed by laws that are susceptible to rational understanding. By applying these laws we extend our knowledge of, and therefore our influence over, the environment. The science of Newton and Descartes, albeit unwittingly, reduced the status of men to that of helpless cogs in a machine whose functioning had been preordained from the day of its creation. There seemed to be no phenomena which could not be explained in terms of mechanical models, subject to long-established principles.

## THE PARADIGM OF OBJECTIVITY

In his book *The Structure of Scientific Revolutions* (1970), T.S. Kuhn theorised that behind all current work in the sciences – behind the rules and assumptions of what he terms 'normal science' – there lurks a 'paradigm'. This paradigm is a conceptual ideal which informs the thinking of a given society, directs its interests and establishes for that society a strong sense of its own objectivity. 'Normal science' works with an implicit faith in this paradigm and plods on, 'problem-solving' at low theoretical pressure, until it reaches a problem it cannot solve within that paradigm. This brings about a crisis of conceptuality and a 'revolutionary science' is created.

Kuhn implicitly questions the dominant paradigm of objectivity in our society and the Popperian orthodoxy of the traditional hypothetico-deductive methodology of 'normal science', in favour of a 'revolutionary science'. A paradigm is only in place until a better one replaces it, with the implication that objectivity is not external as we had taken it to be but only a temporary paradigm. Like others before him such as Galileo and Newton, who questioned the ruling scientific paradigm of the day, Kuhn's view outraged many 'objective' scientists, particularly in his view of the long

and arduous training required of scientists as an exercise in theological indoctrination and dogma, for the underlying premise of
objectivity is that it is totally open to reasoned criticism at all levels.


## SOME PRINCIPLES OF MODERN PHYSICS

The 'new physics', which is about quantum physics and relativity,
is in fact nearly a century old. Quantum mechanics, a branch of
physics, began with Max Planck's theory of quanta in 1900 and
Albert Einstein's special theory of relativity in 1905. Quantum theory
is closely linked with philosophy and also perception. Gary Zukav,
in *The Dancing Wu Li Masters* (1979), presents an excellent overview
of developments in advanced physics. In his view, physics is inseparable from philosophy. Modern physics deals with events at both the
atomic and subatomic level. The smallest object that we can see,
even under a microscope, contains millions of atoms. At the subatomic level the particles that make up atoms are studied. A subatomic particle cannot be pictured as a thing. We must therefore
abandon the idea of a subatomic particle as an object. Quantum
mechanics views subatomic particles as 'tendencies to exist' or 'tendencies to happen'. How strong these tendencies are is expressed in
terms of probabilities. At this subatomic level, mass and energy
change unceasingly into each other. The development of physics in
the twentieth century has included the study of complementarity,
the uncertainty principle, quantum field theory and the Copenhagen
Interpretation of quantum mechanics. These produce insights into
the nature of reality.

   The Copenhagen Interpretation of Quantum Mechanics was formulated in 1927 by a group of physicists meeting in 1927 at the
Fifth Solvay Congress in Brussels. Henry Stapp (1972) outlines some
of the major conclusions of this Conference in his article, 'The
Copenhagen Interpretation and the Nature of Space-Time'. The term
reflects the dominant influence of Niels Bohr who came from Copenhagen. Essentially, the Copenhagen Interpretation marks the emergence of the new physics as a consistent way of viewing the world
and it remains the most influential interpretation of quantum mechanics. The importance of the Copenhagen Interpretation lies in the
fact that, for the first time, scientists attempting to formulate a consistent physics were forced by their own findings to acknowledge
that a complete understanding of reality lies beyond the capabilities of rational thought. The Copenhagen Interpretation states that

reality is not as it appears. It says that what we perceive to be physical reality is actually our cognitive construction of it. This cognitive
construction may appear to be substantive, but the physical world
itself is not. An implication of this is that parts of our being or
psyche, which includes for example our irrational side, which science
had ignored since the 1700s, could merge again with the rational
part of our psyche recognised by science. Another crucial implication is that a concept such as mind not synonymous with the physical
brain can exist.

Another interpretation derived from quantum mechanics is the
Many Worlds Interpretation of quantum mechanics. According to
this theory, whenever a choice is made in the universe between
one possible event and another, the universe splits into different
branches representing different coexisting realities. In the Many
Worlds theory the world is continuously splitting into separate and
mutually inaccessible branches, each of which contains different
editions of the same actors performing different acts at the same time,
on different stages which somehow are located in the same place.

In physics, the principle of local causes says that what happens in
one area does not depend upon variables subject to the control of an
experimenter in a distant space-separated area. However, quantum
mechanics concludes that what happens in one area does depend
upon variables subject to the control of an experimenter in a distant
space-separated area. Thus, in 1927, at the Fifth Solvay Conference
in Brussels, perhaps the most famous gathering of physicists in history formulated the Copenhagen Interpretation and decided that it
might not ever be possible to construct a model of reality.

Bohr's principle of complementarity addresses the underlying
relation of physics to consciousness. The experimenter's choice of
experiment determines which mutually exclusive aspect of the same
phenomenon will manifest itself. Heisenberg's Uncertainty Principle
demonstrates that we cannot observe a phenomenon without changing it. The physical properties which we observe in the 'external'
world are enmeshed in our own perceptions.

Quantum mechanics does not replace Newtonian physics, it includes
it. Quantum mechanics shows us that we are not as separate from
the rest of the world as we once thought. Particle physics shows
us that the rest of the world is not a 'thing' resting passively 'out
there'. It is in a state of continual creation, transformation and
annihilation. Each different experience is capable of changing us in
such ways that we can never again view the world as we did before.
For example, the study of relativity theory can lead us to the experience that space and time are only mental constructions. There

is no one single 'experience' of physics, as the experience is always changing.

There are many implications of quantum mechanics. For example, as Zukav points out, the organic and inorganic are linked.

> Some biologists believe that a single plant cell carries within it the capability to reproduce the entire plant. Similarly, the philosophical implication of quantum mechanics is that all the things in our universe (including us) that appear to exist independently are actually parts of one all-encompassing organic pattern, and that no parts of that pattern are ever really separate from it or from each other.
>
> (1979: 72–3)

Another implication of quantum mechanics is that not only do we influence our reality, but that also to some degree, we actually create it. According to quantum mechanics we can know either the momentum of a particle or its position but not both; we then choose which of these two properties we want to determine. In this way we can create certain properties because we choose to measure those properties. For example, it is possible that we create something that has position, like a particle, because we are intent on determining position and it is impossible to determine position without having some thing occupying the position that we want to determine. Quantum physicists thus address issues such as whether a particle with momentum exists before an experiment was conducted to measure its momentum; or whether a particle with position exists before an experiment was set up to measure its position; or did any particles exist at all before we thought about them and measured them. In other words, did we in fact create the very particles that we are experimenting with.

Zukav quotes John Wheeler:

> May the universe in some strange sense be 'brought into being' by the participation of those who participate? . . . The vital act is the act of participation. 'Participator' is the incontrovertible new concept given by quantum mechanics. It strikes down the term 'observer' of classical theory, the man who stands safely behind the thick glass wall and watches what goes on without taking part. It can't be done, quantum mechanics says.
>
> (in Zukav 1979: 54)

Quantum mechanics shows that we cannot observe something without changing it. If we observe a certain particle collision experiment, not only do we have no way of proving that the result would have been the same if we had not been watching it, all that we know indicates that it would not have been the same, because the result that we got was affected by the fact that we were looking for it. Some experiments show that light is wave-like, others show equally well that it is particle-like. If we want to demonstrate that light is one or the other, we only need to select the appropriate experiment.

> 'Reality' is what we take to be true. What we take to be true is what we believe. What we believe is based upon our percep-tions. What we perceive depends upon what we look for. What we look for depends upon what we think. What we think depends upon what we perceive. What we perceive determines what we believe. What we believe determines what we take to be true. What we take to be true is our reality.
>
> (Zukav 1979: 328)

The central focus of this process initially is what we think.

There are fundamental differences between Newtonian science and quantum mechanics. Newtonian physics is about things that we can picture, and describes things – individual objects in space and their change in time – whereas quantum mechanics is about things that we cannot picture, and is based on the behaviour of subatomic particles and systems not directly observable. Newtonian physics predicts events, and strives for absolute truths. Quantum mechanics tells us that we cannot predict subatomic phenomena with any certainty. We can only predict their probabilities.

Newtonian physics claims to be based on 'absolute truth', whereas quantum mechanics claims only to correlate experience correctly. Newtonian physics is based on the idea of laws which govern phe-nomena and the power inherent in understanding them, but it leads to helplessness in the face of the Great Machine which is the Universe. Quantum mechanics is based upon the idea of minimal knowledge of future phenomena – to knowing probabilities – but it leads to the possibility that our reality is what we choose to make it. Another fundamental difference between the old and new phys-ics is that old physics assumes that there is an external world which exists apart from us. It also assumes that we can observe, measure, and speculate about the external world without changing it. Quan-tum mechanics does not assume an objective reality apart from our experience. Further, it claims that we cannot observe something without changing it.

## CRITICISM OF THE TRADITIONAL SCIENTIFIC
## PARADIGM FROM WITHIN PSYCHOLOGY
## AND PHILOSOPHY

Although the classical scientific model has remained the main paradigm for psychology to the present day, there have been developments in philosophy and psychology that are in line with the
developments in modern physics. Poole (1972), in his book *Towards
Deep Subjectivity*, argues that the principles of empiricism and objectivity that are derived from classic sciences are built on fundamentally
false premises. Drawing on a tradition of thought from Kierkegaard
and Husserl to Laing and Chomsky, Poole argues that what is needed
is a commitment to subjective personal values rather than the attempt
to avoid subjective thought (even if we could). According to Poole,
if we view our attempts to be objective to be a search for truth then
for a science to be truly objective, it must contain the subjective, as
subjectivity is an essential part of our humanity.

'Meaning and interpretation belong together inseparably. Anything which visibly has a meaning is in that same instant invested
with an interpretation by each and every onlooker' (1972: 6). The
meaning attributed to what we select to be significant will vary
according to our moral presuppositions, the relative position of
our vantage point. Interpretation is always instant, and any act an
embodied intention. Poole (1972: 44) points out that objectivity
is that which is commonly received as objectively valid: all the
attitudes, presuppositions, unquestioned assumptions typical of any
given society. Objectivity implies the acceptance of the dominant
social, ethical and religious view in that society. Thus, objectivity is
tautological in that objectivity in any society gets defined in terms
of the political and social status quo. Objectivity is the dominant
objectivity of a given society. Objectivity is no more and no less
than the belief in objectivity as such.

Poole points out the coincidence of the power status quo and the
objective status quo, that is, the bonding of intellectual and political
objectivity within the existing power structure. The facts which are
recognised are those congruent with the prevailing political objectivity. Thus, anyone who does not see or accept the 'obvious' as the
obvious will be taken to have an impaired sense of objectivity or
even be suffering from some sort of delusion. Society's reactions
will vary from ignoring the individual to psychiatric treatment. When
there is pressure for a change in the nature of objectivity, by those
who maintain the status quo, then objectivity is redefined overnight. Thinkers who do not see objectivity objectively, be they Galileo
or Chomsky, threaten the prevailing objectivity.

## STRUCTURES OF OBJECTIVITY

Poole considers three major structures of objectivity. These are first an unquestioning grasp of 'facts' (data, and the quantifiability of data). Second, a refusal to make public the justification for its acts and decisions. Third, an inbuilt tendency to account for the parts rather than the whole.

Considering the first: objectivity contends that 'facts' have to be accepted and the status of these facts should not be questioned. Just as physics and mathematics have facts, so, the argument goes, all human endeavour which claims to be objective should adopt the impersonal stance of the traditional scientist. It claims that facts can exist in an objective, context-free way, even when the facts are about human beings. This emphasis on facts regarding human life is behind the impersonal rhetoric of the military, where human tragedy is concealed in military jargon. For example, 'taking out' means killing. Those that question the status of facts when placed in their human context, such as Chomsky, are dismissed or con-sidered a threat to objectivity. The attitude of acceptance results in our accepting the unacceptable. For example, research findings pointing out that there is more evidence of schizophrenia amongst the black population of Nottingham are considered a fact. (See, for example, Harrison et al. 1989; Harrison 1990; Owens et al. 1991; Dauncey et al. 1993.) This is a fact that we are all supposed to discuss objectively and rationally.

It is also implicitly assumed that an objective discussion of the fact of increased incidence would not in itself lead to the necessity of looking at the historical, economic, social and political context within which black people live in Nottingham. It would not lead to looking at the context of the role of the mental illness model, psy-chiatry and psychiatric diagnostic classification systems, or the eco-nomic interests of drug companies whose interest it is to fund much psychiatric research and claim to show that they have just the right medicine to cure this illness. Neither would it lead to the necessity of changing the context – this is taken to be a matter for the gov-ernment of the day. However, the facts do concern such issues. The facts are taken to be objective. Suggestions that they only have the status of facts in the sense that they represent the state of affairs existing at the moment, and that these facts could be changed into non-facts are treated as unscientific, unobjective and are dismissed as irrational. The facts of human suffering are non-facts for objec-tivity – they are merely subjective.

The second element of objectivity is that it believes that it is not called upon to justify publicly the policies and actions for which it is responsible. It refuses to question the moral criteria which govern its decisions. Objectivity sets itself up as impersonal, and refuses all subjective critique. Criticism of objectivity in our society is called 'subjective', 'old-fashioned', 'communist', '60s thinking', or whatever the current putdown might be.

Third, objectivity is selective about what it intends to consider. It selects only those parts of a problem which are either quantifiable or empirical or both. It retreats from the general to the particular, from the complex to the simple and from the adequate to the banal. The belief in the quantifiability of data and the advent of the computer has furthered this tendency, so that it is possible to refuse to discuss the human aspect of almost any subject.

Objectivity has ended up as the equivalent of that fragment of rationality which is commonly called scientific. In scientific objectivity, the thinker is excluded from the thought, and the personal involvement of the thinker is denied. Great efforts are made to exclude subjectivity from endeavours, while all ethical criteria are cut off from the pure scientific effort. This is the split of objectivity which Marcuse (1964) refers to in his book *One Dimensional Man*.

## THE PARADIGM OF OBJECTIVITY IN PSYCHOLOGY

The current paradigm of objectivity in the sciences which is materialist-determinist-behaviourist-positivist dates back at least three centuries. The structure of this paradigm may be viewed as a set of ideal assumptions. The nature of this may be seen in Roger Poole's reference to the entry on 'Behaviourism' in the Encyclopaedia Britannica. This lists the precursors of behaviourism as including materialist and mechanistic philosophy in the seventeenth century; the English empiricists of the eighteenth and nineteenth centuries; the French materialist philosophers; the dominance of the mechanical world-view in the physical science of the eighteenth and nineteenth centuries; and the positivism of the French sociologist–philosopher Auguste Comte, who explicitly repudiated introspection as a basis for psychology in 1838. The Encyclopaedia Britannica further lists as influences J.B. Watson, the father of theoretical behaviourism; animal psychology; objective biology; Russian reflexology; and American philosophic pragmatism. It asserts that behaviourism is primarily an extension of the methods of animal psychology to the study of humans. Watson himself urged in 1913 that psychology should discard all reference to consciousness and no longer delude itself into thinking that mental state is the object of observation.

Hence, psychology was to become 'a purely objective, experimental branch of natural science'.

## CHALLENGES TO OBJECTIVITY FROM WITHIN PSYCHOLOGY AND PHILOSOPHY

Poole points out that whole areas of subjective experience have never been made the subject of a suitably subjective investigation by objectivity, and the prevailing objectivism ignores what it cannot quantify. The behaviourist B.F. Skinner is explicit about this paradigm in saying that we can only know what we can measure. However, two movements this century have significantly challenged the premises of objectivity from within psychology and philosophy, namely phenomenology and Gestalt theory. Both these theories and their derivatives deal with the totality of phenomena, not just the composite parts. Edmund Husserl (1859–1938), a German mathematician and philosopher, was the founder of phenomenology. Paul Ricoeur (1967) in his analysis of Husserl's phenomenology describes how Husserl in his work *Logical Investigations* (1901) departed from empiricism and positivism, rejecting false objectivity or objectivism, as he called it, and became interested in the way we confer meaning upon the world.

Husserl's views are revolutionary in Kuhn's sense, in consciously reversing three centuries of paradigms in his emphasis on the subjectively experienced world. A central tenet in Husserl's work is the idea of perspectives. Although we are all conscious that there is only one world, we also see it differently, interpret it differently, and attribute different meanings to it at various times. The world to Husserl is a communalised set of perspectives. He states, 'Each individual . . . has different aspects, different sides, perspectives, etc. . . . but in each case these are taken from the same total system of multiplicities of which each individual is constantly conscious' (1970: 164).

Husserl further makes the intrinsic connection between subjectivity and intentionality, that is, our power of conferring meaning. It is with attention to how we confer meaning and interpret the world that the huge task of reintegrating subjectivity into objective research begins. Intentionality is a hypothesis which we test out and confirm and disconfirm. Further, the fact that we confer meaning onto the world, instead of it imposing one meaning onto us, implies that we are active participants in this process. What is in question here is not just the mechanics of perception – the brain receives information when light hits the retina. However, the information sent to the brain is processed, and a hypothesis about what the eye is seeing transmitted rather than direct information about what is 'out there'. Husserl's description of the problem of subjectivity is crucial in defining a new and adequate objectivity. To him, if the world we live in and confer meaning upon, and in which we build up intersubjectivity with others, is to be the subject of our enquiry then it should be made just that – the subject of enquiry and not the object. Husserl stated: 'One must finally achieve the insight that no objective science, no matter how exact, explains or ever can explain anything in a serious sense' (1970: 163). This is revolutionary in Kuhn's sense as he points to the possibility of an achieved and adequate objectivity in his attempts to integrate subjectivity (the way we confer meaning and interpret the world) and objectivity. This also points to the challenge of integrating subjectivity and objective research.

Husserl inspired many philosophers, including Heidegger, Sartre and Merleau-Ponty. His work was also the precursor of later work within psychology like that of Allport in the 1930s on perceptual set, in which the human being is seen as an ever-active agent in the process of hypothesis-testing to derive a version of reality. Similarly, George Kelly's work in the 1950s, which greatly influenced an important group of followers in this country, relies on us forming meaning through our active process of construing the world. Like Husserl and Allport, Kelly points out that this does not leave us individually in solitary isolation, as there are also shared hypotheses or constructs which then enable us to share a social meaning. Husserl states: 'Thus in general the world exists not only for isolated men but for the community of men; and this is due to the fact that even what is straightforwardly perceptual is communalised' (1970: 165).

Following in this tradition, there have been notable examples of works that step outside the confines of traditional science. This is seen, for example, in the New Paradigm research of Alan Radley and John Shotter in psychology, and in perhaps the best-known example, the work of R.D. Laing and his associates (Laing 1960; Laing and Esterson 1964). Here, space is measured not in feet and inches, but as it is experienced by a suffering schizophrenic. This is achieved through the study of the totality, and by working from the inside. It is not objective in the typical impoverished sense, but takes objectivity seriously by examining subjectivity subjectively.

Kierkegaard, like Husserl, makes a subjective objection to objectivity. Kierkegaard's philosophy of subjectivity, as he develops it in *Concluding Unscientific Postscript* (1941), expands upon Husserl's concept of subjectivity as a meaning-conferring process (intentionality) by integrating subjectivity directly into the ethical sphere. 'The only reality that exists for the existing individual is his own ethical reality. To every other reality he stands in a cognitive relation; but true knowledge consists in translating the real into the possible' (1941: 280).

To Kierkegaard all objective knowledge is subservient to the use we intend to make of it. The use we make of it necessarily involves us as ethical beings. An achievement in physics or biology, Kierkegaard would argue, is itself real but neutral as all its possibilities lie before it. True knowledge consists of translating the real into the possible. Then it must be questioned what we are to do with this achievement and to what possible future should it be directed. This leads us to consider the use made of scientific discoveries as being an intrinsic part of the process of science. For example, in translating the real into the possible, as in the political use of science, objective science and objective military strategy might very well fail to meet the standards of an adequate objectivity according to Kierkegaard's view of science. The success of a technique is, in its use, capable of being a failure of adequate objectivity. The facts about modern warfare alone are enough to convince most of us of the total irrationality of what is presented as objectivity, whether or not it is claimed to be of strategic, ideological or of political necessity.

Chomsky is the historical successor to the philosophical concerns of Husserl and Kierkegaard. Like Kierkegaard, he knows that he has a duty to knowledge which exceeds the demands of the academic and professional world. He stresses the necessity to move beyond a 'merely cognitive' relation to his knowledge and to establish knowledge in an ethical relationship to the world. Chomsky's work is another subjective objection to objectivity. His book *American Power and the New Mandarins* (1968) is an exercise that shows that the combination of objective study of perspectives and personal ethical commitment is possible. As Husserl comments, no objective science, however exact, explains or can ever explain anything in a serious sense.

We were presented with horrifying accounts of warfare in, for example, the chemical warfare in Vietnam described by Noam Chomsky in *American Power and the New Mandarins* (1968), in Askoy and Robins' (1992) account of the technological Gulf War, and in the detailed, cold nightly accounts on television of the Gulf War and massacres in the Balkans. These highlight the status of 'facts' in relation to objectivity. Although the descriptions of Chomsky and Askoy and Robins are full of detailed facts, there is not one which is free of a moral implication. There is no fact to which, as readers, we can stand in an objective relationship. Seen from the Pentagon or Whitehall these facts were seen to be objective and strategic necessities. What are facts of horror to the ordinary human being are facts of objective necessity for government administrations. Facts, as Poole points out, have a modality and are different according to the perspective from which we view them. Seen from where Chomsky and Askoy and Robins see them, the facts of the war amount to war crimes, if not crimes against humanity, totally unobjective and indefensible. However, we again have to question whether these are indeed the same facts.

## REFLEXIVITY AS AN ISSUE FOR CLINICAL PSYCHOLOGY

The issue of reflexivity is apparent throughout the development of psychology. Earlier on, nineteenth-century psychology was controlled and produced by a limited selection of the population – of white, educated males through whose 'objective' eyes the rest of the species was studied. From their position they set out to define sub-disciplines such as race psychology, to perceive turbulent crowds as being the product of regressive psychological forces and to view non-heterosexuality as pathological. However, this monopoly, although not extinguished, has been eroded and many of the 'objects' of studies have now gradually entered the discipline and helped influence the discourse, for example in the areas of race, gender and sexual orientation. The groups which had once been defined as problems to be objectively studied are now to a greater extent incorporated into the discipline and change the nature of the discourse reflexively, so that the agenda is now focused on our attitudes to race, sexuality and gender and the origins of these attitudes. By the late 1930s race psychology – concerned with racial psychological differences – had given way to studies of racism – the obsession with racial differences. By the end of the 1960s studies on the psychology of women had similarly been transformed. Likewise, in the early 1970s the American Psychiatric Association overnight reversed its view on homosexuality so that the research problem changed from 'homosexuality' to 'homophobia'. Highlighting the cultural relativity of society's definition of what is mentally ill and the weakness of the psychiatric medical illness model, Albee (1996) points out thousands of citizens of homosexual orientation in the USA were changed overnight from being defined as psychiatrically ill to sane, as the American Psychiatric Association dropped its classification of homosexuality as a psychiatric disorder.

Apart from the world of the senses, seventeenth-century rationalism left one other vital element out of its philosophy – that of the thinker him- or herself. The thinker was excluded from what he thought. Everything that belonged to him other than his pure presence as thinking mind, as an ethical being, was swept out as a secondary quality or later, in behaviourism, as an 'intervening variable'. Galileo's importance rests in his efforts to quantify or measure the phenomena of the external world. Once a relationship is discovered, like the acceleration of a falling object, it does not matter who drops the object, what object is dropped or where the dropping takes place. The results are always the same whether the experiment takes place in different countries and different times by experimenters with completely different belief systems. Facts like these convinced philosophers that the physical universe obeys its own laws regardless of its inhabitants. Even if two people were dropped instead of stones the results would be the same regardless of the feelings or thoughts of the people so unfortunately dropped, as universal laws are impersonal. It was precisely this impersonality that inspired scientists to strive for 'absolute objectivity'.

However, it was not the thinker as rationalist mathematician who was thrown out, but the whole person, the thinker as a human being endowed with sensitivity, personality, commitments, etc. Other factors were seen as unfortunate intervening variables to be controlled if not completely discarded. But this objectivity was a fantasy concerned only with impersonal knowledge. Excluded man became the ideal, and exclusiveness was the aim. However, adequacy is not met if the thinker is omitted from his own philosophical line of argument to this extent. The refusal to treat the totality of problems and focus on selected bits of problems is a failure of adequate objectivity. However, adequacy, as Poole defines it and as Chomsky demands, is 'the study of the totality of problems, objective and subjective, by the whole thinker, taking into account all the evidence, both quantifiable and unquantifiable' (Poole 1972: 108–9). According to quantum mechanics there is no such thing as objectivity. We cannot take ourselves out of the picture. We are a part of nature, and when we study nature there is no way around that fact that nature is studying itself. Hence physics may be seen as a branch of psychology or the other way round.

Carl Jung, the Swiss analytical psychologist, wrote: 'The psychological rule says that when an inner situation is not made conscious, it happens outside, as fate. That is to say, when the individual remains undivided and does not become conscious of his inner contradictions, the world must perforce act out the conflict and be torn into opposite halves' (1978: 70–1). In a parallel way the physicist Pauli stated: 'From an inner center, then psyche seems to move outward, in the sense of an extroversion, into the physical world' (1955: 175).

The concept of scientific objectivity rests upon the assumption of an external world which is 'out there' as opposed to an 'I' which is 'in here'. The task of the scientist is to observe the 'out there' as objectively as possible. To observe something objectively means to see it as it would appear to an observer who has no prejudices about what he observes. However, the problem here is that the person who carries such an attitude *is* prejudiced, in that he/she is prejudiced to be 'objective', that is, without a preformed opinion. An opinion is a point of view. The point of view that we can be without a point of view is in fact a point of view. The decision itself to study one segment of reality instead of another is a subjective expression of the researcher who makes it. It affects his/her perceptions of reality.

In *The Shaping of Modern Psychology* (1987), Hearnshaw points out that psychology is an unusual science as it is inherently reflexive. However, the issue of reflexivity poses problems for psychology if psychology is defined within the positivist science framework. For example, the implication of reflexivity, as George Kelly (1955) emphasised, is that psychological theories should be able to explain their own production and also that the psychological character of psychologists affects the work they produce. This creates a basic problem for the discipline of psychology because in the process of psychologising, the mind has by definition to turn back on itself. As we have seen, in its striving for scientific status, psychology attempted to model its scientific paradigm on that of the physical sciences. This led to attempts to objectify its subject matter, assuming it to have fixed characteristics which were then amenable to scientific investigation. The analogy between using the laws of chemistry to create new chemical compounds and using, for example, the laws of learning to direct the course of the learning process is dubious, because chemicals do not read or write books about chemistry. The problem is that the technological application of psychological laws is itself a psychological activity; that is, investigating psychological phenomena is itself a psychological process. The investigator cannot stand outside or divorce him/herself from psychological processes. As such, the relationship between the investigator and the subject of the investigation is different from the relationship between the investigator and his/her subject matter in the physical sciences. However, confronting this dilemma means confronting the claims of the scientific status of psychology within the narrow traditional view of science. In many ways it has been the quest for scientific status at the expense of considerations of reflexivity which has limited the development of psychology as a discipline.

Richards (1993) outlines five main issues in relation to psychology and reflexivity. These are first the scientific status problem, due to the fact that scientific behaviour is part of our subject matter. The second problem revolves around the dilemma that psychology is directly a product of its subject matter. Third, research on psychological phenomena is an aspect of that phenomenon. The fourth dilemma arises from the fact that psychology can actually create its own subject matter. Fifth, psychological research poses psychological process problems. Other issues revolving around the nature of reflexivity emphasise, as Kelly (1955) points out, that psychological theories should be able to account for their own production.

First Richards addresses the issue of psychology in relation to science. Carrying out the process of science is itself a form of human behaviour, and is thus itself a legitimate area of investigation by psychology as the science of human behaviour. However, scientific behaviour is not an objective neutral activity as is implied in the positivist tradition. As we have discussed, psychology has followed a positivist philosophy of science. Richards outlines how over the past 20 years increasing attention has been given to the psychological aspects of scientific behaviour from the interpretation of experimental findings to theory construction and priorities of research, which include perception, personality, cognition, communication, small group dynamics and organisational psychology. These psychological aspects are illustrated, for example, in questions of how scientists really derive their theories; in definitions of research findings; in the social psychological processes determining peer group evaluation; and in the limitation of the scientist and science's thinking within the culturally available conceptual repertoire. In addition there are professional, political and social factors which influence not just the selection of the content of research which is carried out, but the entire research process itself – from what is perceived and selected or ignored in the course of the investigation, to the selection, analysis, interpretation and presentation of the findings. This places the profession of psychology in a paradox for it has striven for a traditional scientific status which lends it authority; yet as a discipline aiming to understand human behaviour, including scientific behaviour, it is led to question the viability of the traditional scientific model.

A second dilemma regarding reflexivity concerns psychology's relationship to its subject matter. Psychology is the product of its subject matter which means that psychological theories and findings are not only about the psychological but are themselves instances of the psychological. This has implications for the evaluation of psychological work, for the evaluators will be influenced by how, for example, the work they are evaluating is similar to their own psychological framework.

The third reflexivity paradox Richards points out concerns psychological processes in the context of research. Psychological research on a topic is an aspect of that topic. It is not only that research programmes in science are socially determined but that psychological work on understanding a process is itself an aspect of the evolution of the very process. Related to this is a self-constituting paradox. Psychology creates its own subject matter in that, as Kurt Danziger (1990) points out, psychology is actively engaged in moulding and creating the very thing it studies. What is being studied is the same thing as that doing the studying or even the capacity to do that studying. For example, additional understanding of perception changes perception and determines the nature of that change.

## REFLEXIVITY AND PERSONAL THERAPY

Freud underlined the importance of personal therapy as far as the practice of psychoanalysis was concerned, stating in 'Analysis terminable and interminable': 'But where and how is the poor wretch to acquire the ideal qualifications which he will need in this profession? The answer is in an analysis of himself, with which his preparation for his future activity begins' (1937: 246).

In the USA, personal therapy is far more common among clinical psychologists (Prochaska and Norcross 1983; Norcross, Prochaska and Gallagher 1989). Further, American clinicians rate personal therapy as second only to practical experience as the main contributor to their professional development (Rachelson and Clance 1980). As we discussed earlier, behaviour therapy established a strong hold on the development of clinical psychology in this county for professional and pragmatic reasons (in that it was important in securing psychology an independent professional status within the NHS); and also for academic reasons, fitting in with the British empirical intellectual traditions and with the existing scientist–researcher role of clinical psychology, to which it could be neatly added both in the training courses and in clinical practice. The implications of the scientist–researcher model generally and that of behaviour therapy in particular are important in understanding the context in which issues central to psychotherapy training and practice – such as subjectivity, reflexivity and personal training – have been viewed in the training and clinical practice of psychologists. Behaviour therapy claims to be founded on the scientific basis of learning theory. From this perspective, its practitioners can be viewed as objective scientists who make empirical observations and apply their research-based scientific knowledge to formulate hypotheses, make interventions and proceed with the solutions of the presenting problems. The clinical psychologist's role in this model is essentially that of an applied experimental scientist, with clients or patients viewed as the objects of experimental investigation. Issues relating to the subjectivity of the clinician, the patient or the interaction between them are not seen as having any relevance in this model or, when they do unfortunately arise in the course of the human interaction, are explained and dismissed either within the terms of the theory or as nuisance, extraneous variables. As the name implies its focus is on objectively measurable behaviour. Subjective processes such as thoughts and emotions may be ignored or relegated to secondary consequences of behaviour. The basic behaviourist stance is: change the behaviour – thoughts and feelings will follow.

Norcross et al. (1992c), in a study of the personal therapy of a sample of British clinical psychologists, point out that despite evidence of the prevalence of personal therapy for practitioners, there are few published papers on the topic of personal therapy of therapists and even fewer on the personal therapy of clinical psychologists. They point out that the aim of the psychotherapist's personal therapy is to enhance the effectiveness of subsequent therapeutic work. As part of a larger study of British clinical psychologists, Norcross et al. (1992c) explored the issue of personal therapy of clinical psychologists. They found that compared to their British counterparts, many more American psychologists had sought personal therapy (see, for example, Norcross et al. 1989). This finding, the authors suggest, could be due to the stronger allegiance to behaviourism and cognitivism amongst British clinical psychologists. The majority of the sample in this study claimed personal and professional benefit from their therapy, as well as a heightened awareness of the importance of the therapeutic relationship and nurturing interpersonal skills. Norcross et al. (1992c) suggest that this increased awareness may translate into clinical practice. Having personal therapy has been shown to be associated with the clinician's ability to display empathy, warmth and genuineness (Peebles 1980), and an increased emphasis on the personal relationship in therapy (Wogan

and Norcross 1985). These factors gained from personal therapy
have been shown in the literature to be essential for effective psychological treatment (Greenberg and Staller 1981) and are crucial to
the patient–therapist relationship at least in the practice of insight-
oriented therapy.

The Training Committee of the British Psychological Society sets
criteria by which courses are accredited. However, this has been criticised by, for example, Pilgrim and Treacher because it emphasises
structural criteria rather than addressing the underlying dilemmas
involved in the training of clinical psychologists, like the question of
personal work as a necessary component of training. Pilgrim and
Treacher (1992) point out that the scientist–practitioner model generally, and the influence of behaviour therapy specifically, may be
responsible for the emphasis on the acquisition of theoretical knowledge and skills rather than the exploration of issues of personal
growth and self-knowledge, necessary in understanding the role of
the person in therapy.

Writing from a clinical psychologist trainee's point of view, Morgan
(1993) views the most important part of training as a clinical psychologist as the development of self-awareness, while knowledge
of psychological therapies and their application is essential but
insufficient. While recognising the depth and scope of clinical psychology training, Morgan believes training would be enhanced by
the provision of personal therapy, and outlines three main reasons
why personal therapy should be part of clinical psychology training.
First, the development of self-understanding and the direct experience of being a client, as several studies suggest, enhances clinical
work (Garfield and Kurtz 1976; Peebles 1980; Norcross *et al.* 1992c).
Second, therapy would provide personal support and alleviate stress
during training. Walsh *et al.* (1991) point to the danger that without
personal work trainees will emerge as clinicians with a 'disability
in self-care', the burnt-out professionals described by Rippere and
Williams (1985). In the context of personal therapy, trainees would
also have the opportunity to further their knowledge of the therapeutic relationship, and of their own attitudes and dynamics as they
influence their work with clients. Third, without the experience of
being in the role of patient, Morgan points to the danger of clinicians setting themselves apart from clients who may be seen as
needy recipients in relation to the therapist's role of the holder of
knowledge.

Milne (1989) points out the inconsistency between training and
clinical practice in so far as the model of training largely ignores
personal issues which might have an effect on the trainee, while

emphasis is given to the development of a sound knowledge base and clinical techniques rather than self-awareness. The Committee on Training in Clinical Psychology (CTCP) includes personal support in its Criteria for the Assessment of Post-Graduate Training Courses in Clinical Psychology (CTCP 1991). Courses are requested to be 'alert to personal issues which bear on a trainee's professional performance' and to give 'assistance in obtaining appropriate help' (1991: 14). However, they do not give suggestions as to how best to accomplish this. Attempts have been made on some training courses to address the issue of personal training, such as the use of personal development counselling for clinical psychology trainees. Eayrs *et al.* (1992) describe the setting up of a personal support model for trainees on the North Wales In-Service Training Course in Clinical Psychology. On the Birmingham Clinical Psychology Training Course, Cushway *et al.* (1993) set up a three-tier system of personal support which included a system of personal and appraisal tutors, a personal awareness group, and the opportunity for personal therapy from crisis intervention to longer-term therapy. Trainees also offered their own suggestions for stress reduction, which ranged from keeping travel time to a minimum, to suggesting better information and communication systems between course staff and trainees, to encouraging trainees to create their own support systems. A general finding from the inclusion of personal work in training is that trainees find the experience both personally and professionally valuable.

## IMPLICATIONS OF REFLEXIVITY IN CLINICAL PRACTICE

The issue of reflexivity has implications for clinical practice. Richards (1993) points out that the limits of our understanding of others are bounded by the limitations of one's own understanding of oneself. He points out that the most influential psychological thinkers such as Freud, Jung and even Skinner reflexively explored themselves in the context of their theories. Another point of view, including that of Karl Marx, would widen this definition to include our capacity to go beyond the given, in our capacity, for example, to imagine and to think about our thinking – itself a reflexive process – in setting the limitations of our understanding of human nature. Richards points out that it is only by attending to the problems of reflexivity that we will be able to further our goals of increased understanding of the psychological. However, Richards warns of the routinised ploy of reflexivity sometimes found in the practice of counselling and psychotherapy, of reflexively turning a statement back on itself: for example, the client saying that he is angry with the therapist, the therapist saying this is displaced anger with himself, etc. in a routine of meta-commentary.

Reflexivity has implications not just for the clinician and the process of psychotherapy or counselling, but for the whole organisational context within which practitioners work. As Meikle (1989) discusses, in his paper 'Reality, reflexivity and the NHS', it is all too easy in an era of market forces to forget about issues such as reflexivity and to accept without challenge a particular view of reality, rendering all other accounts of reality redundant. Frequently, clinical psychologists in the NHS are urged to respond to reality. Meikle discusses the notion of a reality, endorsed implicitly if not explicitly by Brown et al. (1988a), who suggest that if it is part of the psychologist's skills to adapt to the world as it is and respond to reality, this would mean a definition of clinical psychology which is market-led, contract-based, competitive, high-profile and marketed. Meikle questions the stance of there being one objective reality rendering all other accounts of reality redundant, stating:

> [E]very scientist, every philosopher, indeed anyone whose aim has been to advance knowledge has striven towards this discovery since the dawn of history. Plato in his shadowy cave, Descartes in his lonely hut and Berkeley in his ephemeral see, Democritus among his speculative atoms, Newton in his orchard and Einstein from somewhere dependent on your vantage point, all sought it in vain and with methodologies now exposed as suspect. But now the truth is out and Brown et al. are among the enlightened.
>
> (Meikle 1989: 32)

If this is indeed a true finding, Meikle suggests that the authors abide by the rules surrounding the declaration of scientific discovery enabling us to assess the validity of this finding. Even if psychological methods yield knowledge which is different from that of the physical sciences, we are still engaged in procedures which derive their validity from a body of knowledge. Meikle points out the difficulties inherent in defining an 'objective reality', and comments that a significant part of our knowledge is concerned with how both individuals and societies fail to reach an appreciation of 'reality'.

If we are to remain truly scientific, Meikle urges we should view with caution 'anyone who would claim a hot-line to reality or would attempt to collapse existing alternative realities into a single monolithic structure without good scientific justification' (1989: 33). This process may be seen in the current market force vocabulary favoured by the new management system in the NHS, where reality is defined in terms such as 'good marketing', 'cost-effectiveness', etc. Meikle highlights the difficulty in being truly scientific – if science is broadly defined as a quest for truth – in the current climate of the NHS. He states:

> [T]he soil in which science seeks to thrive can be either fertile or barren. Government, cultures, powerful individuals or other sponsors can all make things more or less difficult for those who seek the truth for its own sake. But when this happens it is a consequence of someone's choice and policy, not a change in reality and to represent it otherwise is dishonest, particularly for psychologists who know so much about these processes. The current 'market' philosophy is dogma, not reality, and underlying reality does not change to suit dogma. There is therefore a crucial difference here over which science has to take a stance if it is to survive.
>
> (1989: 33)

Clinical psychologists are increasingly being encouraged to justify our existence and to demonstrate our value by being responsive to the needs and requests of mental health service managers and to provide services accordingly. Meikle draws attention to the assumption that it is managers and not clinicians who best know the needs of the clients (or consumers, in the new market jargon). This is a different philosophy from that where clinicians assessed and responded to clients' needs using their professional judgement within the context of academic freedom, which the NHS provided and could continue to provide if the government chose. Changes in the freedom to carry out truly scientific research reflect changes in the policies and choices of the powerful, not a change in 'reality'. Meikle highlights the moral dimension of a 'free' science, stating:

> The possession of scientific knowledge and the derived technology seem to me to imply a moral responsibility for ensuring that they are applied in the interests of clients and humanity in general. To compromise this responsibility by surrendering it to managers whose concerns may be altogether different is to put in jeopardy an important trust.
>
> (1989: 34)

Meikle argues that psychologists are in a better position than most to articulate what is going on, and that as responsible professionals we cannot just forget what we know to be true for the sake of economic survival. He states: 'fugue and amnesia are, as we

know, uneasy and precarious states' (p. 34). Although recognising
the lack of power of psychologists in the current NHS, Meikle urges
us to be reflexive and take for ourselves the advice we often give
to clients 'that in order to achieve something worthwhile and triumph over anxiety, we may have to endure some discomfort and
unpopularity. We can oppose market dogma before we take to the
life-rafts. We need not embrace it' (p. 34).

Attempting to reduce everything to one reality or unreflectively
asserting the importance of one reality over the others has many
crucial implications. For example, it affects the language we use and
ultimately our thoughts and perceptions. Currently, by translating
everything into market force language we even begin to lose the
language in which we can articulate and debate. Meikle gives salu-
tary historical examples of situations where scientists either tried
to ignore the uses to which their discoveries were put, or were
put into situations over which they had no control. For example,
industrial chemists who sold gas to the Nazis in wartime Germany
were following the line of adapting to reality and responding to the
requirements of their managers. Similarly, their modern-day British
equivalents manufacturing and selling weapons of death and mass
destruction are seen as adapting to the real world encouraged by
government policy, and applauded for improving Britain's balance of payments and thus contributing to our economic recovery.
How often, when weapon manufacturers and suppliers are called to
account, the reasons given include adapting to the real world, in the
guise of 'If we didn't supply them, someone else would'. Doubtless,
survivors of the gas chambers and Iraqi conscripts in the Gulf War
would testify that one person's reality is another person's hell.

We all have a responsibility in defining our social and political
reality. If everyone opposed or disagreed with certain government
policies they would remain solitary fantasies. The most striking comment on the NHS reforms was cited by a dialogue on the satirical
Rory Bremner Show, where the interviewee could only conclude
that some of the NHS reforms were instigated as a bet. It is indeed
difficult to know if reality as currently defined has now over-
taken satire.

### PERSPECTIVE REALITY AND THE EVOLUTION OF
### A SUBJECTIVE METHODOLOGY

The major philosophical task of our age was seen by Husserl to be
the evolution of a subjective method which would take account of

the perspectival world and of intersubjectivity in the cultural and moral communities in which we live. The basic truth of perceptual experience is that what we see is directly dependent upon the perspective from which we see it. Our experience of the outer world modifies that structure and affects the way it works. In a process of selection and exclusion, a world-view will be filtered through the hopes and fears, the expectations and the experiences of the individual. The end result is a set of perspectives which have been multiply modified in the transmission. There is, as Poole points out, not truth only truths according to one's perspectives. This is similar, as we have seen, to the concepts developed in the 1930s by Allport's concept of perceptual set and in the 1950s by Kelly's personal construct theory.

What Poole terms as subjective reflection, or subjective methodology, consists of first analysing and then recognising perspectival reality and the relativity of criteria. Objectivity, with its preconceptions about the monolithic nature of truth, the facts, etc., believes that there is only one solution to any given problem or state of affairs. This implies a conceptual distortion from the outset. Subjective reflection works with subjective tools. Sympathy, empathy and antipathy, for example, are not tools which would be allowed at any point in objective analysis. In addition, Poole points out, some major structures of subjective thinking are personal commitment, ethical concern, desire to treat the totality, necessity of taking account of the reality of perspectival variation and distortion, the use of unquantifiable evidence, comparison, interrelation and description. Roger Poole concludes his book on deep subjectivity in this way:

> Deep subjectivity emerges finally then as a concern for objectivity, for a full, real and adequate objectivity. In order to express this concern, it has to discover (first of all) and then to trust to (even harder) a space of personally won philosophical commitment.
>
> Deep subjectivity operates from within a philosophical space with the tools of subjective analysis and critique. It thus affects and challenges the world of objectivity and sets up a more acceptable standard of objectivity beside it.
>
> (1972: 152)

## THE CHALLENGE OF SUBJECTIVITY TO THE PRACTICE OF PSYCHOLOGY AND COUNSELLING

We have seen in this chapter how traditional classic science has influenced the development of modern psychology and influenced the current theories and practices of its derivative professions such as clinical psychology and counselling psychology. Clinical psychology can continue with the old scientific paradigm, adding yet more research papers albeit adapting their focus to accommodate the new managerial demands of the NHS. One of the effects of the professionalism of clinical psychology is a concern for status and respectability, which results in the reinforcement of the status quo. To this has been added another factor, which is the current political context of the NHS with its philosophy of free market individualism and managerialism. The philosophical, political and moral concerns which should be included in the study of the circumstances of human beings are sacrificed to the altar of professionalism. To effect a radical change in the approach of clinical psychology to its discipline would fundamentally challenge their present concerns and way of working. There is not likely to be much encouragement for such changes in the managerial structure of the NHS, nor from many individual clinical psychologists who in this era of employment insecurity would understandably be concerned with preserving their jobs.

Counselling psychology is a newer profession and draws on other theoretical models as well as those derived from academic psychology. However, in so far as both counselling and clinical psychology base their theory and practice on traditional notions of science they both ignore and deny essential elements concerning the study of humanity. Counselling and clinical psychology are presented with a choice: either to remain with traditional notions of science or to face the challenge of integrating subjectivity and all its philosophical, ethical as well as methodological implications into their theory and practice.

Mental health care workers, including psychologists working in the NHS, are required to offer briefer treatment to a wider range of patients in order to reduce waiting lists and help provide better care in the community for those with longer-term mental health needs discharged to the community after the closure of the mental hospitals. Likewise in their research concerns, clinical psychologists are increasingly being professionally acquiescent in serving the requirements of their paymasters. Research increasingly has to be of direct relevance and use to the health service. Such research is often in the form of service evaluation in its different forms. (I sometimes wonder how many negative findings are presented to health service managers, or if indeed despite the evidence of our senses, health services to patients are in fact improving dramatically up and down the country as they are said to be). There is correspondingly, as we shall see in Chapter Four, an increasing tendency on courses for adding additional components such as managerial and diverse therapeutic skills to go on being added, to provide the required 'skills mix' according to the fashion of the day.

Counselling does not have the historical professional legacy regarding objective research as does clinical psychology. Further, the more specific focus of its concerns, of human relationships, as we shall see in Chapter Four, makes it more readily amenable to the exploration of subjective understandings.

It would be refreshing to see if counselling psychologists were authentic in their attempts to provide a necessary service. Counselling psychology has a choice. It can follow in the footsteps of clinical psychology in seeking professional status and respectability. Indeed it may in many ways gain from its association with traditional clinical psychology in benefiting from the professional gains and recognition clinical psychology has obtained after many and often difficult years of struggle for recognition in the health service. It may present itself to health service managers and to GP fundholders as a more individualistic, easier to manage and cheaper option than clinical psychology. This would be especially so in areas such as primary mental health care, where counselling psychologists could present themselves as just competitors in a field where they may have specialised knowledge of an important function of psychological services, namely counselling. Alternatively, counselling psychology could face up to the challenge of subjectivity, which as a discipline it is ideally suited to do. Counselling psychology would then be a truly authentic and worthwhile endeavour. Attempting to face the challenge of subjectivity is a difficult challenge but the act of attempting it is vital.

## · FOUR ·

# Specific issues in counselling in psychological services

## TRAINING IN CLINICAL AND COUNSELLING PSYCHOLOGY

Both professions of clinical psychology and counselling psychology require post-graduate training. To become either a chartered clinical or counselling psychologist, it is first necessary to complete a BPS-accredited first degree. The counselling psychology training is through the BPS's Diploma in Counselling Psychology or, alternatively, through taking a Society-accredited post-graduate training course. These courses will allow candidates to be exempt from all or part of the Diploma. As it is a new profession at present there is a 'grandfather clause' enabling psychologists with suitable experience in the field of counselling to obtain a Statement of Equivalence to the Diploma in Counselling Psychology and to use the term Chartered Counselling Psychologist. As the Diploma and post-graduate courses are becoming more established the 'grandfather clause' ends in January 1997. Clinical psychology training takes an additional three years after completion of a BPS-accredited undergraduate degree, and must be undertaken through a Society-accredited training course. Places are in short supply, with around 20 applicants for each place, and often a first or an upper second class degree is required. Also important is relevant experience, either before or after graduation, and an understanding of the profession. Frequently, potential applicants gain this experience by working as psychology assistants. After over 10 years of discussion within the profession, the Whitley Council rules changed in 1992 with the result that all clinical psychology training programmes became three-year courses. Starting with the intake of 1992, all trainees have to complete at least three years of suitably supervised training before being eligible for Grade A posts. The move to three-year structures on courses has been accompanied by increased calls for changes from MSc and Diploma qualifications to doctoral degrees. As clinical psychology training has a longer-established background than counselling psychology, more has been written on both the training process and evaluation of training. We will first examine the training requirements for clinical psychology before looking at the requirements for counselling psychology.

## TRAINING ISSUES IN CLINICAL PSYCHOLOGY

The fundamental purpose of the Committee on Training in Clinical Psychology (CTCP) is the accreditation of courses and the promotion of good practice within clinical psychology training. The main business of the Committee is to discuss and finalise the reports arising from the five-year cycle of accreditation visits to courses. As well as accrediting individual courses, the Committee has the brief of implementing the British Psychological Society's policies regarding clinical psychology training. The whole area of 'qualifications' is an issue. For example, in January 1994 the Committee noted the proposals from some 10 different training courses for clinical doctoral degrees (e.g. DClinPsy) and it is reviewing the implications, for clinical psychology training, of the widespread move to doctoral qualification. The Committee is concerned that clinical psychology training should generally reflect the demand for clinical psychology services within the NHS, and as such has expanded its role in relation to regional health authorities, who currently have the ultimate responsibility for commissioning clinical psychology training.

Since 1980 there has been a clearing house system in order to help applicants apply for clinical psychology courses. A handbook is published annually which describes the courses, which have to be accredited by the Training Committee of the British Psychological Society. However, these criteria are mainly structural and concern the organisation of the courses. There is a great deal of variability between the courses as to philosophy and content. Some of the main issues that revolve around training courses are the degree to which they adhere to the scientist–practitioner model, and the degree to which they adhere to an eclectic rather than a behavioural model. Other issues emerge such as the question of whether clinical psychologists can be adequately trained without undergoing some personal therapy, and whether the variability and range of training and the trend towards eclecticism results in a professional identity confusion.

Clinical psychologists will have studied on a three-year degree course in psychology before undertaking their professional clinical psychology training. This post-graduate training consists of an additional three years specifically in the theoretical and practical applications of clinical psychology. This is usually university-based and until recently led to an MSc in Clinical Psychology. An increasing trend over the last few years is for these courses to be extended into doctoral courses. During this training knowledge of a broad range of therapies is emphasised so that clinical psychologists are able, as far as possible, to assess and plan the most appropriate therapy for their future clients. One element of training is an acknowledgement of the limitations of trainees' knowledge and experience, and the appropriateness of referring on to other professionals when necessary. Some clinical psychologists specialise further after training, and take post-qualification courses in, for example, counselling or in psychotherapy.

A major difficulty is that clinical psychologists are a scarce resource in the NHS. The total profession numbered only 2,500 in 1989 and only 179 training places were available. Over the last decade there has been an increasing demand from health care providers for clinical psychologists to contribute to the continuously changing organisational and therapeutic needs of the NHS. A series of manpower surveys has been carried out, and these have shown both the expansion of clinical psychology services and the shortfall in the supply of qualified staff (Scrivens and Charlton 1985; Whitehead and Parry 1986). The number of vacant posts is a problem for the development of clinical psychology generally, especially so in services with the highest vacancy rates, such as services for people with learning disabilities, older adults and people with severe mental health problems. The acknowledgement of these difficulties brought about a major national review of the profession which examined models of service delivery and future targets for training (MPAG 1990). It is clear that if the demand for clinical psychologists is to be met, then there has to be a significant increase in the number trained. The MPAG report recommended a short-term increase in training places for England from 152 places funded by the NHS in 1989 to targets of 258 and 303 for 1990 and 1991. However, these targets were not met as shown by a survey by Richardson (1992) indicating only 163 for 1990 and 191 for 1991. As Turpin et al.

(1993) point out, there are many reasons for the failure to achieve the MPAG targets. For example, the publication of the MPAG report coincided with the major reforms within the NHS.

Courses differ as to the extent to which they expect students to have previous work experience outside the educational setting before embarking on a post-graduate course in clinical psychology. In their clinical training, psychologists are expected to acquire a broad range of psychological therapies and approaches which reflect the multi-dimensional nature of personal experience and the influences upon it. Courses may differ in the emphasis they may place on a particular model or theory, but they are required to provide knowledge of a range of models including behavioural, supportive, cognitive and psychodynamic approaches. Some courses reflect the tendency towards eclecticism.

The form of clinical psychology training in Britain is that of generic training. All courses require that trainees should undertake clinical placements under supervision in specialisms such as child health, adult mental health and learning disabilities. Some courses require additional compulsory placements. Over time, training courses have developed in parallel with the changing role of clinical psychology itself. For example, as clinical psychologists have become more involved in areas such as psychotherapy and in work with clients with complex and long-term difficulties, so training courses have adapted and have become increasingly eclectic in order to meet the necessary training requirements. As is the case in medicine, new courses are added as the professional or knowledge base expands, with little consideration given to how this information is to be assimilated or integrated. The workload demanded by the courses, together with the consequent scarcity of time and limited financial resources of most trainees, is one of the factors frequently mentioned that prevents the consideration of adding a further, and often expensive component such as personal therapy to the already overstretched syllabuses.

Although all courses have to conform to a number of criteria in order to gain accreditation by the Training Committee of the BPS, they are variable as to emphasis of content and goals of training. One major dimension on which courses may be compared is the degree of adherence to the scientist–practitioner or to the eclectic model. Although some argue that the resultant variability is the profession's strength, others point to the individual trainee being left in a state of confusion within the context of a wide range of contradictory opinions within the profession. For example, David Smail (1982) points out that the eclectic blandness of many courses can lead to a homogenised and sterilised version of clinical psychology, lacking in both commitment and passion.

## THE CONTENT OF CLINICAL PSYCHOLOGY COURSES

The Committee on Training in Clinical Psychology of the BPS outlines the criteria for accreditation by the BPS of post-graduate training courses in clinical psychology (1995). The BPS delineates certain roles in the training of clinical psychologists, such as the role of supervisors and that of coordinator of training or course organiser. The content of clinical psychology training courses in Britain can be divided into three main components. These are the academic component, the clinical component of supervised clinical experience and the research component. According to the model of clinical psychology these three components of academic, clinical and research experience should be closely interrelated. However, a frequent difficulty expressed by trainees is the difficulty of integrating the academic and clinical components. The clinical skills taught by different courses will to some degree vary according to the theoretical preference of the course. Exposure to core clinical models and skills cannot be left to supervised placement alone, given the inevitable variations between supervisors and the time constraints on supervised placements. Thus, as part of the academic programme the teaching of core clinical skills is alongside academic and theoretical perspectives, psychological and psychotherapeutic models, research ideas and the development of fundamental clinical strategies, techniques and insights. This to some degree ensures the exposure of trainees to the core clinical models and skills.

A survey by Frosh and Levinson (1990) conducted amongst clinical psychologists with supervisory responsibilities on the North West Thames course aimed to identify the skills which are generally thought to be central to clinical psychology training and practice. A range of skills was nominated by the supervisors, which were then categorised into four main headings: assessment, therapeutic, professional and personal. The components of these four main areas, together with the percentage figure of supervisors in this sample who rated the skill as central to the training of clinical psychologists, were as follows.

Eight elements came under the general heading of *assessment skills*.

1 Basic assessment methods: 37 per cent (e.g. elicitation of baseline data, administering psychometric tests, specialist test and interpreting results)

2 Basic assessment interviewing: 26 per cent (e.g. interviewing for clinically relevant information)
3 Hypothesising and problem formulation: 17 per cent
4 Cognitive assessment of children and adults: 6 per cent
5 Basic observational principles: 6 per cent
6 Behavioural assessment: 6 per cent
7 Assessing children and families: 0 per cent
8 Information on tests and background psychometric rationale: 0 per cent.

The components of the second main category were concerned with *therapeutic skills.*

1 Listening, counselling and psychotherapeutic skills: 54 per cent
2 Knowledge of common behavioural and cognitive procedures: 49 per cent
3 Basic therapeutic interviewing and awareness of range of interview styles: 29 per cent
4 Marital and family therapy: 11 per cent
5 Forming empathic working relationships with clients: 11 per cent (e.g. developing and maintaining rapport)
6 Developing a problem-solving/hypothesis-testing approach: 9 per cent (e.g. generating hypotheses, making formulations)
7 Group therapy: 9 per cent
8 Consultative: 6 per cent (including knowledge of how organisational, institutional and professional systems work)
9 Interviewing children and families: 0 per cent.

The third category involved *professional skills.*

1 Record-keeping, report- and letter-writing: 23 per cent
2 Multi-disciplinary and teamwork: 23 per cent
3 Social and communication skills with colleagues and clients: 17 per cent
4 Combining research and practitioner roles: 11 per cent
5 Understanding group processes: 0 per cent.

The final category referred to *personal skills.*

1 Maintaining emotional detachment and empathy: 11 per cent
2 Self-knowledge: 6 per cent (e.g. the capacity to explore one's own feelings and thoughts).

As well as nominating the skills which they saw as central to the training of clinical psychologists, the supervisors were asked to nominate the skills according to two additional criteria: whether they thought it necessary for trainees to have learnt the skills before the placement, and whether they would be expected to learn the skills during the placement. Thus skills such as assessing children and families and the understanding of group processes, although not seen as central to the training of clinical psychologists, were identified as skills which a trainee should expect to learn during a placement. Other elements such as information on tests and background psychometric rationale were seen as necessary for the trainee to have learnt before the placement.

The second part of Frosh and Levinson's questionnaire elicited supervisors' views on the role of the course in offering clinical skills training. It suggested a range of views concerning the respective roles of course work and placements. Some supervisors, reflecting the apprenticeship model of training, viewed clinical skills as the province of clinical supervision, although most suggested that all the skills identified could be introduced on the academic programme but refined during the placement. The preferred model was one in which the academic course provided a theoretical background to clinical skills, together with the opportunity for trainees to practice skills in a supportive setting with feedback from trainers and peers. On placement, trainees could then learn about the application and development of these skills in various settings.

Frosh and Levinson's survey demonstrates that clinical supervisors are willing to identify a range of skills which they view as being central to the training of clinical psychologists. Many of these skills are in the traditional core areas of clinical psychological practice, techniques of formal assessment, and behavioural and cognitive interventions. However, the authors also comment on a notable emphasis on interviewing, both for assessment and therapeutic purposes, and on counselling and psychotherapeutic skills. In fact counselling and psychotherapeutic skills were the most nominated set of therapeutic skills. Some of the apparent inconsistencies in the questionnaire results have to do with the discrepancies between ratings of the importance of clinical skills of various kinds, and of the provision for training in these skills offered on placement. Thus some of the best provision was for skills not rated particularly highly in terms of importance. For example, 43 per cent of supervisors said that trainees would receive experience in consultative, organisational/institutional and professional systems work, but only 6 per cent nominated this as a central clinical skill. Similarly, while 40 per cent of supervisors offered experience in multi-disciplinary and team-work, only 23 per cent nominated this as a core skill. With reference to clinical practice, 49 per cent viewed knowledge of common behavioural and cognitive procedures as a central skill, and 37 per cent thought these skills should have been taught prior to the placement. However, only 23 per cent actually offered training in this model of work.

Only 11 per cent of supervisors regarded the combining of research and practitioner roles either as a skill to be learnt on placement or even as one which should have been previously taught. Again this highlights the issue of the research basis of professional identity. The emphasis by training courses on research is frequently not reflected in the supervisory practice of trained clinical psychologists. It seems from this survey that clinical psychologists view themselves as needing considerable ability in interviewing and formal assessment techniques, alongside expertise in some of a wide range of therapeutic techniques. Further, it is of interest to note that although many psychologists currently work in teams of one kind or another, it seems that clinical psychologists still regard face-to-face assessment and therapeutic interventions with clients as their central tasks.

Research is an element frequently stressed in the training courses. The stress is on a knowledge of the whole process of research. However, as we have seen, a continuing issue is how much and what kind of research qualified clinical psychologists carry out, and the extent to which they use research findings in their daily practice. However, the ability to interpret research findings and make sense of research papers, even if they do not all directly conduct research in their daily practice, is still stressed as an important component of the clinical psychologist's role.

Considering the clinical component in clinical psychology training, the BPS stipulates that supervised clinical experience must normally extend over at least a continuous three-year period. At least 50 per cent (338–400 days) of the total course time must be on placement with supervised clinical experience. During the course of training the range of clinical experience must be gained in service for five categories: adults with psychological disorders; children and adolescents with psychological disorders; adults and children with learning disability; and elderly people with psychological disorders. In addition to these four, an elective experience is required to provide the trainee with the opportunity to acquire further specialist skills. The criteria for an elective experience include, for example, experience with a particular client group such as people with neuropsychological problems or people with chronic mental illness; within particular settings, for example, forensic services; or intensive experience with a particular therapeutic technique such as psychodynamic psychotherapy, family therapy, behavioural or cognitive therapy. The BPS details the exact requirements of supervised clinical experience in terms of time spent and assessment. For example, clinical placements have to ensure that there is enough time to gain the relevant experience, and placements should be of at least four months' duration.

Clinical experience needs to be planned in a developmental sequence to allow trainees to develop their core skills through experience with different groups. The aims of clinical placements are to ensure that trainees have experience in the full range of psychological work in health settings. This should include applying a variety of psychological models to a wide range of clinical problems across the age spectrum and in a variety of settings. Core placements will involve direct experience with clients and indirect work with carers and others. There is a need for experience of working in multi-disciplinary settings and for some involvement in the planning and organisation of services. Trainees should gain understanding of the psychology department in which they are working and the NHS generally. Trainees should develop skills in assessment, formulation, intervention, evaluation and reporting. There must be enough time and experience through the placements to ensure that these are developed adequately. The overall amount of time allocated to clinical experience should be 50–60 per cent of the total time available. Enough time should be allocated to the main client groups so that the full range of core experience may be gained. Core experience is distinguished from placements, since the same placement may provide experience of more than one client group and it may be necessary to have more than one placement to gain all the required experience with a particular client group.

For their core training, all trainees should obtain experience with children and adolescents, adults, elderly people and people with learning disabilities. Core experience in child and adolescent problems should provide trainees with opportunities to work with children and young people with a variety of problems, including developmental, emotional and behavioural, and also across the full age range. Assessment work should be broadly based, including but not confined to assessment of intelligence and attainment. There should be experience of treatment both of individual children and of the child within the family. Placements should enable trainees to understand the organisational context of services for children, and provide experience of liaising with other agencies. Further, trainees should have the opportunity to understand the problems experienced by children who have been physically and/or sexually abused and the difficulties of working with such children and their families.

### Core training experiences in clinical psychology placements

Core experience in adult psychological problems should give trainees supervised experience with a range of clinical approaches and techniques of assessment and intervention. There should be experience with a range of psychological problems including acute, severe and long-term problems with a range of severity and across the life span. Placements should enable trainees to understand the organisational context of services for adults.

Core experience in work with elderly people should include assessment of and intervention in both functional and organic problems. There should be both direct work with elderly people and indirect work with families and other carers. Trainees should be alerted to the ways in which various psychotherapeutic and behavioural interventions may need to be adapted when used with this client group as well as gaining some knowledge of therapies devised specifically for use with older people.

Core experience in work with people with learning disabilities should include: assessment and interventions; both direct work with handicapped people and indirect work with their carers; work in residential and day-care settings; work with families and work as a part of a multi-disciplinary team. Experience should be gained with people with mild and severe degrees of disability and with both children and adults. The trainee should gain experience of working in a service specifically for people with learning disabilities.

Trainees should also have a specialist experience which consolidates and develops their existing experience. It could be specialist regarding client group, setting and/or therapeutic orientation. This might include, for example, neurological disorders, behavioural medicine, primary health care, adolescent services, rehabilitation, forensic services, therapeutic communities, dynamic psychotherapy, family therapy or social or education services.

The guidelines also detail the research experiences necessary for trainee clinical psychologists on their clinical placements. Trainees should have experience of small-scale service-oriented research in at least one of their placements. The placement should include teaching and supervised experience of a range of methods of assessment

and clinical investigation. This should include structured interviewing, observation of behaviour and psychometric methods
where appropriate. Trainees during the course of their placements
should gain knowledge of the theory and practice of a wide range
of psychological interventions and therapies. It is expected that the
training course would include supervisors representing a wide variety
of approaches. In addition, thorough supervised experience in more
than one approach should be provided at a level sufficient for trainees
to achieve competence in their use. Furthermore, supervised experience of treatment spanning at least six months should be provided
at some stage for all trainees.

In addition to the above clinical requirements, the Guidelines also
cover other areas which should be covered during clinical placements.
For example, at least some placements should provide experience
of working with patients in close cooperation with other members
of a multi-disciplinary team. Trainees should have supervised experience during placements of teaching and/or training other staff.

## RESEARCH COMPONENT IN CLINICAL PSYCHOLOGY TRAINING

The third component of training is concerned with the assessment
of research competence. The BPS believes that knowledge and competence in psychological research is a hallmark of a clinical psychologist. Trainees are required to complete a research dissertation
reporting a substantial piece of research. The aims of the research project are to provide trainees with experience of completing research
within a clinical context, and also to foster the development of
research awareness and skills. The topic for research must address
a problem of relevance to the practice of clinical psychology. For
example, a consumer satisfaction survey should be of a group either
receiving some form of psychological help or with known or predicted psychological needs. Examples of projects include single-case
experiments to evaluate treatment efficacy, small-scale surveys,
analysis of data routinely collected by a service, and small pieces of
quantitative research. As well as considering ethical issues raised
by the research, trainees are required to ensure that the research
design, execution, analysis and interpretation should be of a high
standard and appropriate to the research problem and they should
be prepared to justify their methods at the oral examination. The
BPS outlines precise details of the presentation and format of the
dissertation according to conventional scientific criteria.

### *Legacy of the scientific–practitioner model in clinical psychology training*

Although courses have moved away from the narrow behavioural paradigm to a more eclectic trend, this does not solve the problems inherent in the scientist–practitioner model. A further difficulty is an eclectic approach presented without a sense of integration, with each and every theory duly presented and criticised in the name of academic freedom. The eclectic approach of many courses is also a difficulty for the cultivation of the scientist–practitioner psychologist. Eclecticism carries with it difficulties not just of pure information overload, but also of having to assimilate a wide variety of models, giving rise to the emotionally as well as intellectually difficult task of having to hold sometimes contradictory views of persons and the world, without succumbing to a crisis of dissonance or existential paralysis. There is also a danger that the traditional academic critical appraisal of theories is at the expense of personal knowledge of one's own feelings and intuition, and of the creativity engendered by philosophical or theoretical commitment.

## TENSION BETWEEN THE SCIENTIFIC–PRACTITIONER AND PSYCHOTHERAPEUTIC MODELS IN TRAINING AND PRACTICE

I have shown in earlier chapters that clinical psychology has traditionally emphasised its research basis. The profession has generally promoted the research aspect of a clinical psychologist's role relative to the therapeutic role and the practical knowledge gained from direct client contact. However, there has been much discussion about the success of clinical psychology courses in producing scientist–practitioners, at least in the sense of pure research. This is due to two main factors. First, competent research training is long and arduous, and it is debatable whether this degree of competence can be gained within the time allocated to it on clinical psychology courses. Furthermore, as Eysenck originally pointed out, there are inherent occupational difficulties in trying to combine the role of the scientist and the clinician. As we have seen in Chapter Three, these difficulties are compounded by the occupational pressures currently operating within the NHS which do not encourage a culture where the process of research can be carried out in any meaningful sense of the word.

The complicated and difficult role of the clinical psychologist within the NHS is currently characterised by a culture of continuous change

and uncertainties, which has made the trainee role even more demanding, insecure, confusing and personally vulnerable. However,
as Pilgrim and Treacher (1992) point out, the profession of clinical
psychology has stressed its scientific basis and has not valued self-
reflexivity. They emphasise the historical roots of this, pointing out
how a male-dominated profession sought to establish a role by
stressing its scientific and diagnostic skills and credentials in the process of understanding patients' distress. As such, historically it could
ill afford to pay attention to the profession's and practitioners' own
human vulnerabilities. This legacy has left its mark in the paradox
that a profession focused on caring for others psychologically is
often neglectful of its own practitioners, and uncaring of its trainees
as they attempt a role which is increasingly diffuse and personally
threatening.

However, the historical debate in clinical psychology between the
scientific–practitioner and psychotherapeutic role of clinical psychology has continued throughout the development of psychology. Some
clinical psychologists, especially those with a psychodynamic background or those who have undertaken post-qualification psychodynamic training, such as Crockatt (1976) and Mollon (1989), take
a very different view of the development of clinical psychology from
the scientist–practitioner model as proposed by Eysenck. Crockatt
(1976) advocates that clinical psychology should place the clinical,
therapeutic role before developing the assessment and research roles
and the more recent roles of teacher and consultant. He views the
central role of a clinical psychologist as that of therapist, specialising
in the practice and development of methods of psychological help
for those suffering from psychological distress. Crockatt cites Koch
(1974) who argues that the adoption of the scientist–practitioner
model reflects an inappropriate view of science as applied to psychology in the nineteenth century. Koch points out that many
psychologists have applied the methods of natural science to social
and human events to the exclusion of any other form of knowledge.
Koch argues that the early experimentalists' concern that psychology should be adequate to science overrode their commitment that
it should be adequate to the person. In this way the institutionalisation of psychology preceded its content, and the methods of psychology preceded an adequate consideration of problems.

Using Koch's argument Crockatt (1976) questions how clinical
psychological research and assessment can be in any way relevant
or meaningful if it is carried out by people who separate themselves
from the phenomena they claim to study, that is, the experience of
psychological distress. Mollon (1989) points out the danger that
academic psychology is used by clinical psychologists as a defence

against coming into emotional contact with clients and their emotional pain. The danger that comes from a clinician attempting to distance him- or herself is, in Mollon's view, the development of manipulative and technique-oriented prescriptive therapies based on an illusion of omnipotence. Developing the clinical and therapeutic role of clinical psychology could ultimately lead to more meaningful and relevant research activities and teacher, supervisor and consultant roles.

Mollon (1989) discusses the issue of identity confusion that can beset the clinical psychologist. He points out that the lack of agreement about the central task of clinical psychology can result in a sense of a lack of identity. Furthermore, Mollon points out, clinical psychologists often have a weak sense of historical lineage as the history of psychology is too broad and diverse for them to immediately identify with. Mollon argues that there are two ways of achieving a professional identity: one is through an omnipotent assumption of identity based on 'projective identification'; the other is based on the slow and sometimes painful process of learning and development. He gives an illustration of projective identification in his description of a small girl dressing up in adult clothes, playing with a doll which she describes as being her baby and pretending that she is her mother. In this case the little girl has a lot of development and learning to go through before she in reality can become a mother. The false assumption of characteristics inherent in projective identification may be seen not just in the individual but in groups and institutions. When the psychologist is facing a difficult task or role without adequate guidance and supervision, the tendency is to resort to projective identification, to avoid the pain of learning and gradual development. The desired identity can be omnipotently enhanced.

This situation, Mollon claims, often characterises that of the trainee clinical psychologist. He or she does not have enough time in training to develop and learn, and at the same time is not encouraged to express doubts or personal difficulties. As Pilgrim and Treacher point out, unless the supervisor has been trained in models which recognise the exploration of personal issues there is a tendency for their own experience of supervision to be repeated with their own supervisees. However, other psychologists, such as behaviour therapists with an adherence to the scientist–practitioner model of Eysenck and Shapiro, can express a strong sense of identity without tackling any of the issues revolving around reflexivity and personal exploration.

Mollon discusses the question whether clinical psychology training often encourages a detached intellectual stance rather than one which fosters an emotional contact with the patient. The relative brevity of clinical training does not allow genuine growth and learning to take place. He does not view clinical psychology training as incorporating an apprenticeship model, at least in the intensive, long-term analytical sense. However, it may be argued that clinical training does involve supervision albeit of shorter duration and carried out by a sequence of different supervisors working in different specialisms. It therefore could be said to contain elements of an apprenticeship model.

Mollon views the attempts to distance oneself from the emotional distress experienced by patients, for example in the application of techniques and strategies to manipulate or modify behaviour, as containing elements of manic and obsessional controlling states of mind. Behaviour therapy in his view is an example of a manipulative and prescriptive therapy based on a delusion of omnipotence. Mollon looks from a psychodynamic perspective at why clinical psychologists embraced behaviour therapy. He derides the tendency towards eclecticism as merely the putting together of different scraps of information so that each individual psychologist collates a pseudo-original mix of assorted therapies. This he views as the consequence of the denial of inheritance and the avoidance of the apprenticeship model. A difficulty in Mollon's perspective is his view that psychoanalysis is the only tradition that psychologists should be encouraged to follow, whereas Corsini points out there are currently at least 15 major approaches to psychotherapy (Corsini and Wedding 1989). Mollon disregards the historical context that confronted the development of clinical psychology as an independent profession, as I have outlined and as is described for example by Smail (1973) and Pilgrim and Treacher (1992). He also disregards the practicalities of training for most aspirant practitioners in terms of psychoanalytic training being both costly and lengthy, and predominantly London-based.

## TRAINEES' DIFFICULTIES IN CLINICAL PSYCHOLOGY TRAINING

In a paper written by a first-year trainee clinical psychologist, Nikki Gorsuch (1994) sets out some of the issues confronted by trainees in the early days of training. Gorsuch describes the difficulties in acknowledging the confusion experienced in the role of a new trainee and in adopting a professional identity as a psychologist. Behind the reticence of Gorsuch's peer group there lay considerable uncertainty and anxiety. This reticence was due to several factors. For example, there was little encouragement to express these feelings, no forum for expressing doubt and no exploration of the way their work was affecting them at a personal level. In addition, there was an investment in being 'knowledgeable' – which quality had got them their places on the course. The pressure within the health service was to be effective and efficient. Gorsuch describes the difficulty in role identity and notes that although the current trend is towards viewing psychologists as a supervisory resource, the identity of psychologists seems to shift according to the structures they find themselves in. Discussing how clinical psychology's internal coherence derives from its basis in academic psychology, Gorsuch comments that this can often seem too broad a background for psychologists to relate their immediate concerns to.

Another difficulty lay in attempting to combine academic and clinical ways of understanding. Neatly presented theories can easily demoralise trainees when contrasted with the unpredictable reality of clinical sessions. Gorsuch writes:

> Presumably the emphasis on theory was not necessarily because of bad course organisation but because it is actually very difficult to talk about how to work with a particular human being and translate theory into a living relationship. Yet speaking in the patient's language is what we need to learn.
>
> (1994: 11)

Gorsuch goes on to describe the difficulties experienced by trainees as they struggle with the issues of personal motivation and professional role, stating; 'More than in any other job, the instruments with which we work are our selves; our own histories and individuality cannot be left out of it. Yet, at the same time, we are each of us striving to cast ourselves in a common mould' (1994: 11). She considers personal motivations, recollecting reading a booklet when applying for clinical training, which recommended that when the applicant was asked the inevitable question at interview as to why they wanted to become clinical psychologists, on no account should they give the reply that it was because they wanted to help people. However, that is just what many applicants wish to do. Other motives may include identification with clients, a wish to be needed, or to be in the role of rescuing others. However, trainees are rarely encouraged on courses to explore and acknowledge such motives or consider the implications of these in their work with clients. Gorsuch suggests that there may be a collective wish to deny our own investment as if in so doing our validity or competence as therapists and status as professionals is somehow undermined.

By emphasising the theoretical and the technical, training courses can often distance trainees from their clients' pain. However, rarely do courses set up a structure where this issue may be addressed so that the individual trainees do not become overwhelmed by it. Gorsuch raises another important issue which revolves around the psychologist's role in the alleviation of distress. Distress, as I discuss fully in Chapter Six, is also embedded in a social and cultural context. It may be, as psychologists such as David Smail emphasise, a sign that something is amiss not with the individual but with the larger social context. To view the role of the clinical psychologist as helping to bring about a better adjustment brings about the danger that psychologists ignore the causal societal determinants of distress, and act in a role that serves only to conserve the status quo.

## POST-QUALIFICATION TRAINING IN
## CLINICAL PSYCHOLOGY

In recent years there has been increasing evidence of clinical psychologists acknowledging the need to continue to develop their knowledge and skills throughout their careers. This ranges from the necessity of acquiring new skills such as in supervision of trainees, personal and career development, the development of specialist knowledge and the maintenance of good professional standards. As Green (1992) points out, the pattern of post-qualification training has tended to be diverse and driven primarily by the interests of individual clinical psychologists resulting in what Green terms 'a healthy catholic repertoire' (1995: 37) of the content of post-qualification training. Green continues:

> However, the political passion of the current era is that professional education in the NHS should be driven by employers' priorities. Just as the skills profile of the workforce as a whole needs to match the business requirements of the organizations the post-qualification training of the individual practitioner should be linked to the specific quality and quantity of health care contracts. So, for example, doctors may be directed to develop skills in keyhole surgery or psychologists required to become competent in time-limited focused psychotherapy. The NHS has sought to create a managerial culture in which organizational goals can be translated into operationally defined targets for individual workers using an individual performance review (IPR) system. When you know what you are supposed

to be achieving over the next year or so, it should be a deal easier to work out what training you will require to enable you to meet those expectations.

(1995: 37–8)

As well as the clinical training, the profession is also committed to post-qualification training. 'Psychologists shall endeavour to maintain and develop their professional competence' (BPS 1993: Section 2,1). The Division of Clinical Psychology Standing Committee on Post-Qualification Training has sought to be facilitative rather then prescriptive in its approach. Continuous professional development is a voluntary activity. In 1990 the DCP Standing Committee on Post-Qualification Training reported on the broad findings of a survey carried out in Britain in order to guide its own initiatives in this area. It reported that post-qualification training was organised at a regional level in England and at a national level in Wales, Scotland and the six counties of Northern Ireland. This has the advantage of being able to pool resources from geographical areas large enough to provide local teachers or trainers. However, since the survey was carried out, reorganisation of the NHS has meant that many of the structures which supported continuing professional development, such as district departments and regional post-qualification training committees, have either disappeared, or no longer control or have access to financial resources to fund these activities. Currently post-qualification training is mainly organised around three or four events a year, often lasting a day or more on appropriate topics. These topics broadly fall into three categories: current issues, skill acquisition (both clinical and professional) and academic updating. Additionally many clinical psychologists are encouraged to attend conferences or events run by the British Psychological Society, other professional bodies and universities.

At district, area, or department level, many heads of service support staff development, for example holding regular departmental seminars. The findings of the survey indicated that there was a host of post-qualification training potentially available to clinical psychologists. The survey also notes arrangements for the training of supervisors which is invariably undertaken by the local training courses, for example through the setting up of supervisors' workshops. Other local initiatives include the opportunity for staff members in Dumfries and Galloway to register for a two-year post-qualification course in therapeutic psychology based at the department; in Grampian, staff members are encouraged to register for a post-graduate diploma in psychotherapy; and in the North

Warwickshire NHS Trust, staff members are given the opportunity to attend the two-year part-time introductory course in cognitive-analytic therapy based at the clinical psychology department. In other departments, such as at Leicester and at Tayside, staff members are encouraged to register for part-time PhDs.

A wide range of training opportunities exists in spite of poor financial provision and only passive support from the health service. Funds available are small and funding arrangements vary greatly between trusts, districts and areas. Some have their own budget for courses, conferences and post-qualification training, while some districts are top-sliced or charged for post-qualification events. Some regions have a post-qualification budget, not usually dedicating a particular sum to a particular profession. Sometimes funds are also made available in kind, so that regional or national facilities are often made available free of charge and some regions do fund a portion of regional tutors' time for post-qualification purposes. Frequently, staff are able to obtain sufficient paid leave of absence in order to attend a reasonable number of events. The problem is often whether the appropriate kind of training is available for each individual clinical psychologist in a particular area. Hayes (1992) published the results of a national survey on the views of the Divisions and Special Groups of the BPS on continuing professional development. One major conclusion of this survey was that 'continuing professional development is multi-faceted, and variable. It is much more than just attending short courses' (1992: 509).

## TRAINING IN COUNSELLING PSYCHOLOGY

Training in Counselling Psychology is by means of either the BPS Diploma in Counselling Psychology or by the increasingly preferred option of a post-graduate three-year training course leading to a MSc or Doctorate in Counselling Psychology. Compared to courses in clinical psychology, these courses are new, although expanding in number at a rapid rate. One reason for this is the different funding arrangements and criteria for acceptance on clinical and counselling psychology courses with counselling courses accepting a wider range of applicants dependent on private funding, compared to the entry criteria for clinical psychology courses dependent on government-NHS funding. The development of the structure of training in counselling psychology seems to be following the pattern of clinical psychology from the initial training via the BPS diploma to a tendency for courses to award MScs and, latterly, doctorates.

Because of the more recent development of counselling psychology, the BPS has focused on detailed accounts of training for the Diploma in Counselling Psychology rather than on the content and structure of training courses as it does for clinical psychology. The Diploma in Counselling Psychology serves as a guideline for the development of courses and, as the BPS states in the Regulations and Syllabus for the Diploma in Counselling Psychology (1996), the Diploma represents a means through which psychologists in the field of counselling psychology can achieve Chartered status. It does so by providing a yardstick against which the experience and qualifications of psychologists can be assessed.

There are five main components of the Diploma in Counselling Psychology. The BPS's Regulations and Syllabus for the Diploma in Counselling Psychology (1996) give a detailed account of the nature of the components as well as detailed minimum time spent engaged in or number of practical requirements necessary. Part One covers practical competence, psychological counselling skills, personal development, academic competence and overall competence. Part Two expands on these, substituting research competence for overall competence. The examining board's concern is to bring psychological knowledge and ways of understanding into close and useful relationship with psychological therapy practice.

> In this, the Board recognises that the counselling psychologist will need to make good use of existing formal knowledge, but will also have to come to rely on and develop their personal ways of knowing, sensing and acting. This concern with personally grounded knowing (with personal enquiry, exploration and development) allows counselling psychology to make a distinctive contribution to psychological science and its modes of enquiry.
>
> (1996: 1)

The Diploma is concerned with four main issues. First, it emphasises the importance of a variety of perspectives and kinds of knowledge both to contribute to clients, and to use to make sense of the counselling process and context. Second, it is concerned with

> encouraging continuing personal development and personal enquiry so that practitioners are familiar with the counselling process from the perspective of the client as well as the practitioner, and are experienced in the subtle disciplines by which problems and feelings are transformed into issues, understanding

and methods which then become available for practical testing
and use.

(p. 1)

A third concern is to encourage 'subjective and objective, qualitative and quantitative modes of investigation; the interactive, interpre-
tative, discursive, and other fluid feature of the counselling psychology
situation' (p. 2). The fourth concern revolves around training in the
expressive communication of what is going on to others using a
variety of different forms of reference from counselling psychologists. 'In this, it will be necessary to have a command of metaphor
and other figurative aspects of language, as well as skills in the
analysis and ordering of complex events' (p. 2). Finally, the Diploma is concerned with seeking a model of psychological enquiry
which is suitable for the interpersonal, complex nature of human
relationships as people 'meet and negotiate the terms in which they
can understand themselves and their words, particularly in forms of
meeting such as psychological counselling' (p. 2).

The syllabus of the Diploma is presented as a series of issues or
topics, although the concrete details of the syllabus are a matter for
each individual training course. The syllabus is divided into two
main parts. Part One consists of three main areas of psychological
knowledge, which includes an integration of fundamental psychological knowledge with understanding in counselling psychology;
a broad overview of the main schools of counselling psychology
including dynamic, cognitive/behavioural, humanistic, existential and
integrative schools; theories of the counselling psychology relationship and issues concerning 'normality' and 'abnormality'. The second
area of study concerns research and evaluation including process and
outcome research of psychological interventions. The third area concerns counselling psychology practice, which includes assessment
strategies and planning and structuring sessions. Part Two of the
syllabus is divided into two broad areas. The first area, that of psychological perspectives on clients and their concerns, outlines first a
knowledge of psychological theories of counselling and psychotherapy
and a comparative and evaluative overview of the main theoretical
schools. Second, a focus is on clients including the effects of culture,
contextual influences and the nature of counselling approaches
to individuals, groups, family, systems and organisations. Third the
concerns of counselling psychology are those of normal life span
development, life stressors and traumatic events and the impact
of ill health.

The second area of the syllabus first focuses on professional identity and boundaries, including counselling psychology in the public and private sector; second, research and evaluation including an overview of a broad range of quantitative and qualitative strategies. This is followed by the study of the process of psychological counselling including an understanding from a variety of theoretical perspectives, developmental phases in the therapeutic process and the contribution of the therapist's personality, style and self-awareness to the enabling of the counselling process.

### The personal development component in counselling psychology training

The BPS Regulations and Syllabus for the Diploma in Counselling Psychology (1996) require that counselling psychologists should have undertaken at least 40 hours of personal psychological counselling. This should ideally be provided by an experienced counselling psychologist with specialist training in personal counselling. In addition to personal counselling, a personal diary must be kept by candidates for the Diploma.

> The diary might include background factors and personal or philosophical issues, which are experienced as having a bearing on choosing this profession, and how such factors inform one's way of working, including the articulation of their professional identity and guiding values in their practice.
>
> (1996: 8–9)

According to the BPS the personal diary is not formally assessed but it provides evidence of the candidate's ability to reflect on their own training experiences.

## ROLES OF TRAINING COORDINATOR, SUPERVISORS AND PERSONAL COUNSELLING PSYCHOLOGIST IN COUNSELLING PSYCHOLOGY TRAINING

In their regulations for the Diploma in Counselling Psychology, the BPS delineates the roles of coordinator of training, supervisors and personal counselling psychologist. It is worth noting that the guidelines for training in clinical psychology only delineate the roles of supervisors and coordinator of training. The inclusion of the role of personal counselling psychologist in counselling psychology training highlights the crucial difference in importance placed on the value of personal work in counselling psychology training. The coordinator of training in counselling psychology has a similar role to the coordinator in clinical psychology training in the overall planning and coordination of training. In counselling psychology, the coordinator is responsible for providing guidance and support for the candidate throughout the course of the Diploma, and for taking overall responsibility for the candidate's preparation for the Diploma. In counselling psychology training there is also a requirement of the course coordinator of training regarding the personal issues of trainees. The coordinator of training and other tutors and supervisors should be alert to personal issues which bear on the candidate's professional performance and academic achievement. Considering the supervision of client work, it is the responsibility of the supervisor to organise regular supervision sessions with their candidate and see that the candidate maintains a log of their counselling practice, and keep a diary which reflects their developing state as a professional. A research supervisor is responsible for the supervision of the candidate's research work and, like the previous two roles, reports to the coordinator of training on the progress of candidates. Finally, the role of the personal psychological counsellor is delineated. It is the responsibility of the candidate to approach a person suitable to undertake this task. The relationship between the counsellor and candidate is a confidential one and exists for the benefit and personal growth of the candidate.

## THE EMPHASIS ON RELATIONSHIPS IN COUNSELLING PSYCHOLOGY TRAINING

Counselling psychology courses place more emphasis than clinical psychology courses on relationships and interrelationships as they apply to clinical experience, both in relation to the psychologist's relationship to clients and to other colleagues.

### *Counselling psychologists' relationship to self and clients*

The BPS delineates the role of counselling psychologist through its Guidelines for the Professional Practice of Counselling Psychology (1995a). The Guidelines first set out the practitioner's responsibilities and obligations to self and client. The first issue is that of competence, in that practitioners should offer their best practice while recognising and not practising beyond their limitations in current training and ability, and continue throughout their careers to maintain and advance their knowledge and skills. The second issue deals with fitness to practise, with practitioners obliged to maintain an effective level of personal functioning. Should the practitioner feel unable to work effectively, help and advice will be sought from the supervisor/professional consultant. The supervision/consultancy relationship is a key element in this process.

The third issue deals with respect for clients' autonomy, the counsellor being mindful of the power dynamics of the professional/client relationship and respectful of a diversity of beliefs and values. Further, the Guidelines state: 'In view of the personal and often intense nature of the therapeutic relationship practitioners will take particular care to avoid exploiting their clients financially, sexually, emotionally or in any other way' (1995a: 4). Therapeutic relationships preclude sexual relationships and boundary issues need to be carefully considered. Any concerns need to be discussed with the supervisor/consultant and it is the practitioner's responsibility to define and maintain clear and appropriate boundaries. Fourth, the Guidelines deal with contracting. Practitioners are responsible for making clear and explicit contracts and need to inform clients of any financial liability before it is incurred.

### Counselling psychologists' relationship to self and colleagues

The Guidelines next set out the practitioner's responsibilities and obligations to self and colleagues. They outline responsibilities of the practitioner as trainer and the practitioner as researcher. They also outline the responsibilities of supervision and consultative support, which is a contractually negotiated relationship between practitioners with the purpose of supporting, evaluating and developing professional practice. There is an ethical requirement for every practitioner to have regular supervision or consultative support from a suitably qualified co-professional. This supervisory contract needs to be clearly defined, confidential and proportional to the volume of work and appropriate to the experience of the supervisees. The expectation for individual supervision is of 1.5 hours per month for a minimal caseload. The Guidelines stress the importance of the supervisory relationship being clearly distinguished from any line-management responsibilities. Another area of responsibility is concerned with boundaries and dual relationships in supervision and training. The Guidelines state:

As in client/practitioner relationships, the personal and often intense nature of supervision and training relationships in counselling/psychotherapy require practitioners to be especially sensitive to boundary issues and particularly careful in the area of dual relationships. Sexual relationships are precluded. Trainers and supervisors should avoid therapeutic contracts with trainees and supervisees. It is the responsibility of the practitioner to establish and maintain appropriate boundaries and to make complaints procedures available to trainees and supervisees.

(1995a: 7)

## THE ISSUE OF PERSONAL TRAINING IN CLINICAL PSYCHOLOGY

Post-graduate courses in clinical psychology vary in whether or not they expect students to engage in their own personal therapy. A major problem is that to be accepted for a post-graduate course, because of severe competition, there tends to be an emphasis on academic excellence, competence and coping. Little scope is allowed for personal exploration, so that some courses emphasise intellectual and personal competence alone. Yet personal therapy or self-development can often lead to invaluable elements in good counselling, such as awareness of inner dilemmas and conflicts, personal motivation, and personal vulnerabilities. Most post-qualification courses now contain some elements of personal therapy either in the form of individual therapy or in group work.

There is a growing body of opinion which indicates that the person of the therapist is a crucial element in effective therapy (Malan 1979; Storr 1979; Edwards 1985; Kottler 1986; Walsh 1990). Such writings highlight the relationship between caring for others and the ability to deal with one's own feelings. For example, if the therapist ignores an uncomfortable emotion so may the client, and such feelings may then be projected or denied. Caring for and helping others can be an effective way of hiding personal needs, denying one's own difficulties and reinforcing fantasies of omnipotence. If the therapist's emotional needs are met in the process of caring for clients, this itself can lead to resistance to seeking help to deal with one's own emotional issues. Therapists may be unaware of what motives drew them into their chosen work and may care for clients as they themselves would like to be cared for, unaware that this is in fact not what the client needs. Since the success of therapy often depends on finding the right therapist as much as finding the right school of therapy, it is important that the therapist be as effective as the technique of therapy is supposed to be.

Despite the apparent diversity of clinical psychology training courses as they have evolved over the last 40 years, still too little attention is given on training courses to exploring the role of the person in therapy. Although applicants have to undergo rigorous recruitment requirements based on examination result, interviews and other selection procedures, once accepted on a course it is too often assumed that trainees will gain the necessary knowledge and competence solely through the acquisition of information, skills and techniques. They are assumed to be people with no genuine diffi-culties, or who experience no problems in learning to survive in a role which requires coping with the distress of others. Not only has the scientist–practitioner model encouraged the practitioner to dis-tance him- or herself from the distress of the client but, as Mollon describes, it also distances the practitioner from his or her own distress. A basic assumption inherent in most clinical psychology training courses is, as Mollon (1989) points out, that psychologists should be healthy enough not to need help themselves, a naive assumption which implies that clients and psychologists can be clearly differentiated into two distinct categories.

Mollon's view is that the defensive position implicit in the denial of the need for personal work helps explain the current flight into management by many clinical psychologists. Based on projective identification, this flight is seen by Mollon as an essentially manic defence involving contempt and denigration of clinical skills. How-ever, Pilgrim and Treacher point out that the flight into manage-ment could be a response to political pressure over which the profession has no control.

Although there has been much subsequent work on the subject-ive nature of the experimenter, experimental psychologists tend not to consider the experimenter as a significant variable in influ-encing the results of their experiments. Although Shapiro (1963) advocated more single-case studies, these reinforced the notion of the objective scientist formulating hypotheses and applying tech-niques based on these hypotheses, rather than any consideration of the subject of the clinician or interaction between client and clinician. The influence of experimental psychology was likewise reflected in the ignoring of the person of the psychologist as a significant variable in clinical training. This was further emphasised by Eysenck's work, purporting to show the ineffectiveness of psy-choanalysis as a form of treatment, which helped create an intellec-tual climate that discouraged the consideration of psychoanalytic views of the client–therapist relationship. This was also true of most clinical psychology training courses, at least in their earlier days.

Historically, clinical psychologists were only peripherally involved with clients, but gradually their role as therapists and as consultants to people undertaking therapy has grown. Over the last 40 years, clinical psychology courses have changed to reflect this changing role. Opinion differs whether they have changed enough for them to equip new trainees for their new roles. Some writers, such as Crockatt (1976) and Mollon (1989, 1991), take the view that more change is desirable in courses to enable trainees to carry out their therapeutic roles. Others disagree while still others debate whether clinical psychologists should have embraced the treatment or therapeutic role at all. Some clinical psychologists point out that although many of the criticisms of the training courses are valid, nevertheless it is at post-qualification level, when the trainee has attained a basic grade post, that certain elements not covered in training may be made up later, when further specialisation can be undertaken. Houston *et al.* (1989) point to the great variability of training experiences, with some trainees stating that their post-qualification requirements were being met, while a minority reported that they were not.

One major reason for this is the different roles that may be performed by clinical psychologists. For example, if trainees are primarily interested in specialising in research work, they will not seek out the depth of learning and understanding necessary for working with clients, where therapeutic needs require a well-trained psychotherapist. Some clinical psychology specialisms require depth of therapeutic knowledge and understanding necessary for one-to-one client work; but other specialisms such as learning difficulties and work with older adults involve a different emphasis, with the clinician often working more with staff and other carers in a supportive consultancy role.

## PERSONAL SUPPORT IN CLINICAL PSYCHOLOGY TRAINING

The neglect of personal work in much training is reinforced by many factors. One is that in the current situation in the NHS each profession jostles to show off its knowledge base and what it purports to offer. It is not politic to emphasise the issue of personal vulnerabilities and other difficulties in training, especially when even more resources are required for these additional components. Even after training, there is little recognition of the need for personal

support, and little provision of it once qualified (Nichols 1988; Walsh
*et al.* 1991; Nichols *et al.* 1992). A survey by Walsh (1990) demonstrated that in her sample of 95 clinical psychologists, 51 per cent
had arrangements for professional support, but only 11 per cent
had effective provision of personal support. Nichols *et al.* (1992)
point to a general acceptance of this position by qualified clinical
psychologists, and observe the necessity not just of professional but
also of personal support for clinical psychologists. They state:

> In psychological therapy there is a continual exposure to the
> distress, frustrations, defeat and heightened emotional func-
> tioning of others. This exposure is made more burdensome by
> the basic interpersonal position of the psychological therapist,
> that is, as one whose task is to empathise and share in the
> perceptions and feelings of another person. In these terms psy-
> chological therapy, despite its various rewards for the therapist,
> can only be seen as a source of continual exposure to low-key
> stressors. Consequently, our argument has been that those
> working in the field should see themselves as people at risk and
> practise self-care in its various forms.
>
> (1992: 29)

Of these 'various forms' the authors emphasise the necessity
of preventive personal support. Although there is some degree of
overlap between the content of personal support and support for
professional issues, regarding personal support, attention primarily
focuses on the personal experience of the therapist. 'Hence a central
objective in personal support is to monitor the impact of the process
of giving therapy and the effect which this has on the therapist's
own psychological state and interpersonal functioning' (1992: 29).
They point out the difference between the conventional view of
support work based simply on unburdening and problem-solving,
and the use of support sessions to meet the psychological therapist's
ongoing professional obligation to take care of his or her emotional
and physical state. Contextual issues are vital for this process of self-
enquiry to occur, requiring, for example, the resources of skilled
and trusted colleagues and the setting up of support networks,
support groups or reciprocal support pairs. The authors stress the
importance of the therapeutic environment in order for this to take
place, a key ingredient being an atmosphere of absolute safety. Yet
this is a feature that is often missing from departmental meetings or
discussions of professional issues. It is interesting to note that the
model on the Tavistock clinical psychology course included weekly
supervision on client and professional work and also a weekly

personal tutorial, with a different staff member, where the trainee was encouraged to explore individual and interpersonal issues between him- or herself and clients. These one-to-one weekly sessions as they related to the trainee's work were kept as a distinct part of the training course, separate from the trainee's personal therapy sessions which took place outside the course setting.

Commenting on Walsh, Nichols and Cormack's description (1991) of a defensive set of attitudes by qualified clinical psychologists to personal work, Nichols *et al.* (1992) suggest that this is partly due to the attitude on training courses to personal work. Nichols (1988) pointed out that the graduates of British MSc clinical training courses receive little or no training in minimising stress, maintaining self-care or acquiring appropriate support for themselves. Furthermore, in a survey of clinical psychology trainees, Cushway (1988) points out that certain courses impose such excessive burdens on trainees that the training itself becomes a survival test. In her survey, the incidence of psychological distress among clinical psychology trainees was 57 per cent of the sample, a good proportion of whom viewed their difficulties as specifically brought about by the course.

Nichols *et al.* (1992) see the imposed model of work style, and the absence of encouragement of self-care and preventive support as an integral part of training, as a failure. Again it is the historical context within which British clinical psychology developed which helps explain this. Most of the older British training courses originated within the behavioural model, where attention to personal feelings and the feeling process was minimised or even discredited. Mollon (1989) discusses the position taken by prominent British psychologists in formulating the rationale and content of the early British training courses. For example, he cites Eysenck (1949), who argued that clinical psychology training was about 'competence in the fields of diagnosis and/or research but that therapy is something which is essentially alien to clinical psychology'. Thus in the early training courses there was often no recognition of the need to include personal development as a component. Nichols *et al.* (1992) observe that the denial of feeling was both taught and modelled. Trainees who emerged from these courses carried within them the attitudes conveyed on the courses, unless they managed to distance themselves from their trainers' views. These graduates who trained in the 1970s are now themselves in influential training roles, and may still fail to understand the importance of personal work. Thus they may have a retarding effect on the encouragement of both personal understanding and of development and personal support systems, both in their clinical departments and in the training courses.

Nichols *et al.* (1992) point out two further factors in preventing psychologists from paying attention to their own personal support. These are to do with the problem of unexplored ambivalence towards the client role, and the problem of destructive modelling. There is a tendency to view support work as only something for clinicians who are stressed and problem-laden. They comment that support work becomes associated with actual therapy. Walsh *et al.* (1991) report that a significant proportion of clinical psychologists seem to fear becoming a client. Nicholls *et al.* explore feelings and attitudes towards this issue, and say that although usually masked by compassion and a powerful sense of a need to care, a number of negative perceptions and feelings towards clients may be identified. They found, for example, that the notion of being a client was closely linked with constructs such as 'less coping', 'less able', 'less powerful', 'less competent', 'lost', 'defeated', 'a burden' and 'a source of strain'. Nichols *et al.* suggest that this accounts for the ambivalence seen in the apparent reluctance of clinical psychologists to seek personal support with colleagues.

Other issues include the fear that what is implied by personal support is becoming a burden on one's colleagues. It seems that many clinical psychologists may not have been encouraged in their training to accept their own needs as legitimate. It is difficult to allow others to recognise and meet these needs in reciprocal self-care. A second issue concerns that of destructive modelling. The early post-qualification years are also a time of continuous training. Nichols *et al.* discovered that newly qualified psychologists often perceive their department's ethos as one of anxious productivity where emphasis was given to accumulating and tolerating extremely heavy workloads. In this atmosphere notions of self-care are viewed as a threat to productivity. Those seeking personal support are moreover sometimes seen as weak or not coping. Thus the whole issue of personal support is bound up with career implications as well as a loss of regard by one's colleagues. Similarly, Walsh (1990) reported that only 11 per cent of her sample indicated that they would like to be involved in personal support work with close colleagues. However, other research, like Nichols *et al.* (1992) and Cormack, Nichols and Walsh (1991), suggests a change in this perspective, favouring improved systems of personal support amongst newly trained clinical psychologists.

Although professional burn-out is recognised within the caring professions (Rippere and Williams 1985) Walsh (1990) points out that little has been written about how psychologists cope with this particular problem. Penzer (1984) and Nichols (1988) comment that

although psychologists teach self-care to other professionals they
fail to practise what they preach. Some work has been carried out
exploring the obstacles perceived by clinical psychologists in seeking
personal support (Walsh 1990; Walsh *et al.* 1991; Nichols *et al.* 1992).

Commenting on what is essentially a damaging and defensive set
of attitudes, Nichols *et al.* suggest that this may reflect the attitudes
to personal work found on many training courses. Walsh (1990)
discusses two factors which discourage clinical psychologists from
confronting their own vulnerabilities. The first is the result of the
confused nature of their professional ethos. Although the practice
of psychology revolves around the world of emotions, the professional background is academic, emphasising objectivity in the
applied scientist role as opposed to the subjective world of the
practitioner. Walsh views the conflict between objectivity and emotion as setting up a contradiction within the clinical psychologist
that may mitigate against the process of self-care. The second factor
she views as revolving around the relationship between the profession and the climate in the NHS. Psychologists, along with other
NHS professionals, are increasingly placed under intolerable pressure to provide client care around targets of efficiency and economy.
In this climate notions of self-care often have little place in current
requirements for larger caseloads, more rapid client turnover, and
the pressure to reduce waiting times and waiting lists.


## SUPERVISION

The Committee on Training in Clinical Psychology of the BPS publishes a rigorous set of *Guidelines on clinical supervision* (BPS 1992a).
In these Guidelines, a reference is made to the role of the clinical
supervisor regarding the personal support of the trainee. Item 7.4
states:

> Supervisors should be prepared to discuss seriously and sympa-
> thetically with the trainee any general issues of relationships
> with patients or staff that arise during clinical work. Super-
> visors should be sensitive to any personal issues that arise for
> the trainees in relation to clients and be prepared to discuss
> these in a supportive way when they are considered to affect
> the trainee's work. The range of personal issues that can be
> raised by clinical work is wide and includes, for example, over-
> involvement, dealing with anger and despair, workload and time
> management problems.
>
> (Clinical Psychology Forum 1992: 33)

Clinical Psychology Forum (1992: 31–4) details ten items. The first guideline refers to the qualifications of supervisors, and specifies that supervisors should themselves have been qualified at least two years. Second, training courses should organise regular supervision workshops, which the BPS expects supervisors to attend, aimed at both new and experienced supervisors. The guidelines note the importance of supervisors keeping abreast of theoretical, research and professional developments in their fields of work. The next three criteria involve the allocation to, the setting up of and the content of placements. The BPS states that there should be an explicit procedure for allocating trainees to clinical placements. Both supervisors and trainees should understand this procedure and know how to influence decisions regarding clinical placements. Information should be provided about different placements. Although primacy should be given to general training needs, individual needs and interests should also be considered, especially in the allocation of specialist placements. Regarding the setting up of placements, the BPS notes that both supervisor and trainee should meet before the start of the placement to discuss the trainee's needs, interests and previous experience as well as mutual expectations and joint aims of the placement. The supervisor should ensure that the trainee has access to physical resources, e.g. desk space.

The BPS publishes guidelines for the content of particular placements in the Criteria for the Assessment of Courses (1992b). Both these and local training course placement content requirements should be taken into account in providing placement experiences for the trainee. The trainee's experience, expertise and level of training should also be taken into account. The BPS states that supervisors should ensure that the trainee has an appropriate amount of clinical work, and that enough space is left for planning and reflection upon the work. The time should be balanced, that is, spent on work at different levels such as direct client work, and indirect and organisational work, recognising that the balance will vary according to the stage of training and the type of placement.

Clinical supervision is the next item of the guidelines. The guidelines state that formal, scheduled supervision should take place at least weekly and be of at least an hour's duration, although longer supervision will usually be needed. Additionally, supervisors should make themselves available for informal discussion of matters that arise between formal supervision sessions. The total contact between trainee and supervisor should be at least three hours weekly and will need to be considerably longer at the beginning of training. The supervisor should ensure that the trainee has adequate reading time and should recommend appropriate reading material. Supervisors should help facilitate the trainee to integrate the theory and practice and should help trainees develop a scholarly and critical approach to their clinical work. As well as discussing clinical work the guidelines note that it is essential that trainees and supervisors have opportunities to observe each other's work. The BPS stresses that some form of mutual observation of clinical work is essential, whether this is by direct observation, or by other methods such as joint clinical work, audio- or videotapes or the use of a one-way screen. This provides the trainee with a learning opportunity and enables the supervisor to give the trainee accurate and constructive feedback.

The seventh criterion involves the quality of clinical supervision which depends upon many factors. The BPS notes that care taken in the early stages to develop a good relationship will enhance the quality of clinical supervision. Supervisors should be prepared to adapt their style to the stage of training of the trainee, with a detailed description of basic clinical procedures and techniques as appropriate. The guidelines recognise that supervisors and trainees may have a different orientation and interests, and recommend that trainees should be encouraged to view this as an opportunity for learning, with the supervisor showing flexibility and facilitating the trainee's development. In cases where the supervisor has serious doubts about the trainee's approach, he or she should fully explain the reasons for their doubts. The supervisor should also be prepared to listen and to discuss with the trainee general issues of relationships with patients or staff that arise during clinical work. Furthermore, as I have already stated, the supervisor should be sensitive and supportive to the trainee regarding personal issues that arise in relation to clients and to clinical work generally.

The eighth item in the guidelines describes how clinical reports and communication (both written and oral) should be presented. The ninth guideline concerns review meetings and feedback. It emphasises that there should be a mid-placement review involving the trainee, supervisor and training staff member. Relevant details are given as to how this should be carried out, with the aim of providing an opportunity for assessment of progress, feedback to the trainee and reappraisal of aims. It should also provide an opportunity for the trainee to discuss placement concerns. The guidelines note that both supervisor and trainee have a responsibility to the course and the profession to give feedback about the quality of the placement and the supervision. At the end of the placement a written assessment is made by the supervisor, which should be seen by the trainee. Feedback should be given to the trainee who should have the opportunity to comment on the placement. The trainee's views should be recorded formally as part of the general evaluation of the placement. At this stage, the supervisor should help the trainee to identify gaps in his or her experience, to facilitate planning for future placements arranged by the person coordinating placements.

The final guideline concerns the assessment of clinical competence. It emphasises that supervisors should be familiar with the examination and continuous assessment requirements for trainees and the guidelines and regulations for these. Supervisors should also be familiar with the criteria for passing and failing placements set by the course and with the appeals procedures. If the supervisor has concerns about the trainee's competence, the trainee should be told the nature of these concerns which should be discussed with the placement coordinator.

Although it may not be so close a relationship as that in traditional psychotherapy training, there is an element of apprenticeship in clinical psychology training. Pilgrim and Treacher report, in an analysis of trainees' accounts of their training, that many trainees view this relationship as teaching them most about their future role. The problem is often that the academic teaching they receive may not seem relevant to their role in clinical settings. A further issue regarding the experience of learning through supervision is that because of the requirement to have varied experiences in different specialities, clinical placements are not long enough. Trainees have a number of different supervisors, leading to a sense of fragmentation. Furthermore, the breadth of psychological knowledge, with its plurality of approaches and the eclecticism of clinical practice, can lead to a further sense of fragmentation and lack of cohesive professional identity for the trainee clinical psychologist.

Although the Committee on Training in Clinical Psychology has published guidelines for supervision, a study by Sharrock and Hunt (1986) points to the variability of the quality of clinical supervision. Circulating all the clinical psychology training courses in Britain, the authors asked trainees to rate their experience of current supervision on three dimensions. The results indicate that trainees' experience of supervision was positive on these three dimensions. The mean scores on a 7-point rating scale were: satisfaction 5.4, usefulness 5.6 and relaxed atmosphere 5.5. The results of this study indicate a positive attitude to clinical psychology training, at least as far as supervision is concerned. However, 18 per cent of the respondents indicated dissatisfaction with their supervision, and there was a tendency for older trainees to be more dissatisfied than

younger ones. Twenty-one of the 88 respondents claimed not to
receive regular supervision, despite the CTCP regulation that the minimum amount of supervision should be an hour a week. Although
a majority of trainees observed some of their supervisor's work, 28
did not, and 20 were not observed by their supervisors. It is interesting to note that the findings of this study point to a high corre-
lation between items gauged to assess the 'atmosphere of supervision'
and 'satisfaction', and the four aspects of supervision that significantly contributed to trainees' overall satisfaction. These were: empathy
to trainees' emotional needs, sufficiency of supervision, tactful use of
criticism and focus on specific details of cases.

Supervision is not only important to the *training* of clinical psychologists, it also constitutes a significant part of the role of many
clinical psychologists in their ongoing practice. However, as Hirons
and Velleman (1993) point out, relatively little is known about the
process of supervision or the factors that contribute to good supervision. In an exploratory study, Hirons and Velleman tape-recorded
the formal supervision sessions of six first-year clinical psychology
trainees and their adult mental health supervisors. Data from supervisors and trainees was obtained regarding helpful and unhelpful
events (Elliott 1979) that occurred during the sessions, as well as
measures of effective supervision. This study identifies four main
features as helpful. Consistent with other studies (e.g. Kennard *et al.*
1987), direct guidance on clinical work was identified as being helpful
by both trainees and supervisors. This was provided by supervisors
in a number of different ways. One of the helpful aspects of direct
guidance lies in the ability of supervisors to help trainees to express
their opinions, and this is in line with research such as that by
Holloway and Wampold (1983), who point out that trainees' satisfaction is linked to the supervisor's role being one of solicitation of
ideas from the trainee. Joint problem-solving, reassurance, and link-
ing theory and practice were also identified as contributing to effective supervision. There was agreement between supervisors and
trainees as to the helpfulness of these four elements of supervision.

However, there was a difference in the views of supervisors and
trainees in relation to feedback, with supervisors reporting this to
be more important to effective supervision than did trainees. This
finding is in line with results of other studies in this field. In their
report on a questionnaire survey of beginning counselling psychologists, Worthington and Roehlke (1987) comment on this difference
of views between trainees and supervisors, suggesting that in the
early stages of their training trainees are more interested in learning
what to do with their clients than in receiving feedback on their

performance, especially if that feedback is negative. Worthington and Roehlke suggest that trainees are more likely to value feedback as they progress through their training. Commenting on the differences between the opinions of supervisors and trainees, Loganbill *et al.* (1982) suggest that at the start of their training, trainees may not be aware of their own deficiencies.

Amongst the most unhelpful features of supervision elicited in Hirons and Velleman's study (1993) are lack of direction in therapy, the supervisor telling the trainee what to do, and the trainee being talked to as if he or she were a client. Commenting on the last, the authors point out that being talked to as if one were a client was ranked as the single most likely factor presenting a block to effective supervision. They give two possible reasons for this. First, they point to a general agreement (e.g. Eckstein and Wallerstein 1972) that supervision should not be therapy; and second, they suggest that such an approach might undermine the cooperative elements of supervision which trainees seem to value.

A paper by Bacon (1992) illustrates the supervisory process where the core elements in the model of supervision are based on a systemic approach developed from family therapy. She considers placement supervision as a joint experience for both supervisor and trainee, who:

> embark on an exploration or journey during which, if all goes well, they will eventually be travelling together through the same perceived landscape. Since each will have very different starting points, in terms of prior experience, learning and values, the journey primarily involves communicating and understanding these differences in order to create common ground upon which the work of the trainee during the placement can be based. During the journey each may be looking out of different windows, and the train will also present them with several alternative vantage points.
>
> (1992: 24)

Eventually this results in a more comprehensive perspective. Although Bacon points out that the landscape of each placement is largely determined by individual characteristics, there are nevertheless discernible stages in the process. The first stage is negotiating the placement, including a discussion of how the supervisor can best meet the present needs of the trainee. This needs to take in to consideration the trainee's prior professional and personally relevant experiences. Other issues include the degree of independence expected by the supervisor, and the supervisor's expectations and formal requirements and personal preferences. The second stage involves taking on a new framework, beginning with the trainee largely observing the supervisor. This is followed by observed practice within the context of support and feedback from the supervisor, before both trainee and supervisor are ready for the trainee to work independently. Bacon recognises that at this stage issues of control are likely to rise with the process moving developmentally from dependence to separation. The consequent issues of power and responsibility need to be acknowledged and discussed throughout the supervisory process.

The result of the findings of studies on supervision such as those of Hirons and Velleman (1993), Worthington and Roehlke (1987) and Bacon (1992), seem therefore to indicate that supervision is most effective when the process is carried out in a supportive environment, where trainees are actively encouraged to form and express their own opinions *before* the supervisor provides them with advice and guidance, and where the supervisor's guidance is given in a way which is neither threatening nor undermining, and facilitates the trainees to make links between theory and practice.

## TRAINING IN SUPERVISION IN CLINICAL PSYCHOLOGY TRAINING

Supervision is a complex and sensitive issue, as it brings up topics of professional and personal competencies. In Hirons and Velleman's study (1993), there was a low level of agreement amongst supervisors as to which types of event contributed to effective supervision. There are many possible reasons for the lack of consensus amongst supervisors, such as uncertainty as to the aims as well as the means of supervision. This itself could mirror the personal view of the individual supervisor of what clinical psychology is or should be, or be a reflection of the supervisor passing on a model of supervision gained in his or her own supervision as a trainee. Additionally, it may be argued that there are as many different models of supervision as there are models and theoretical systems within the broad field of clinical psychology. As clinical and counselling psychology training courses do not insist on the adoption of one model, it is likely that the particular model or integration of models acquired by any particular supervisor will be reflected in their supervisory style.

Compared to the amount of time supervision can take up in the role of the qualified clinical psychologist, relatively little attention is given to the formal training of the process of supervision on train-ing courses. Although there is no clear consensus as to the exact nature of supervisor training (see, for example, Dent and Milne 1987) research findings eliciting the most important elements for effective supervision have implications for the training of super-visors in the facilitation of knowledge of these elements.

One check on the quality of supervision of clinical psychologists in training is that courses have to meet criteria of accreditation set by the BPS. In the Criteria for the Assessment of Postgraduate Train-ing Courses in Clinical Psychology (CTCP) (BPS 1991b), one of the criteria for course accreditation is that supervisors of clinical psy-chology trainees should periodically attend refresher workshops. An article by Milne (1994) describes such a refresher workshop, organised around the theme of 'quality supervision' in the northern region. Milne defined the criteria for assessing 'quality' in relation to the topical 'quality assurance', following the elements specified by Maxwell (1984). These are 'access', 'relevance to need', 'effective-ness', 'equity', 'social acceptability' and 'efficiency'. It is worth sum-marising these criteria as they are viewed as the factors contributing to good clinical psychology supervision.

First, Milne notes that an accessible supervisor is fundamental to a clinical psychology training. This includes the time that a super-visor allocates to the trainee, the content of their comments during supervision, especially self-disclosure, and the process of supervi-sion. An accessible supervision process mirrors the 'analytic atti-tude' described by Moldowsky (1980), which is characterised by a respect for the trainee's autonomy, 'discovering with' rather than 'knowing in advance', and a genuine interest and acceptance. In many ways, these criteria are reminiscent of Rogers' core thera-peutic conditions. The placement itself plays a part in determining access to quality supervision. A placement can provide opportunities to participate in a whole range of interactive activities such as team-work and meetings that provide a high level of 'social' access. On the other hand the trainee can experience low 'physical' access when there is no desk space available, or secretaries or telephones are inaccessible. Milne emphasises that access is determined by the trainee as well as the supervisor, because the trainee also influences the process of supervision in either a facilitative, constructive man-ner or in various ways that may impede the process. Milne cites Kadushin's work (1968) on the games people play in supervision, which describes trainee strategies of avoiding or regulating super-vision. Kadushin gives the example of how the trainee may mani-pulate the supervisor's demands ('It seems daft that you should waste your precious time observing me with my first few clients, since I could learn so much more just by studying your sophisticated style and wise clinical judgement'; Milne 1994: 18), while the supervisor may wish to reduce the power disparity ('You have a valid general point on observing me with my first few clients, but it fails to acknowledge the findings of my recent article on client reactivity to non-participant observation'; Milne 1994: 18).

Milne describes the second component of good supervision as revolving around relevant needs, which includes a consideration of the respective needs of the trainee, supervisor, training course and the BPS. Milne notes the range of different learning needs that have to be considered, including skills, knowledge, attitudes, confidence and personal development, as well as a shared need between the trainee and supervisor to form a 'learning alliance'. There is a need to adapt supervision to the learning style of the trainee, whether, for example, the trainee learns best through practical experience or by first proceeding with more direction and the conceptual provision of clear models. Learning opportunities such as teaching should be adapted to the needs of the trainee. Milne suggests that a collaborative supervision agreement should be reviewed at the very least halfway through the placement, thus enabling its clarification and revision. He goes on to describe the teaching of supervisors, through such means as role-play and feedback, with opportunities for supervisors to enhance their effectiveness.

The fourth criterion outlined by Milne is the consideration of equity: a fair relationship implies open recognition of significant power or resource differences between supervisor and trainee. These differences include not just the fact that part of the supervisor's role is to evaluate the trainee, but also the supervisor's greater status, ability and experience. It also includes the process by which each deals with differences of opinion, for example, whether the supervisor overrides a trainee's objection to a particular situation or whether the trainee feels able to argue his or her case. Another dimension of equity is concerned with the sharing of information at different levels. Optimal supervision depends on both the trainee and the supervisor being self-disclosing, such as in disclosing feelings of threat when confronted with a particular client or feelings of doubt about their competencies. The fifth component of the supervision workshop revolves around consideration of the criterion of social acceptability. Milne adopts Nguyen, Atkinson and Stegner's (1983) multi-dimensional model of client satisfaction for use with supervisees. This defines satisfaction using such criteria as the type, competence, quantity, process and outcomes of supervision. Other components regarding the acceptability of supervision include consideration of other supervisors, as in the peer review process, the training course and the BPS through its accreditation function.

Milne's final criterion is that of efficiency. He points to numerous ways in which the learning of trainees can be facilitated. These include better use of available time through prioritisation, and by the trainee taking responsibility for more of the preparatory work. Milne points out that there are other opportunities for learning besides the traditional approach to supervision, which are less costly in time and effort: for example, joint work with other staff and other trainees. Furthermore, as Milne and Britton (1994) suggest, the process of supervision may become easier with increased knowledge and experience, and it may be helpful for a range of supervisors to meet to share approaches and ideas.

Milne (1991) raises questions regarding the costs and benefits of supervision and the issue of supervisors providing placements for clinical psychology trainees in the context of the recent changes in the NHS. Some of the consequences of these recent developments include increased work pressure, role expansion and heightened awareness of the issues of the costs involved in allocating time between the NHS and training courses. A working paper of the 1989 White Paper *Working for Patients* (*Working Paper 10*) outlined NHS policy towards education and training in separating the providers of clinical psychology training (e.g. universities) and purchasers (the regional health authorities). In this model the training course would purchase placements from local district health authorities and would have to convince the regional health authority that appropriate placements could be organised. Such a model would not normally be necessary or desirable, because the distinction between purchaser and provider is difficult to draw at the placement level; for example, the trainee provides a service while on placement.

Supervision is a complex phenomenon and there are many motivational forces that come into play that may determine competence as well as satisfaction and dissatisfaction with the supervisory role. Hawkins and Shohet (1989) emphasise the natural career progression into supervision and its related status enhancement. Supervision is not only cited in most clinical psychologist job descriptions, but is a criterion used in the career grading structure, with status as well as financial implications. Hawkins and Shohet consider the possibility that supervision may serve as an escape from, or be a way of revitalising, clinical work.

A survey conducted by Milne (1991) with clinical psychology supervisors in the northern region, on their perception of the costs and benefits of supervision, gives some indication of their satisfactions and dissatisfactions. A total of 21 kinds of benefits were mentioned, the most frequently cited being intellectual stimulation (28 per cent of all the benefits mentioned), followed by learning from the trainee (12 per cent), the company of a colleague (9 per cent) and deriving satisfaction from supervision (7 per cent). There were a total of 19 perceived costs of supervision, the most frequently cited being time (40 per cent of responses), followed by effort (10 per cent), impact on other duties (10 per cent) and preparation for the trainee (10 per cent). When asked to consider the overall balance between costs and benefits, supervisors judged the benefits to be slightly more than the costs. Their clinical psychology managers viewed the benefits even more favourably. One reason for this may be to do with recruitment. Managers may have thought that the trainee would be more likely to apply for a post in their department or unit once qualified. However, considering the relationship between training placement and subsequent employment over the previous five years in the northern region, Milne concluded that there was no significant association between placement and subsequent employment. Supervisors were asked whether they saw any significant changes over the last two years regarding costs and benefits. While the majority (74 per cent) did not, the remainder thought the changes that had occurred had been for the worse and increased the costs to them of supervision (22 per cent). The new developments cited include taking on more management duties and difficulties in justifying supervision time to others in their place of work. The second part of the questionnaire required supervisors to rate 20 factors considered to be relevant to supervision. Of these, the six most important factors were the amount of time available, routine work demands, the trainee's response to supervision, support from others, lack of room/facilities, and supervision training.

This chapter has outlined the main features of clinical training in counselling and clinical psychology. There is a difference of emphasis in the content of training in clinical and counselling psychology, with clinical psychology courses having to provide training in a much wider range of psychological specialisms and topics, given the generic training required of clinical psychologists. Counselling psychology focuses in depth at primarily one aspect of psychological practice – that of counselling and its related issues. There are also differences in emphasis in the two syllabuses even when discussing the same topic. For example, even though both have a research component, research matters are interwoven with the subject matter of clinical psychology as a legacy of the scientist–practitioner model and the research requirements more stringent.

Counselling psychology, on the other hand, focuses on human relationships and interactions drawing on disciplines and psychotherapeutic models other than academic psychology as its knowledge base. This is also reflected in the greater emphasis in counselling psychology on personal development and the delineation of roles such as personal tutor, while elaborating far more on concerns to do with interpersonal issues in supervisory and training relationships. In particular the nature of the supervisory role is different in counselling from that in clinical psychology, with supervision seen as a necessary requirement throughout not just the training but the practice of the counselling psychologist. Furthermore, the training of clinical psychologists is still largely geared to working in the public sector, especially the NHS within which it developed. The NHS has not been the context in which counselling psychology has developed, and this is reflected in differences in the training courses of clinical and in counselling psychology, for example, in the NHS health care is free at the point of delivery and the clinical psychologist does not deal directly in financial transactions with the client, whereas more counselling psychologists are employed in private practice or work with private organisations. Thus, issues such as the financial implications of the therapeutic contract as well as a consideration of a wider range of employment contexts are found more in counselling psychology than in clinical psychology training courses. In particular, there are specific issues which are different in the two professions. Personal training is seen as being of critical importance in the training and practice of counselling psychology. However, as we have seen, due to the historical legacy of the scientist–practitioner model in clinical psychology, personal training is not viewed as a necessary requirement for clinical psychologists. Instead, clinical psychology emphasises far more the research and academic basis of its profession, drawing from its main knowledge base of academic psychology. Reflecting its commitment to research, there is far more research work carried out by clinical psychologists than counselling psychologists into many of the issues described in this chapter, such as the efficacy of supervision, personal training, training in supervision, research itself, as well as clinical psychologists' own efficacy in various clinical and organisational settings. However, this may reflect a time factor, in that counselling psychology is a relatively new profession. It is interesting to note that clinical psychology, a profession that theoretically does not set much store by the concept of reflexivity, has nevertheless been prepared to examine and evaluate itself and its related activities, at least within its own scientific paradigm. In the next chapter we will move on to explore the relationship between clinical psychologists and counsellors, and with others working in the field of mental health.

# · FIVE ·

# *Professional relationships in counselling in psychological services*

## THE NATURE OF PROFESSIONS

Before we explore the specific relationships between professions, it is important to elucidate the nature of professions themselves. Pilgrim and Treacher (1992) point out that professions pursue their own interests, not those of their clients much of the time. Accounts of professions which depend upon practitioners themselves will be limited to professional rhetoric and to a set of positive attributions proferred for the profession's own advancement. There is frequently an uncritical assumption that professions exist merely to provide a disinterested service to the public based upon a set of specific personal skills and attributes. However, Pilgrim and Treacher outline two strategies used by leaders of occupational groups to corner the market in relation to certain client types. They work towards claiming to have a mandate to have a special legitimate control over that group – either through state powers or through an informal acceptance of a unique knowledge base or both. If successful, this produces closure around the activities and the relations with clients, which excludes other workers making similar bids. Then the profession will resist encroachment from new bids. It will also seek to dominate nearby professional groups, which helps resist encroachment and ensures and amplifies the social and financial status of the dominant profession. A fully fledged profession has control over its own training, in order to regulate its own professional boundaries, and it tends to lengthen that training increasingly in order to justify its special expertise. It also regulates its boundaries by being in control of its activities in relation to its client group.

## *Relations with applied psychologists in other settings*

Contemporary psychology services have developed in the context of historical relationships with others in the field of applied psychology. At the beginning of the century changes in the ways of managing or regulating the population were emerging which were to provide new social opportunities for psychological applications. The development and application of psychology, in military, industrial and educational settings during and after the two world wars, was an essentially conservative endeavour which legitimised the individualisation of social and economic relationships by working within a psychological framework. During wartime, efficiency in the manufacture of weapons was demanded while post-war developments in industrial psychology focused on the relationship between efficiency and stress. Social and political problems, such as conflict of interests between owners and alienated labour, were reformulated as problems within or between individuals, such as stress, neurosis or adjustment to be solved or managed by psychological techniques. Applied psychology was offering an instant solution for what were essentially political tensions.

After compulsory schooling was introduced in Britain in 1876, there was concern that slower pupils would affect the performance of brighter pupils. Thus the segregative solution for the mentally disabled was extended to the field of education. In 1913 the Mental Deficiency Act was introduced, recommending that each local authority should diagnose and detain their own 'defectives'. A medical classification was introduced which distinguished 'idiots', 'imbeciles', 'feeble minded' and 'moral imbeciles'. London County Council had decided to appoint the psychologist Cyril Burt, who pioneered the application of the Galtonian tradition of classification and measurement to the educational testing of children. Thus, the profession of educational psychology in Britain was founded with applied psychologists working in the field of education for local authorities. It is interesting to note that, from its beginnings, educational psychology was established outside medical jurisdiction. The underlying empiricist ideology of applied psychology was applied to the field of mental disorder when, in the 1950s, Eysenck, Burt's pupil, was to incorporate intelligence- and personality-testing into the first professional practices of British clinical psychology. Here, psychologists, like their medical colleagues, played a political role in terms of the management and control of the population, at the same time disowning such a role by pointing to their objective scientific training and qualifications.

The categorising and labelling of individuals was derived from the dominant British tradition of empiricism, which defined the limits of what was defined as the acceptable psychology of the day. In the words of Jack Tizard

> [T]hose who were using psychology in industry, education and the clinical field drew from the prevailing psychological theory of the time the lesson that to apply psychology was to assign individuals to a point in a multi-dimensional matrix. This, it was thought, would enable them to be sorted into appropriate categories, for which there were appropriate educational or occupational niches, or appropriate forms of remedial treatment.
>
> (quoted in Holland 1978: 176)

A Marxist analysis of the professions highlights the collusion between state and the professions to effect social control and regulate the population. The work of Galton and Burt is an example of this. The framing of social relations as individual characteristics is a danger of applied psychology, as we shall see in the next chapter.

### The development of the relationship with psychiatry

The ideology of the new National Health Service – health care financed from general taxation delivered free at the time of need – was to have important consequences for the post-war health professions. Science and egalitarianism were important strands in the political climate of the 1950s. This was particularly so for those like clinical psychology, which did not resort to any legal means to establish its legitimacy, although there was limited chartering in terms of mental testing following a report of the BPS Professional Standards Committee in 1934, which warned of the problem of unqualified people abusing tests. However, it was science that was viewed as the main sign of professional credibility.

In the atmosphere of egalitarianism, the hierarchical and authoritarian relationships associated with medical dominance were antithetical to the values of psychology graduates socialised in the post-war period, making conflict with the medical profession inevitable. Further, clinical psychology changed its area of concern from being mainly research/psychometrics to include therapy, thus entering an area where conflict with psychiatry was more likely.

### The role of psychometrics in psychologists' relationship with psychiatrists

Psychologists in the early 1950s defined their role as being a diagnostic assistant role before encompassing behaviour therapy.

However, the psychometric emphasis of the Galtonian tradition had put post-war psychologists in a difficult position. The diagnostic role meant that psychologists could communicate meaningfully with psychiatrists by means of a supposedly common language, and such diagnostic services fitted in with the medical role. Psychiatry viewed the psychology role as that of the medical ancillary, whose main role was to assist in arriving at a diagnostic category into which the patient could be fitted. Eysenck's original position (1949) emphasised a division of labour with psychologists responsible for diagnostic help and research design, the psychiatrist responsible for carrying out therapy and the social worker for investigation of social conditions. He accepted a division of labour which thus implicitly endorsed the professional dominance of psychiatry. A reductionist view of mental illness underlined his acceptance of the primacy of the psychiatrist's role in providing therapy. Eysenck quotes Dr D.G. Wright, an eminent US psychiatrist, who emphasised that

> the psychiatrist's part in defining the kind of pathological processes at work must be decisive. A great many pathological processes have significance only to the physician, and are in the first place illnesses which, although manifested by emotional and mental symptoms, are caused directly by injuries, diseases, and other organic processes in the brain.
>
> (Eysenck 1949: 174)

By adopting a conforming role which avoided conflict with psychiatry, Eysenck helped to create a milieu which enabled clinical psychology to develop. He stressed that psychiatrists and clinical psychologists were allies in that

> the emergence of a large, well-qualified group of clinical psychologists will be of considerable usefulness to the psychiatrists . . . The old and always untenable view which regarded psychiatrists and psychologists in some sense as rivals is surely ready to be thrown on the scrap heap . . . the more effectively psychiatrists and psychologists learn to work together the greater that prestige and the higher that status are likely to be.
>
> (Eysenck 1950: 723)

However, David Smail (1973), referring to the state of the relationship between psychiatry and psychology during the period that Eysenck was commenting upon, comes to a different conclusion from that of Eysenck. According to Smail, clinical psychologists were overshadowed by a medical guild whose powers did not allow psychologists anything but a secondary role. The physical methods of treatment seen as the appropriate form of treatment for mental disorders made it necessary to possess a medical degree, and the non-physical methods, which were mostly derived from the psycho-analytic school, could only be practised by people (mostly doctors) who had undergone long and expensive training. In other words, as Smail comments, the licence to practise treatment was based on a system where authority was granted to would-be healers on the basis of their membership of the right medical club.

Although Eysenck avoided the issue of medical dominance he, together with Cyril Burt, was willing to attack the scientific credentials of medicine. As psychologists they were attempting to establish that it was the scientific training of psychologists that was crucial in determining control of fields which were not central to the task of medicine and psychiatry:

> the closer this integration, the more likely is the ultimate emergence of that unified body of knowledge which alone will be worthy of being called a science of psychology, and of that agreed body of principles of pathology, prognosis and treatment which alone will be worthy of being called the applied science of psychiatry.
>
> (Eysenck 1950: 725)

Eysenck discarded his early efforts to solve the division of labour between psychologists and psychiatrists by psychiatry taking the major role in providing therapy. Eysenck, in the context of attacking psychoanalysis as being ineffective and for unnecessarily involving sustained personal reflection on the part of practitioners, at first emphasised that a research role was incompatible with the role of a therapist. However, he changed his stance when behaviour therapy, which he took a major role in popularising, began to compete with psychoanalysis as a major method of therapy. Behaviour therapy could be attached to the scientist–diagnostician model without very much difficulty. As it claimed to be based on scientific principles, behaviour therapy was ideal for extending the role of psychology into the field of psychotherapy. However, by the 1970s, when the Maudsley influence had seemed to reach a strong enough position to exclude verbal psychotherapies from being seen as part of the role of clinical psychologists permanently, new psychologists were being offered cultural stimulation for the interest in this very practice. This social context facilitated clinical psychology in expanding and also to incorporate areas of concern which it had previously tended to criticise or avoid. However, the profession still had to retain its professional credibility as it had consistently emphasised

its scientific basis to justify its occupational status. Thus a complete
acceptance of psychotherapy to the exclusion of psychometrics and
behaviour therapy was unlikely. The outcome was a compromise in
the form of eclecticism.

### Dissatisfaction of clinical psychologists with their role in relation to psychiatry

By the 1970s, only a minority of psychologists were content to practise solely as diagnostic aides for psychiatrists. The majority were
growing restless with the limitations of being subordinate to the
medical profession. Tensions were becoming more highly visible as
practitioners became more numerous. In the early 1960s there were
fewer than 200 clinical psychologists in England and Wales, and
1,200 by 1982. The dissatisfaction was dealt with by the Trethowan
Report, *The Role of Psychologists in the Health Service* (DHSS 1977). This
expansion together with members' assurance of being graduate
scientists didn't make an easy life for psychiatry. The legitimacy of
psychiatry had been challenged since the anti-psychiatry movement
of the 1960s, from both within and outside the profession, in the
wider cultural context of the time, in which mental health became
a popular focus for 'counter-cultural' interest.

Since then, conceptual critiques of 'mental illness' (Ingleby 1980),
and psychiatry's loss of its traditional base with the closure of the
large mental hospitals, have made psychiatric theory and practice vulnerable. However, psychologists did not respond uniformly to psychiatry. Psychiatry was protected by the legal mandate it claimed: the
1959 Mental Health Act enabled psychiatrists to claim that they had
the leadership role in the field of mental health as a function of
their legal responsibilities. The strategies that professions subordinate to psychiatry, such as social work and nursing, then developed
were determined essentially by this primary medical mandate to
have authority over patients and non-medical colleagues alike. In a
wider study of these strategies, Goldie (1977) points out that non-
medical professionals took up three main positions: of compliance,
eclecticism or radical opposition. Individual psychologists could be
found negotiating the first role by continuing to be psychometri-
cians. The second role – negotiating a local division of labour so that
they would define a role confined to neurotic patients, leaving the
psychotic to psychiatrists – was the position favoured by Eysenck,
who emphasised the appropriateness on scientific grounds of psychologists treating neurotic complaints using variants of behaviour
therapy. This threatened encroachment onto the medical terrain of
treatment was received badly by psychiatric colleagues, provoking

Maudsley psychiatrists into attempting to recover their therapeutic authority. For example, Aubrey Lewis, the director of the Maudsley, encouraged Isaac Marks and Michael Gelder to secure the behaviour therapy terrain by the development of a medically led training course for nurse therapists.

The third position was that of challenging medical theory and practice by entering into conflict with psychiatric colleagues, or by leaving the hospital to practise independently of consultant authority. Concerning the latter, many psychologists sought to work in primary care or non-psychiatric settings. In these settings, conflict was less likely in relation to the medical profession because there was a clearer distance in terms of role expectations. For instance, psychologists were not impinging on the role of GPs, as they might psychiatrists. Further, this relationship was also useful for GPs, who did not always hold a positive view of their psychiatric colleagues; or thought that they could prescribe just as well.

### Avoidance of psychiatric domination

It was the Trethowan Report (DHSS 1977) which gave psychologists confidence to break away from psychiatry. We have seen the disputes clinical psychology had with psychiatry when the therapeutic monopoly established in 1858 by medical practitioners was challenged by clinical psychologists in the late 1950s in relation to behaviour therapy. Psychiatry resisted this encroachment, as is seen, for example, in the writings of Isaac Marks at the Maudsley, but was only partially successful in warding off psychologists. The Trethowan Committee tried to negotiate an end to these hostilities by recommending the informal recognition of the profession's independent status. The DCP then sought formal recognition by the state of this independence in its bid for chartering.

Clinical psychologists also worked more with client groups distant from psychiatry in particular primary care and medical settings where they formed working relationships with physicians and surgeons. Ed Miller, summarised the change during the late 1980s:

> There has been a steady moving away from the traditional links with psychiatry and more towards new client groups – behavioural medicine, primary care, physical medicine. Also the profession has got itself involved more at a national level in what people might mistakenly believe to be the centre of power, the Department of Health.
>
> (cited in Pilgrim 1990: 157)

During the late 1980s and early 1990s the BPS tried to secure relationships with Royal Colleges based on equality rather than on dominance. This was facilitated by two major factors. First, in being granted independence by the Trethowan Report, psychologists were associated with the more mature profession of medicine. The second major factor, as Petchey (1986: 87–101) highlights, was the Griffiths Report, which was the result of an inquiry into NHS management, chaired by Roy Griffiths then managing director of Sainsbury's. It was commissioned by Norman Fowler, the Secretary of State for Health and Social Security. The Griffiths Report, which was published in October 1983, attacked the power of the clinical professions and the existing managerial structure of the NHS. Its recommendation of new and increased management structure in the NHS, meant that clinical professionals, whatever their disciplinary background, came together to ward off the threat from the DHSS and its NHS managers. There were some signs of clinical psychologists themselves exercising dominance over other professions in the 1980s when psychologists, despite their manpower shortages, often took up a leadership role. During this period, the DCP also sought to influence psychology input to other professions such as occupational therapy and to increase contact with other occupational groups such as the Police Federation.

## THE EFFECT OF GOVERNMENT POLICIES ON THE RELATIONSHIP BETWEEN WORKERS

### Changes in management policy in the NHS

Since the 1970s the main influence on clinical psychology and the main determinant of its relationships with other professionals has been the legislation passed by successive Conservative governments. Government policies had four significant effects for clinical psychologists working within the NHS. These were first, as mentioned, the incentive to independence of the Trethowan Report. Second, the move to chartering. Third, the destabilising of clinical professions by the Conservative government. Fourth, the effects of deinstitutionalisation, which created new opportunities and threats in terms of working in the community.

By the time Margaret Thatcher was elected, the 1978 Trethowan Report was beginning to have an impact on the actions of clinical psychology professional leaders and NHS administrators. Although many of these policies affecting clinical psychology were undone by the Griffiths Report (1983), the emphasis on management introduced by the Trethowan Report was further stressed by the Griffiths Report, which recommended a general management structure affecting all NHS professionals. Petchey (1986), discussing the report, notes that a series of other cost-cutting exercises had already been initiated by the first Thatcher government: the privatisation of support services – catering, laundry and cleaning; the expansion of private medicine via the encouragement of private insurance schemes and increases in NHS fees; and the introduction of charges for spectacles and other services. This was to set in motion a set of cost-cutting and 'value for money' initiatives during the 1980s. One of the most important, which was associated with the Griffiths Report, was an attack on the power of the clinical professions. The Conservative administration of the 1980s saw professions as a threat and increasingly sought to increase its own central powers by replacing traditional professional power with centrally directed managerial power. The NHS was no longer administered, rather it was managed along the lines of private business but directed from the centre. Cash limits in the NHS combined with the anti-clinician message emerging from the Griffiths Report were together attacking the professions.

In line with the anti-professionalism of the political ethos it was evident to the BPS that the government would not support the introduction of legislation to grant full registration of psychologists. Thus the BPS sought a weaker version, that of chartering. Registration proper would have involved new legislation to set up an independent register of practitioners. Chartering involved the BPS itself keeping its own register and did not require new legislation.

The political context hurt all the health professions. For a while clinical psychology, like the BMA and the Royal College of Nurses, cooperated with the Griffiths-based implementation of general managers, as clinical psychologists hoped to fill the posts as much as possible from within their own ranks. However, by 1985 it was obvious that clinical professionals were securing these posts in only a minority of cases. Over 60 per cent were appointed from the ranks of hospital administrators. Campaigns were mounted by nursing and the BMA against the government. The DCP opted for a different survival strategy by avoiding direct confrontation with its state employer and instead requested a manpower review, which the DCP hoped would result in recommendations favourable to clinical psychology. Manpower levels had been of concern for many years with training courses over-subscribed but recruitment to posts difficult due to a shortage of trained clinical psychologists. The review was carried out by the Management Advisory Service (MAS) headed by Derek Mowbray to the NHS on behalf of the Manpower Planning Advisory Group (MPAG) – a committee deployed by the Department of Health to examine manpower levels in the NHS. The MAS presented a draft report to the MPAG in 1989. This report was complimentary about the profession, and even provided suggestions for expansion and increased status. It tried to define psychological expertise and regulate training levels. The report also suggested that psychologists had particular skill levels, as a product of their scientific training, unmatched by others in the NHS; that is, that clinical psychologists were experts at a third level of skill. Level 1 skills were about rapport and simple techniques of counselling clients or stress management. Level 2 skills were about undertaking, cookbook fashion, circumscribed activities such as behaviour therapy. Clinical psychologists, but also lots of other professionals, attained Levels 1 and 2. Mowbray argued that only psychologists can theorise about new problems and how to solve them because of their higher education in academic and applied psychology. This Level 3 marked off clinical psychologists from other workers. They could be unique consultants to theorise, analyse and make suggestions about a variety of psychological issues in a variety of health care settings. This unique role was a function of their broadly based psychological knowledge.

Mowbray also suggested a model which would be 'consultant psychologist led' where the consultant psychologist would be responsible not only for the services provided by other psychologists working in the area but also for coordinating the psychological services provided by certain other disciplines to that client group. He also recommended the expansion of the profession such that by the year 2000 there should be 4,000 clinical psychologists in England alone. The MAS recommendations suggesting a consultancy role for psychologists would have given them a special and protected status in the NHS. However, the government's preferred option was to preserve the status quo while the new legislation in the White Paper *Working for Patients* (1989) set out a new philosophy for the NHS which would define its organisation and its staffing patterns.

Another difficulty was the reality of interdisciplinary rivalry in the mental health professions. As well as clinical psychologists others use psychological knowledge in health care contexts. Medical psychotherapists, social workers, psychiatric nurses, occupational therapists can point to their claimed expertise in cognitive-behavioural, family and dynamic psychotherapy as well as organisational consultancy. Organisational control is already established by others who are unlikely to accept the special authority of psychologists about psychological knowledge. Thus clinical psychology experienced problems achieving closure and legitimacy. Not surprising that faced with such a legitimisation crisis many NHS psychologists have sought refuge whether in private practice, or in trying to gain Griffiths management roles, or by leaving the profession. Further, important legislation was passed which was to affect the NHS drastically. After the Griffiths Report the NHS became market-driven. There was a possibility that other mental health professionals would out-bid psychologists for work once the provider and purchaser functions in the NHS were separated out in the 1990 NHS and Community Care Act. Professionals from one discipline could compete with those from another in selling a treatment package to the local health authority.

The Conservative attack upon clinical professional power explains why the market formula of *Working for Patients* was the preferred government option for NHS staffing compared to professionally influenced options. While the Mowbray formula satisfied professionals it contradicted the new managerialist emphasis of exerting greater control over them. After the Griffiths Report, spending on management consultancies expanded as the Report claimed that inefficiency in the NHS had been due to a failure of management. This led to the hiring of management consultants to recommend corrective action. Between 1979 and 1985 alone DHSS spending on NHS management consultants rose from £411,000 to £13.8 million (Petchey 1986).

### The deskilling of the professions

Pilgrim and Treacher point out that psychology services are no different from other white-collar professions in advanced capitalist states. The notion of 'proletarianisation' affecting the middle class of the late twentieth century has now replaced the notion of 'embourgeoisement' of the 1960s. This issue has been addressed by Carchedi (1977) and Oppenheimer (1975). According to Oppenheimer the drive towards deskilling by management increasingly places white-collar workers in a vulnerable position similar to blue-collar workers. The operationalisation of tasks makes work vulnerable to routinisation and tasks may become reduced to a set of skills which could be learned by others and disseminated outside the profession's boundaries. Once professionals accepted a thoroughly operationalised version of their work, defined by their employers, the employer could then argue that others capable of doing the job might do so in a more cost-effective way. Labour costs can then be kept down by employers and, in the process, the special skills developed by some groups become eroded. The result is deskilling. Hence the notion of the proletarianisation of the middle-class worker. The 'Hands Wanted' of the 1930s is replaced by the 'Skills Wanted' of the 1990s. It is interesting to note that within the NHS the threat to occupational groups first came to blue-collar work – laundry and catering subject to outside tendering resulted in lower wages. Both unions' and NHS professionals' view seemed to be 'Keep your head down, it might not happen to us'. But it did. Even in the name of selfish self-interest, professional collectivity might have stopped the worse ravages to the NHS. However, the cultural ethos of the 1980s and 1990s was one of personal and professional individualisation.

As we explored in Chapter Two, one of the continuing themes in counselling within the context of the psychological services is the issue of professional definitions. The relationship between the role of counsellors and that of clinical psychologists and other professionals working in the field of mental health (sometimes using counselling approaches) remains ambiguous; and probably will remain so, some would argue, until respective roles and competencies are clearly defined. In line with the employment ethos of the country, as I have outlined in this chapter, there is a tendency for job specifications to focus on the particular skills and abilities of a particular person to carry out a particular task or set of tasks, rather than on specifying the employment of a person from a given professional background. There are many dangers inherent in this. This operationalisation of activity ignores the wide breadth of training and expertise in a whole range of pertinent areas which are included in an often lengthy professional training. This internalised knowledge, although not always directly applicable or frequently not articulated, nevertheless forms part of the knowledge base which guides and directs professional practice in myriad ways. However, it is unclear whether in its protests about deskilling a profession is not merely acting to preserve its existing privileges and the status quo. Professions adopted different defensive strategies towards deskilling, such as trying to conceal the exact nature of their activities and defining knowledge as indeterminate, for example; and in claiming special expertise due to scientific training, clinical experience or clinical judgement, in order to resist accountability. It was hoped that such strategies would ward off the jurisdiction of managers and encroachment from other mental health professionals. Clinicians who were concerned only with patient contact and job security struggled simply to survive and keep up flagging morale under conditions of constant organisational changes imposed by the new managerialism.

### The image-makers within and between professions

Thatcherite policies regarding the NHS, with their emphasis on marketing, competition and 'value for money', influenced all the NHS professions. The ethos of self-promotion and competition, which came about as a result of such policies, affected relationships within and between professional groups in the NHS. Pilgrim and Treacher (1992) note that it was a decade when social justice and intellectual integrity were devalued in British society and it showed at all levels. The government began systematically to undermine the existing power of those professions which hitherto had enjoyed relative autonomy from the state. The Tory attack on professional power, along with its legitimisation of competitive individualism, encouraged claims and counter-claims about the unique attributes of every NHS professional group and variety of applied psychology. All implicitly if not explicitly promoted themselves at the expense of their colleagues. Reflecting the wider culture of the 1980s, when government advertising promotions by Saatchi and Saatchi seemed to define reality, clinical psychology as a profession began to be preoccupied with self-promotion and image-building. Self-doubt and differences in opinion were discouraged. The image was that psychology was a thoroughly worked out body of knowledge and its practitioners could be called upon by paymasters to offer expertise on demand. In 1988, the BPS produced a document entitled The Future of the Psychological Sciences: Horizons and Opportunities for British Psychology. This set out to market the profession in a social context where the language and ethos of the marketplace had come to displace other values based upon social justice and intellectual criticism. It seemed that J.B. Priestley's prophecies in his book *The Image Men* (1996) were really an underestimation of what was to happen.

### Relationship of clinical psychology to other mental health professionals

Some clinical psychologists were worried about the competition coming from other groups such as community psychiatric nurses (CPNs). This insecurity prompted them to make even more elaborate claims about their specific expertise. However, after a decade of Thatcherism, self-aggrandisement and not scientific caution characterised the public rhetoric of psychologists. Within psychology departments psychologist managers encouraged this grandiosity, urging staff with such exhortations as 'this is not the time for false modesty', to promote and sell psychology by such means as producing yet more glossy brochures. Glenys Parry outlining what she perceives to be the special feature of clinical psychology and in so doing highlights the role of clinical psychology in relation to other professionals working in the field of mental health:

> Community psychiatric nurses cannot do what we can do. The fact that we have an undergraduate degree and post-graduate qualification does make us different . . . I think that for too long, clinical psychologists pinned their credibility on their cookbook credentials. And yes on these grounds CPNs could, say, offer a similar therapy package to psychologists. But what we should be doing is saying that we can tackle problems that do not have standardised solutions. We can think through from first principles in ways which other professionals cannot. Our strength, which we have got to get across, is that we are special because we combine knowledge of a wider client group, with knowledge about clinical skills, with knowledge about psychological theories. Other professions may be skilled in one of these three areas, but only clinical psychologists can combine all three . . .
>
> (Parry, cited in Pilgrim 1990: 159)

During this era psychologists were vying and competing, with their claims about expertise in the psychological therapies, with others making similar bids. Publicised opportunities for the usefulness were seen in the emotional aftermath of the Zeebrugge ferry sinking in 1987, the Hillsborough football tragedy in 1989, the Dunblane massacre in 1996 – for all the mental health care professions. Further, as Pilgrim and Treacher point out: 'Newly emerging groups making a bid for legitimacy, such as counselling psychologists, announced to the world that they were natural experts in the field' (1992: 159).

> Clinical psychologists do excellent work in their own field, but it is only counselling psychologists whose training in interpersonal and enabling skills specifically equips them to deal with the trauma suffered by victims of disasters. Although some clinical psychologists may possess these skills, it cannot be presumed that it is a major part of their training.
>
> (Noyes, Franklin and Val Baker 1989: 214)

### Competition or collaboration outside the hospital

Another change of policy of the government in the 1980s in relation to deinstitutionalisation resulted in professionals working together outside the hospital. One consequence of this, especially in the new community mental health centres, was the blurring of roles or genericism. While many from all the professions contributed to this trend, those who had no statutory powers or duties, such as clinical psychologists, became vulnerable. Doctors were needed to prescribe drugs and nurses to administer them. Doctors and social workers had statutory duties under the 1983 Mental Health Act when patients were compulsorily detained, and nurses had new holding powers. Psychiatry, psychiatric nursing and social work had guaranteed mandates of practice in the community or in the new district general hospital acute units. This was not the case for psychologists. Also because other mental health professions working in the community increasingly aspired to be applied psychologists, by practising variations of psychological therapy or counselling, a defined role for clinical psychologists was becoming unclear. Although in some localities psychologists negotiated a credible role for themselves, as team leaders, or in supervising others in the team in the psychological therapies, the picture nationally was far from uniform, causing role anxieties for some clinical psychologists in some localities.

### Competition or collaboration from other areas of applied psychology

Within the field of applied psychology there are three branches which, as Street (1992) observes, are potential competitors in a health service encouraged to take on the attributes of a marketplace: they are clinical psychologists, health psychologists and counselling psychologists. There is considerable ambiguity in this area. Street (1992: 34) quotes Marie Johnston, the founding chair of the Health Psychology Section, in identifying health psychology and its boundaries of expertise and competence as 'the application of psychology to the study of health and health care'. However, Street notes the problem with the Health Psychology definition, in that the BPS booklet 'Opportunities and Careers for Psychologists' (1992c) describes clinical psychology as 'the application of psychology in the field of health care'. Furthermore, Street discusses the difficulty, if one is a psychologist, of separating mental from physical health. Similarly, difficulties arise when discussing issues relevant to the relationship between clinical and counselling psychology. An internal threat to the status of clinical psychologists came from within the BPS. In 1979 a working party which had been reviewing the status of counselling suggested the possibility of setting up a new Division of Counselling Psychology. There was already an academic interest group in this topic (i.e. Section, in BPS terms). The possibility of this being converted to Divisional status would legitimise a new applied wing of psychology in competition with clinicians. The DCP minutes (14 April 1980) state their reaction: 'As counselling is a ubiquitous activity, the committee believes that a separate Division within the BPS would be superfluous'. Now the issue about psychological therapies was no longer about what they were, but who owned and controlled them.

Many clinical psychologists feel that their training is neither long enough nor deep enough in counselling or psychotherapy skills to be helpful to the distressed clients who are referred to them. Consequently, many undertake further training. This fact was recognised in the initial setting up of the Special Group in Counselling Psychology, which then became a Division of the BPS in its own right, and where, as we have seen in earlier chapters, the requirements in terms of client contact and supervision are more stringent than those expected for trainee clinical psychologists in a counselling role. Street argues that clinical psychology training has never been and is still not rigorous enough in its teaching of counselling skills.

## THE EMPLOYMENT OF COUNSELLORS

A difficulty for those wishing to employ counsellors is the confusing plethora of counselling training courses and consequent inconsistencies in qualifications of those who call themselves counsellors. No system in any profession can avoid the 'bad apple' effect, but it is a responsibility of the authorities awarding recognition to ensure that appropriate processes and procedures are in place to avoid unsuitable candidates as far as possible. Codes of Conduct and Disciplinary Procedures, although part of the process of ensuring the maintenance of standards, are nevertheless acting after the event. One way of assuring quality is to consider only candidates whose qualifications make them eligible for British Association for Counselling (BAC) approval. However, even this, with its present system of counselling recognition, is not always a guarantee of suitability of candidates. For example, a recent televised report (Watchdog,

BBC1, 1996) reflecting the public concern on standards in counselling documented how a professional comedian known for racist and sexist remarks in his public performances was accepted by the BAC on his written application for membership. This well-publicised incident may well encourage the setting up of more effective procedures of recognition by BAC.

## EMPLOYMENT OF COUNSELLORS IN THE NHS

The issue of where and how counsellors are employed in the NHS is still a developing one. Over the last few years, an increasing number of counsellors have been employed in primary care. Traditionally, GP practices have employed counsellors directly (see the companion volume in this series by East (1995)). An alternative model is for counsellors to be employed by provider units and contracted to primary care purchasers. In some areas this has been managed by clinical psychology services. The formation of the Division of Counselling Psychology has provided another means by which the quality of counselling services can be assured.

Gore (1994) reports on a conference on counselling and primary care organised under the auspices of the Department of Health in December 1993: 'Counselling and Primary Care: Promoting Good Practice'. The conference represented various interest groups in counselling and primary mental health care, including representatives of other professional groups such as psychology and psychiatry. Gore observes that throughout the conference various terms such as 'counsellor', 'psychologist', 'counselling psychologist' tended to be used interchangeably. It was unclear whether the term 'counsellor' was being used generically to refer to any mental health professional, whatever their specific professional background, or whether they were using it in a specific way to denote a theoretical background and form of practice, for example, Rogerian counselling. Gore suggests that there was an avoidance of definition of differences between 'counselling' and 'psychotherapy', 'counselling psychologist' and 'clinical psychologist'. One difficulty inherent in this lack of clarity is the tendency to use the term 'counsellor' as a vague description for anyone providing mental health care. This leads to implications such as the counsellor being able to provide treatment for anyone with any sort of problem.

Counsellors come from varied backgrounds. They may have a background in health or social care and could, for example, be seeking a career change, be returning from a career break, or be seeking alternative employment in the wake of redundancy or the threat of redeployment. Some, although fewer in number, have entered the field of counselling as a career of first choice and apply for posts directly after completing their training. Others include psychology graduates who, because of enormous competition for few places, are unable to gain acceptance on clinical psychology courses. However, the length and quality of counselling training is highly variable, ranging from short introductory courses and certificate courses of 15 to 20 weeks, to validated Diploma or MSc courses lasting two years.

At whatever level the courses award their qualifications, they are generally part-time, and the exact amount of time spent in study and practice is also highly variable. It is not possible at present to take counselling qualifications at their face value. Even after training, the picture is not clear due to the wide variety of terms used to describe practitioners of counselling, as well as the use of terms such as 'counsellor' or 'therapist' to convey different meanings and occupational roles. For example, an RMN-trained nurse with a certificate gained on a nursing course, a diploma or an MA in counselling may be termed 'psychological therapist', 'psychotherapist', 'nurse dynamic therapist', 'nurse therapist', etc., with all the terms being used indiscriminately regardless of the nature of training. Similarly a nurse who attended the corresponding behaviour therapy courses could be termed 'psychological therapist', 'psychotherapist', 'nurse behaviour therapist', etc.

### Employment of counsellors within clinical psychology departments

The current trend is for clinical psychology departments to employ counsellors. For example, Burton and Ramsey (1994) describe how, in the West Hertfordshire Community Trust, the clinical psychology service recruits, selects, supervises and evaluates the work of counsellors based mostly in GP surgeries. In the direct access service for GPs, counsellors engage mainly in short-term work of six sessions or less, and are referred patients with problems such as anxiety, mild depression, bereavement reactions, psychological complications of physical illness, and psychosomatic complaints. In addition, counsellors assess new referrals for their suitability for short-term treatment, undertake short-term treatments and evaluate the effectiveness of their work under the supervision of a qualified clinical psychologist.

Another model obtains in the North Warwickshire NHS Trusts, where professionals with other backgrounds in the NHS, such as psychiatric nursing, and who have had some counselling training are managed by clinical psychologists working in the field of adult mental health in providing counselling sessions at GP practices. Here the counsellors are supervised by clinical psychologists who have undertaken post-qualification psychotherapy training. Other counsellors are employed specifically within particular specialisms such as work with the elderly.

### Counselling psychologists within clinical psychology departments

As outlined by Miller (1994), a number of options are available when employing non-clinical psychologists within psychology departments. Southmead NHS Trust Department of Clinical Psychology project advertised locally for applicants who had a first degree in psychology and a counselling qualification who were, or were eligible to be, accredited by the BAC or the BPS. A distinction was thus made between 'counsellors' (without a first degree in psychology) and 'counselling psychologists'. At the time the two counsellors were employed, there were no salary scales for psychologists employed as counsellors. The counselling psychologists were employed on a six-month contract and were paid on Administration and Clerical pay scales, above the pay level for trainee clinical psychologists and below the floor level for newly qualified clinical psychologists in the service.

In the project, counselling psychologists, working in the GP direct access service, were to receive regular supervision from a qualified clinical psychologist. It was also decided that referrals to the counselling psychologists should be screened by the supervising clinical psychologist, preferably via joint assessment interviews. Thus the model adopted was one in which the services of counselling psychologists were seen to supplement rather than replace those of clinical psychologists, potentially providing GPs with a greater choice of service providers.

### Services provided by counselling psychologists within clinical psychology departments

A study by Miller (1994) outlines the services provided by counselling psychologists to the 47 patients taken off the GP referral waiting list, over a six-month period. The counselling psychologists felt that there were very few clinical problems for which they were unable to offer therapeutic intervention. Most of those who were screened as inappropriate were individuals who were felt to require longer-term therapy than would be possible in the stipulated six-month contract period. Although the sample size of the pilot project is small, with the authors delineating the work of two counsellors with 16 people in active therapy during a two-month period, the counselling psychologists worked with people with a range of presenting problems including child sexual abuse, anger management, marital and family difficulties, depression, anxiety, eating disorders, and grief and bereavement issues. The authors point out that one clinical problem which might be expected to fall outside the remit of the counselling psychologist, where BPS definitions are used, is that of early childhood trauma. This was not reflected in the working practices of the counselling psychologists employed in this study. A difficulty with studies in this area is that the exact qualifications and experience of the counsellors is not described. None of those in active therapy with counselling psychologists during this time period could be classified according to the problem defined in the referral letter as experiencing obsessional-compulsive difficulties, psychosexual problems or needing help with assertiveness or social skills. Clinical problems were defined according to the GP's referral letter. The accuracy with which such letters reflect the concerns of the client is questionable, and as such any assessment of presenting problem made in this way is likely to be limited.

In this study, Miller (1994) does not distinguish between counsellors who have qualifications which are not linked with psychology, either at undergraduate or at post-graduate levels, and those who would be eligible to become chartered counselling psychologists. Collins and Murray (1995) point out that it might be expected that those who can be chartered might more readily be employed by trusts within existing clinical psychology services and that they might share some of the service views of their clinical psychology colleagues. In a pilot project of counselling psychologists within adult mental health clinical psychology services (Collins and Murray 1995) the clinical psychology department employed two counsellors, who also had first degrees in psychology, as a project. As such they were considered to be 'counselling psychologists' due to their undergraduate experience. However, the authors note the subsequent development of the Division of Counselling Psychology and that this definition may not correspond to the Division's requirements.

Collins and Murray (1995) outline the services provided by the counselling psychologists, including their views on the clinical service they were able to offer to clients, and they discuss the attitudes of clinical psychologists working in adult mental health to the future employment of counselling psychologists. Collins and Murray (1995: 8) point out that the BPSs' assumption in the *Directory of Chartered Psychology* (1994), that counselling psychologists are involved in working with people facing 'normal life cycle developmental issues' and by implication with less complex, severe or intractable difficulties is not one which is necessarily held by counselling psychologists themselves. Thus, clinical and counselling psychologists are unable to clarify who does what, where and how. Collins and Murray point out that this lack of clarity could lead to advantages and disadvantages. It may result in a detrimental effect on the marketing of services to purchasers such as GPs, despite the definitions by which clinical and counselling psychology are differentiated by the BPS (1994d), as we outlined in Chapter Two. On the other hand, it may also be the case that the two branches of applied psychology can use this overlapping to their own advantage in retaining the ability to decide themselves on where to direct a referral rather than depend on the judgement of GPs, thus retaining professional autonomy. However, this could probably only be the case if counselling and clinical psychologists join together within health service trusts and develop cooperative working practices which are beneficial to both groups. Services which develop in a piecemeal fashion may be more likely to engender unhelpful interdisciplinary rivalry.

The employment of counsellors by NHS trusts, and whether or not this should be linked with clinical psychology departments, has become an increasingly familiar topic within the profession (Miller 1994). The recognition of counselling psychology as a Division in its own right indicated that within the BPS there is a growing recognition of the professionalisation of counselling. With pressure from the Department of Health to meet the targets identified in *The Health of the Nation* (Marks 1994) the use of those with appropriate qualifications in counselling is becoming a realistic alternative to employing clinical psychologists, given the shortfall in qualified clinical psychologists (Miller 1994).

A growing trend seems to be that unfilled clinical psychology posts can be redesignated as 'counsellor' or 'therapist' posts. These are filled by open competition and attract many applicants. The range of duties, responsibilities and remuneration is highly variable and may or may not take into consideration the applicant's previous career and experience. Salaries may reflect Whitley Council scales, such as clinical scientist, nurse or occupational therapist, or be decided on an ad hoc basis.

There are at present no national guidelines regarding the relationship of clinical psychologists to counsellors. There is a range of
views as to what this relationship should be. At one end of the
debate there are those who question whether clinical psychologists
should get involved in the issue at all as there is a danger, especially
in relation to the employment of counsellors within psychology
departments, that this will dilute the quality of psychological care.
Miller (1994) points out that counsellors or therapists are not clinical psychologists and cannot therefore offer the same breadth and
depth of skilled input. Their employment within clinical psychology departments may lead to a misrepresentation of the nature of
that service. Many interesting questions may be raised regarding
the relationship between clinical psychologists and counsellors, for
example, whether the relationship is going to be one of competition,
collaboration or dominance. One view is that clinical psychologists
are in danger of taking on the role they objected to so strongly in
relation to psychiatry: that is, they may be tempted to limit and
control the development of another profession in order to maintain
their hierarchical dominance. However, other professions have a
right to develop and to offer their expertise. Miller (1994) suggests
that the challenge for clinical psychologists is to welcome them
rather than exclude them.

Counselling may be seen as making a credible and valuable contribution in many areas that have previously been within the field
of clinical psychology. Whatever the arguments, there has been
an increase in the employment of non-clinical psychologists as
counsellors or therapists within clinical psychology departments.
Miller (1994) ascribes three main reasons for the trend to employ
more counsellors within the NHS: the shortage of qualified clinical
psychologists, pressures relating to cost efficiency and the professionalisation of counselling.

The short supply of qualified clinical psychologists and recommendations for an increase in their numbers was emphasised in the
review of clinical psychologists published in the Manpower Planning Advisory Group/Management Advisory Service report (1989).
However, there has not been a substantial increase in the training
of clinical psychologists as recommended by this report, due mainly
to the context of the NHS, which during this period has undergone
reorganisation and change, with general implications for professionals in terms of cost restraint and resource allocation. Traditionally the shortage of clinical psychologists has been made up from
within the psychology departments by the employment of psychology technicians or assistant psychologists. However, psychology

assistants are employed on short-term contracts and typically see the work as a route to gaining later acceptance themselves on a clinical psychology course. This has always been a short-term, unsatisfactory way of dealing with the staff shortage problem, lacking continuity and discouraging the development of maturing skills.

The difficulty for clinical psychologists is that the problem of recruiting qualified staff may lead to the reallocation of resources elsewhere. Miller points out that this process could become a vicious circle, with fewer resources leading to lower prospects of attracting staff, leading to a further loss of resources. On the other hand, counsellors and therapists are increasingly in plentiful supply. They often train at their own expense, which represents a significant saving in economic terms over the lengthy and expensive training of clinical psychologists typically funded by government and health service sources. Government reorganisation of the health service means that the traditional funding of clinical psychology training, as with other post-graduate training courses, based on merit regardless of means, is now uncertain. Counsellors thus represent an attractive option to purchasers of health care, who often have difficulties in obtaining an immediate response from psychology services which are struggling with limited staff to meet ever-increasing demands.

Pressures relating to cost efficiency have therefore led to the increase in the number of counsellors employed in the NHS. Staffing shortages in the NHS generally, and particularly in relation to clinical psychologists, have led to increased expense, with recruitment and retention costs growing faster than inflation and more than the financial resources of the purchasers. This has led to many purchasers considering cheaper solutions in order to achieve a higher level of client contact and a lower cost per case. This has been fuelled by lengthy waiting lists and the development of a consultancy role by clinical psychologists which involves less direct client contact. This may lead managers and also the purchasers of health care to interpret the monthly statistics detailing client contact as indicating fewer clients for more money.

However, well-qualified counsellors and therapists are not necessarily a cheap alternative for purchasers. For example, a nurse behaviour therapist on Grade H may cost as much as a clinical psychologist with several years' experience, and as Miller (1994) suggests the range of work may be significantly narrower. There are, however, cost factors that may make the employment of counsellors to provide services appear more cost-efficient. First, the pay ceiling is lower. Clinical psychology is a profession with a defined career structure with a parallel pay structure. Although the situation may change with government initiatives emphasising local negotiations between NHS managers and health service staff for conditions of pay and employment, these are at present set down for clinical psychologists by the Whitley Council. Counsellors and therapists are less likely to expect salaries comparable to the top of the Grade A or the higher Grade B pay scale of clinical psychologists. Thus although the short-term saving may not be obvious, the long-term salary costs are less. Added to this is the fact that some counsellors are willing to work part-time for lower rates of pay. Related to this factor is another, that counsellors are not organised as a professional body within the NHS with a career and corresponding pay structure. This means the add-on costs related to pay and conditions of employment, such as pension contributions and associated rights, are less costly to the employer. Another factor that may make the employment of counsellors attractive to purchasers is that they are likely to produce a higher proportion of client contacts because their skills are more directly relevant to face-to-face therapy.

The cost of counsellors on the free market is coming down with the upsurge of popularity of counselling courses, with an almost unlimited number of training places. This is due to a number of factors: a reflection of the employment situation generally in Britain; the briefness of training required compared to the lengthy training of many NHS professionals such as those in psychiatry and clinical psychology; the less demanding initial entry requirements to enrol on courses; and counselling as an acceptable second career option with a perceived social status.

Government reorganisation in the health service has encouraged the employment of a greater range of personnel than the traditional professions supplied. Government reorganisation in the field of education has resulted in pressure on educational institutions to generate income from courses. This in turn has led to the proliferation of courses such as counselling with a corresponding proliferation of trainee counsellors. In particular, in areas of the country where there is a glut of counselling training courses, trainees, who may be supervised either on their course, or in exchange for supervision within their NHS placements, are often willing to offer counselling free of any charge in order to meet their course requirements.

Another major factor relevant to the employment of counsellors in the NHS is related to the professionalisation of counselling. One difficulty in the employment of counsellors has been the lack of standardisation in training or experience. Counsellors have attempted to address this issue through increasing professionalisation. The British Association for Counselling (BAC) has defined a rigorous set of requirements for accreditation, outlining the necessary elements of theory and supervised practice. Within the BPS there have been developments, as we have seen, from a Special Group in Counselling Psychology to a Counselling Psychology Division and a BPS Diploma in Counselling Psychology. Nationally the Department of Employment, which is contracting consultants to devise and implement standards for National Vocational Qualifications (NVQs), now accords a significant place to counselling, therapeutic counselling and psychotherapy.

### Competition or collaboration between counselling practitioners and clinical psychologists

Street (1992) discusses two arguments in relation to the potential competition between counselling practitioners and clinical psychologists. The first he identifies as the 'Unrealistic Democratic Argument', which views all those working in the field of mental health as the same, with plenty of work for everybody. But he points out that we are not in fact all the same: 'Counsellors . . . with only a counselling qualification do not have adequate knowledge to distinguish a range of personality and interactive processes in order to appreciate the needs of working with different client groups and complex family problems' (1992: 35). Furthermore, he argues that mental health services for people in distress cannot be built up solely on one model of work seeing one client after another. Rather there have to be other levels and approaches of delivering services that meet the varied needs of psychological health. It could, however, be argued in defence of counselling that there are many theoretical models, and that counselling courses provide training in different modalities.

The other opposite argument Street terms the 'Arrogant Hierarchical Argument'. This holds that 'clinical psychologists are experts in everything and we should supervise the work of less complete professionals such as health and counselling psychologists who will become attached to our departments and have their work directed by us' (1992: 35). This argument, as he points out, puts professional position above the needs of clients and would be to the detriment of the positive development of the practical application of psychology to alleviate distress. One suggestion, as I discuss later, would be to avoid possible professional battles between psychologists by developing a cohesive professional entity for psychologists. This would move in the direction of an applied psychology profession based on recognised core components, with the opportunity to add further specialist qualifications. It is interesting that clinical psychologists frequently point out the undesirability of placing professional protection above the greater consideration of providing the best service for the greatest number of people. However, I wonder, as counselling and psychotherapy courses proliferate and their practitioners become more directed towards professionalism, whether they will be as concerned over issues relevant to the public good as they are with issues concerned with professional advancement. Partly because of their legacy of taking issue with attempts by another profession (psychiatry) to define all matters psychological as psychiatric, and partly due to the historical intertwining of the development of clinical psychology with the development and philosophy of the welfare state and the NHS, clinical psychology as a profession has generally placed the needs of clients above professional protectionism.

I myself have been involved with the development and setting up of a psychotherapy course which is now UKCP-accredited. It was somewhat to my dismay that I saw the earlier egalitarian and democratic philosophy of that course diminish as new practitioners fought desperately to get accredited and, once secure, and waving their newly gained ticket of accreditation as 'real' psychotherapists, took an elitist and protectionist stance. The same newly accredited psychotherapists were eager to maintain that this ticket gave them exclusive rights, for example, in the use of professional titles, etc., and were quick to exclude those who did not have the accrediting piece of paper which they perceived as an exclusive passport to the practice of psychotherapy. Eager for employment as psychotherapists within the new free market NHS, they showed no evidence of consideration of wider contextual issues, either in relation to the NHS and its traditions within the welfare state, or to the situation of clinicians traditionally employed within the NHS. They showed very little evidence of a wider social, historical and political perspective either in their training or current outlook.

This was particularly disappointing as the founder of that particular model of psychotherapy and original inspiration for the establishment and development of the course was not only deeply committed to the principles of the NHS, but had been inspired to develop his model of psychotherapy from a belief that it would provide a better therapy for more people within the NHS. However, when he retired and the quest for professionalism replaced ideological commitment in the development of that particular organisation, I was left with the impression that this part-time training course had succeeded in providing many who hitherto would never have dreamed of obtaining a professional status with a quick passport to professional legitimisation and credibility. This is not to say that many who attended the course are not fine psychotherapists. Many are from mental health backgrounds, and already have a professional training to which they were adding further specialised knowledge. However, I am left questioning the nature of professional commitment and ideological context of much psychotherapy training.

As I have already observed, Street (1992) believes that the training of clinical psychologists is frequently lacking in breadth and depth when it comes to training in counselling, despite clinical psychologists often perceiving themselves as having expertise in this field. According to his survey of one department (Street 1992), the majority of psychologists (16 out of 21) considered that counselling was a major part of their job, and some were advocating the use of training packages to train others. Street does not give details of the training and background of these psychologists, but the point he makes is a valid one, in that he raises the question of how clinical psychologists can be experts in counselling when many do not fulfil the entry requirements of the BPS Division of Counselling Psychology. Gore (1994) suggests that it is inappropriate that psychologists should define for counsellors what they can and cannot do or what they are equipped and trained to do. She points to the need for clinical psychology and counselling psychology to describe clearly their own areas of competence within the field of primary health care.

### The views of clinical and counselling psychologists

In the pilot project carried out by Collins and Murray (1995) the views of the eight clinical psychologists working in adult mental health and those of the two counselling psychologists were ascertained, using a semi-structured short interview consisting of five questions. The results are interesting, although it is difficult to generalise from these findings due to the small sample size. Also in this study, counselling psychologists were defined as such by their undergraduate experience of having a first degree in psychology as well as training in counselling.

First it was questioned what clinical problems counselling psychologists can and cannot deal with. Clinical psychologists believed that counselling psychologists were able to work with a range of clinical problems and that their ways of working might differ from those of clinical psychologists. For example, counselling psychologists were seen to be more interested in process issues in the therapeutic

relationship than in goal-direction. Presumably this reflected the
behavioural background of the clinical psychologists in that particular department. The areas which were felt to be the domain of
clinical psychology were psychometric testing, family therapy and
work in a structured cognitive-behavioural way with clients who
present with obsessional-compulsive problems, severe depression
and anxiety. Those clinical psychologists who worked as part of the
acute psychiatric teams felt that counselling psychologists may not
be trained in psychiatric ways of thinking, and may not be able
to work with clients who have marked or severe psychological disorders. However, counselling psychologists were judged to be helpful in dealing with immediate psychological crises due to major life
events such as divorce and bereavement. Thus there was some
agreement amongst clinical psychologists with the BPS definitions of the differences between counselling and clinical psychology,
although these differences were not viewed in the same way by
the counselling psychologists. Counselling psychologists felt that the
only problems for which they would not offer intervention were
those where the referral agent had made a specific request for
behavioural interventions, as with simple phobias and some anxiety
states. Their replies referred only to one-to-one interventions and
made no mention of whether or not they were able to offer family
or couples counselling. Since the counselling psychologists were
employed within primary care rather than psychiatric teams, there
were no comments made regarding their ability to intervene with
individuals with severe or long-term mental health problems.

The second question asked whether counselling psychologists
should be supervised by clinical psychologists, or if not by whom.
The counselling psychologists felt that they should have a clinical
psychologist as a line manager but stressed the tradition in their
training of having supervision external to the work setting, particularly if expertise could not be provided internally. One felt that the
ideal situation was to have an external supervisor in addition to
contact with a clinical psychologist within the department where
the therapeutic styles of counselling and clinical psychologist were
compatible. A difficulty again is the different possible interpretations applied to the term 'supervision'. Additionally, one view was
that a department of clinical psychology should be committed to
following the same standard of supervision for counsellors as those
required by BAC. Although the majority of the clinical psychologists took the view that counselling psychologists should be
supervised from within the department of clinical psychology, they
recognised the difficulty that this placed clinical psychology above

counselling psychology, which could be viewed as an attempt to limit and control the professional development of counselling psychologists. It was felt that those who offered supervision should have an awareness of the model of counselling employed by the supervisee. The ability of other mental health personnel to act as supervisors, and the wish of counsellors to be supervised by another counselling psychologist, were also acknowledged. The option of counselling psychology developing alongside but separately from clinical psychology services was seen as possibly recreating the problems of overlapping areas of work which have already arisen within multi-disciplinary teamwork.

The third question addressed whether it should be a prerequisite that counsellors should have a first degree in psychology before they are employed by a trust. The counselling psychologists expressed a view that the department was likely to be narrowing the choice of counsellors from whom to select suitable applicants for future employment if a first degree in psychology was a prerequisite in addition to BAC accreditation. Half the clinical psychologists interviewed felt that counsellors should have a psychology degree. Reasons for this included the desirability of appointing counselling psychologists rather than counsellors, a means of screening people applying to work in the service and a way of determining a relationship between the clinical psychology department and counsellors. Those who felt that a psychology degree was not a prerequisite emphasised the importance of taking the individual's training, experience and qualifications into account and felt that such a requirement was discriminatory against other criteria of competence.

Fourth, it was asked whether any problems with appointing counselling psychologists to the department were anticipated. Three of the eight clinical psychologists felt that there could be potential problems in marginalising counselling psychologists by not awarding them equal status. Most felt that there would need to be a clear framework of how the two disciplines would work together which would include an agreed protocol of how to distribute referrals from GPs. Professional rivalry and disparity of pay were two issues which were highlighted by both counselling and clinical psychologists, especially if the working practices of clinical psychologists and counselling psychologists became blurred.

The fifth question highlighted the issue of equal pay for counselling and clinical psychologists. Pay was seen as an important issue by all the clinical psychologists interviewed. Three felt that pay should be equivalent. One felt that this should be done using a separate pay scale from clinical psychology pay scales, while another suggested that equality of pay was unlikely to happen without there being a fall in the salaries of clinical psychologists. Two definitely thought that pay should be greater for clinical psychologists. One quoted the MPAG Report (MPAG 1990) and the fact that clinical psychologists work at a number of different levels, something which counsellors are not trained to do. Another replied that pay should not be equal as long as counselling psychologists were supervised by clinical psychologists. The counselling psychologists felt that they should be paid in accordance with BAC salary guidelines. No reference was made to the role of the BPS in determining pay equivalence or differences.

Clinical psychologists in this study recognise that counsellors have an important role to play in the future structure of mental health services. Their views of the areas of clinical competence of each professional group are broadly in line with those defined by the BPS (1994d). However, it appears that the distinction made between counselling and clinical psychologists – on the basis of the former providing services to those who experience problems related to life events, and the latter to those with more complex, intractable or severe difficulties – is less clearly held by the counselling psychologists. It may be incorrect to assume that all counselling psychologists will wish to interpret their area of clinical competence as a narrow field as defined by clinical psychologists.

## Organisation of counselling services in the NHS

The national trend is for the NHS trusts to employ counsellors. This trend has implications for those currently employed as assistant psychologists who may be hoping to go on to undertake clinical training. Given the difficulty in obtaining a place on a clinical training course, it may become increasingly attractive for those who wish to see clients within the NHS to undertake counselling training and enter the service as a counselling psychologist. Clearly, clinical psychology can no longer assume that it alone has a rightful place in mental health. The way forward will inevitably involve including other applied psychologists working together. The challenge is both to prevent doing to the newly professionalised areas of psychology what was done to clinical psychology by psychiatry (Miller 1994), and also to look upon the developments as a chance to increase the impact of psychology rather than an erosion of our professional basis. It may be that some of the anxieties of clinical psychologists stem from the generic nature of their training which, it has been pointed out, is its strength, but also exposes them to the criticism of being jacks of all trades and masters of none.

A major issue in the provision of counselling within the NHS is how such services should be organised. Gore (1994) notes that, overall, the conclusions derived from the conference 'Counselling and Primary Care: Promoting Good Practice' pointed to the encouragement of the development of quality counselling services run by appropriately trained people who are able to define their areas of competence. However, whether these should be established as separate services or set up within existing services was not clear. Part of this lack of precision is undoubtedly due to the present state of organisation within the NHS, with services being carried out at a more local level, and individual trusts providing services in a variety of different ways. The conference emphasised such issues as appropriate training and supervision, and the necessity for regulatory and accrediting bodies. The position of psychology in these respects is far clearer and better defined than the position of counselling generally. For example, training in applied, educational, clinical, occupational and counselling psychology is well established, with guidelines for content based on the task the practitioner is expected to perform once qualified.

Several reasons have been put forward favouring a positive attitude of clinical psychologists to the employment of counsellors in psychology departments. Many of these reasons revolve around the short supply of clinical psychologists while trying to meet the demands, expectations and quality assurance requirements of both clients and purchasers. First, the MPAG report recommended that clinical psychologists should not undertake work that can be carried out just as well by other staff, providing that adequate support and supervision are available. Second, the needs of clients have to be considered.

Clients' expectations of having their needs met will not be fulfilled if service delivery is solely dependent on clinical psychologists. One of the roles of clinical psychology is to encourage quality in psychological practice by others. Bringing counsellors into psychology departments provides a way of doing this directly. In return, the counsellors benefit from support and supervision. Third, the employment of counsellors fits with the consultancy model of services. The provision of an appropriate level of care depends on enough Level 3 resources to develop, support and monitor the use of psychological skills. Fourth, similar changes are happening in other professions both within the NHS and within other public bodies. Already in health and social services generally an increasing number of staff of varying backgrounds, qualifications and experience are carrying out the work that has historically been the remit of other professions. The argument here regarding psychology services is that if psychologists do not reorganise their own services, they will be carried out by others who are not psychologists.

In the context of similar changes elsewhere in the NHS there may be a certain inevitability about such developments. Thus it is important that clinical psychologists attempt to ensure that they are implemented in ways that enhance rather than diminish psychological care. The advent of the free market means that professional groupings such as counselling, health, occupational and educational psychology also have claims to areas that have traditionally been the preserve of clinical psychologists. National standards and qualifications in areas such as guidance, advice and counselling legitimise these claims. It is both a strength and weakness of clinical psychology that it provides a generic service. However, it may be that the addition of other professional staff will complement both the quantity and expertise offered by the service.

Miller (1994) recommends safeguards and assurances regarding the employment of counsellors and therapists when employed directly in the field of primary care, or when employed under the umbrella of clinical psychology departments. As counsellors and therapists will continue to operate independently in primary care, purchasers must assure themselves both of the appropriateness of their qualifications and also that suitable arrangements are made for their support, review and development. When counsellors and therapists are employed under the umbrella of clinical psychology departments, Miller recommends that the following 10 requirements and assurances should be considered.

He notes that the balance between qualified clinical psychologists and other therapists within a service should be considered. This includes implications for the demand, training and recruitment of clinical psychologists, and has an effect on the assistant psychologist grade. Purchasers should be aware of factors such as the necessity of qualified and experienced clinical psychologists to manage and supervise other therapy staff. They should also note the areas that counsellors and therapists cannot cover, which would normally be undertaken by clinical psychologists. When such staff are employed instead of clinical psychologists, there are other service costs. When employing counsellors a careful examination of their skills and experience is essential, because the training is highly variable and qualifications cannot be taken at face value. As a general guideline, counsellors should be eligible for accreditation by the British Association for Counselling. (In time this may be replaced by NVQ standards.) The roles, job specifications and workloads of counsellors, including job descriptions for voluntary staff, must be defined and documented in job descriptions or contracts. These should include clear statements about accountability. Overall, there should be commitment to further training and development. When the clinical work develops beyond the original qualifications of the counsellor, it is necessary to ensure that the practice of therapy is within acceptable psychological models. Regular and close supervision is necessary. Miller suggests that one to two hours a week should be the minimum, and advises joint screening of new referrals with the supervisor, at least until competence has been demonstrated. Purchasers and clients should be provided with information describing the role of counsellors and therapists, including supervisory arrangements to avoid misunderstanding and misleading expectations. Miller stresses that clients, if they wish, should have the right to see the supervisor.

The BPS has pointed out that a service provided by a firm or practice of 'Chartered Psychologists' need not be solely provided by the chartered psychologists within it. However, these chartered psychologists must be in a position where they can oversee and assume responsibility for the work provided by the service. This same principle may be applied to clinical psychology services. Furthermore, the professional status and the individual and professional career aspirations of counsellors and therapists must be recognised in management and supervisory arrangements. This is to ensure that counsellors do not become second-class citizens.

Finally, counsellors and therapists should have the same opportunities as clinical psychologists for annual professional review and continuing personal and professional development. This is typically carried out by the individual performance review system (IPR). In this the job description is taken as the base, and aims and objectives and the means of attaining these are documented, together with factors that concern professional career development and further training.

## VIEWS OF PURCHASERS OF HEALTH CARE

The views of the purchasers of psychological care regarding the services provided are becoming increasingly important. This is seen in the relationship of GP fundholders to service providers in primary care. Burton and Ramsden (1994) report the findings of a survey carried out in one health authority which was soon to become a

**Table 1** Referral pattern of GPs

| | Direct access service for GPs (%) | Psychiatric unit (%) | Community psychiatric nurses (%) | Counsellors (%) | More than one (%) |
|---|---|---|---|---|---|
| Psychotic problems (e.g. manic-depressive illness and schizophrenia) | 6 | 94 | 36 | 0 | 36 |
| Major depression (endogenous) | 6 | 97 | 39 | 6 | 42 |
| Reactive depression | 6 | 39 | 36 | 64 | 33 |
| Bereavement reactions | 14 | 3 | 28 | 89 | 25 |
| Stress/lifestyle problems | 28 | 3 | 6 | 83 | 19 |
| Eating disorders | 25 | 86 | 6 | 14 | 22 |
| Habit disorders | 64 | 31 | 8 | 11 | 14 |
| Marital problems | 19 | 6 | 3 | 94 | 19 |
| Sexual problems | 33 | 11 | 6 | 69 | 28 |
| Disclosed childhood abuse | 39 | 28 | 6 | 50 | 25 |
| Relationship problems | 22 | 3 | 8 | 92 | 22 |
| Anger and aggression management | 72 | 31 | 8 | 14 | 22 |
| Anxiety, panic attacks and phobias | 78 | 28 | 17 | 17 | 31 |
| Obsessive-compulsive disorder | 64 | 58 | 3 | 6 | 33 |
| Psychosomatic problems | 47 | 25 | 8 | 22 | 14 |
| Adjustment to chronic physical illness | 19 | 6 | 28 | 56 | 25 |
| Personality disorders | 42 | 64 | 19 | 17 | 33 |
| Other | 6 | 3 | 3 | 3 | 0 |

Source: Burton and Ramsden (1994).
Note: The figures shown may add up to more than 100 per cent because multiple responses were possible.

trust, on GP referral patterns to out-patient psychiatry, direct access clinical psychology service, community psychiatric nurses and counsellors. The health authority had a large number of GP fundholders and an increasing number of practice counsellors were offering sessions in GP surgeries. Of the fundholding practices surveyed, 85 per cent had an in-house counsellor (six out of seven practices) and a seventh was intending to employ one. An additional 50 per cent of GPs regularly referred patients to an independent counsellor. The questionnaire, which achieved a 68 per cent response rate, addressed two main questions. First, a series of questions looked at whether GPs would be interested in purchasing a range of direct access clinical psychology services directly. The results of the survey indicated that substantial numbers of GPs were interested in purchasing services for families and children, services for elderly people and mental health promotion directly. Furthermore, approximately half the GPs wanted basic training in psychological therapies and counselling for themselves, and supervision, support and evaluation of their practice counsellors.

The second part of the questionnaire looked at where GPs were likely to refer patients with different diagnoses. A total of 18 different categories of patients were listed, and five referral resources: psychology, direct access service for GPs, a psychiatric unit, community psychiatric nurses, and counsellors. Lastly it was asked whether more than one of these might be used. The results demonstrated that the GPs differed widely in where they referred patients for psychological problems (see Table 1).

There was a wide consensus that patients labelled as psychotic or as having a major depression were referred to the psychiatric unit or to CPNs. In cases of eating disorder, 86 per cent of referrals were made to the psychiatric unit and 25 per cent to psychology services. However, in cases of reactive depression, most referrals were to counsellors and the psychiatric unit, followed by CPNs. Nearly 90 per cent of GPs referred bereavement reactions, and stress and lifestyle problems to counsellors. While the psychology services received the majority of referrals for habit disorders, counsellors received 95 per cent of the marital problems. Counsellors received more sexual problem referrals (38 per cent) more than any other group, and followed by psychology services. Psychology services received the most referrals for anger and aggression management, although this might reflect the existence of a specific cognitive-behavioural group for patients with these problems, set up by this department. Psychology services also received most referrals for anxiety, panic attacks, phobias and obsessive-compulsive disorders.

Whereas psychologists received most of the referrals for psycho-somatic problems, counsellors received more patients where there was need for adjustment to chronic physical illness. There was a mixed referral pattern regarding personality disorder, with half the GPs referring to the psychology services and half to the psychiatric unit. Where childhood abuse had been disclosed, 67 per cent of these cases were referred to counsellors.

Burton and Ramsden view as worrying the fact that counsellors may or may not have the training to prepare them to treat patients with a history of severe, longstanding personality problems. They observe that problems of this nature cannot be effectively remedied in short-term counselling contracts. The psychology services came second with 43 per cent of patients in this category referred to them. Similarly, 95 per cent of respondents indicated that they would refer relationship problems to counsellors, whose skills may or may not be adequate when there is an underlying personality disorder: only 19 per cent of such patients were referred to the psychology services. In the category of personality disorder, the authors note that the referral rate of 24 per cent to counsellors is a cause of concern as again they may or may not have the appropriate training to deal with these difficulties.

Furthermore, Burton and Ramsden comment that those diagnostic categories where the greatest number of multiple referral resources are used – in particular disclosed childhood abuse and personality disorder – indicate the areas in which GPs might need further clarification about the difference between counselling, clinical psychology and psychotherapy. However, as they point out, there is a great diversity in clinical skills, in length and type of training and in levels of experience across these professions in Britain. In some parts of the country, there may be counsellors who are more skilled in helping adult survivors of childhood sexual abuse than some clinical psychologists.

Burton and Ramsden's survey of GP referral patterns shows that referrals are influenced by factors other than just the diagnostic category of the patient and the GP's view of the professional expertise of the available services. These include the following: risk factors (e.g. suicide, children at risk); accessibility (e.g. in-house service for the convenience of patients, lack of negative stigma, ease of follow-up, etc.); the patient's psychological-mindedness; waiting times; chronicity of the problem; the patient's motivation to seek help; the patient's preference; and the presence of physical symptomatology.

Whereas some of these factors favoured referral to counsellors (for example, accessibility where they are employed in-house), others such as the chronicity of the problem influenced preference for the psychology department. The two primary considerations were risk factors, followed closely by waiting times. The comments of respondents recorded by Burton and Ramsden indicate that GPs were very concerned about the waiting times for clinical psychology services. For example, many indicated that psychology services were often needed and that most patients view their problems as urgent, but that waiting times were too long. More worryingly, although the GPs indicate that they would prefer to use psychology services for chronic problems, the lengthy waiting time prompted referrals for this type of problem to counsellors, so that these patients could be seen more quickly.

The results of the survey by Burton and Ramsden highlight the importance of appropriate referral. Each time a psychological therapy fails, it is likely to confirm for the patient the hopelessness of his or her situation. With the employment of counsellors from within psychology departments, the likelihood of patients being referred to the appropriate service will be increased, and the pattern of sequential referrals hopefully reduced. The issue of obtaining the most appropriate referral for a patient so that they receive the best help for their problems is paramount. A close working relationship between the two professions would facilitate the process whereby patients are appropriately referred to either a counsellor or clinical psychologist.

## RELATIONS BETWEEN CLINICAL PSYCHOLOGY AND OTHER STAFF

The clinical work of psychologists frequently involves liaison with other staff involved in the care of the client. Who those staff are varies with different specialisms. For example, in adult acute work, liaison often has to be with a GP or psychiatrist; in working with people with learning difficulties and with the long-term ill, liaison usually involves ward staff, relatives of the client, social services, day-care facilities, and community projects and organisations in the voluntary sector involved with mental health and housing. Good liaison is often crucial to the client's well-being and to the creation of effective counselling situations. The right ethos has to be established before counselling can take place.

### *Training and supervision*

As has been pointed out in earlier chapters and above, a core role of clinical psychologists in the NHS is their involvement in the teaching and supervision of other professionals. This has arisen for ideological and practical reasons. Clinical psychology was developed within the NHS and under the philosophy of the welfare state. It has therefore a commitment to the dispersal of psychological knowledge, including the attendant psychological therapies, in order to provide better psychological care for more people. Practically, there are too few clinical psychologists available to meet the demand of psychological services. One way to provide better psychological care is to train other health care professionals in specific aspects of psychological care and therapies, such as counselling. Psychological interventions are of course made naturally and spontaneously by many different health care professionals. However, clinical psychologists are expected to have a greater depth of understanding of psychological problems.

Teaching counselling can take place in different care settings, both in the hospital and in the community. This can include working with staff in mental health units and with staff working with clients with learning difficulties. Clinical psychologists also teach counselling skills to staff working in a range of other settings such as in physical health, with oncology patients or with coronary care and terminal care patients. Courses range from workshops to one and two years in length, and are delivered to a wide range of professionals, including psychiatrists, hospital nurses, CPNs, social workers, occupational therapists and other related professionals in the NHS.

### Consultancy and staff support

Clinical psychologists provide consultancy and advice to other health care professionals concerning psychological aspects of care. Increasingly they are taking on a consultancy role for management in the NHS setting. Improving service delivery and providing staff with psychological support is another aspect of the role of the clinical psychologist. Work involving the counselling of other staff is often required of clinical psychologists in a period of seemingly constant uncertainty and change within the NHS with its attendant anxieties, unhappiness and insecurities. Counselling is also helpful to mental health workers, whether offered formally or informally, to help them to cope better with the distress with which they are continuously confronted in the course of their work. Counselling enables some understanding of feelings of being overwhelmed, or of helplessness and hopelessness, which are often unacknowledged when working with distressed clients. This is perhaps particularly true when working with certain client groups such as those with long-term difficulties. Such support and acknowledgement of feelings often reduces feelings of isolation, fears of incompetence and enables staff to be in a better position to be able to contain the continuous and sometimes overwhelming despair and distress of others.

Staff support is also provided by clinical psychologists at an institutional level in a ward or other organisational setting. There are many examples of dysfunctional wards, and of dysfunctional coping mechanisms in staff, including splitting, paranoia and denial. These can paralyse effective patient care on a ward. Sometimes, counselling can be used positively in such situations and can facilitate better institutional life. However, there are situations where counselling is either difficult or even impossible because the staff are not prepared to engage in the discourse of psychotherapy, either for themselves or in understanding their work or in the way they view psychotherapy or counselling as an appropriate or useful model in relation to their client group. Counselling is frequently a much more difficult activity to undertake in secure and semi-secure units, and in long-stay wards. Unfortunately too there are also situations where staff claim to be counselling, usually with little or no training, where their practice could not be accommodated even within the broadest definition of counselling.

It is important for the counsellors and psychologists to recognise the limits of their discipline, not only in the appropriateness of counselling for a particular individual but also with regard to its limits in some institutional settings. Counselling can often be perceived as a threat to institutions, particularly when it is feared as likely to undermine the status quo and to attack rigid structures. Sometimes counselling interventions need to be made on different structural levels in order for them to be effective. At other times, as we will address in the next chapter, it needs to be questioned whether counselling is the appropriate intervention at all or rather encourages us to collude in the individualisation of distress.

Clinical psychologists also carry out training to staff working in the voluntary sector, for example, facilitating the setting up of community-based self-help groups. Working in the community, clinical psychologists also help develop community-based self-help groups in specific areas of psychological distress. For example, counselling courses are first of all set up in the clinical psychology department for selected volunteers, often those who have either a professional or personal link with, or have themselves experienced, the specific area of distress. They then set up their own self-help groups, for example for adult survivors of sexual abuse or for those experiencing bereavement, or trying to cope with a symptom of distress such as depression. The volunteers then work as a separate entity in the voluntary sector and thus are able to pass on their psychological understanding and skills to others. In this way more psychological help is made available for those experiencing distress.

Apart from primary care, there are other specialisms in clinical psychology where counselling is frequently practised. These include rehabilitation services, where work is focused on those with long-term difficulties and on work with the elderly. In these specialisms, the therapist typically works not just in one-to-one sessions with clients but is involved in the larger service organisation, working with carers of these clients, such as with staff groups and relatives of the clients. Counselling can take place either directly with the client or with others involved in the care of the client. Increasingly, as in the field of primary care, counsellors are employed in the NHS and are often employed and supervised from within the clinical psychology departments. This, as discussed earlier in this chapter, has implications for cooperative working between counsellors and psychologists.

A primary role for the secondary care services was put forward by the conference on counselling in primary care in December 1993 already discussed. Gore (1994) notes the need to provide support, training and supervision for counsellors working in primary care, and working with clients with more complex or challenging problems within the field of psychiatry. A suggestion made at the conference was for two distinct forms of service, one providing a service for the mentally ill, and a second providing a service for those suffering from emotional ill health. Greater clarity is needed in the relationship between primary and secondary care generally, defining how the sort of people presenting with particular difficulties are best provided for by particular services, in particular settings and by particular types of mental health worker.

This chapter began by an examination of the nature of professions, before exploring relationships within the psychological professions. As I have outlined, these professions developed within a historical and social context which determined the content and structure of the developing psychology professions and influenced their relationship with other mental health professions. This is particularly illustrated in the formation and development of clinical psychology within the NHS, and the relationship between clinical psychology and the longer established profession of psychiatry. Changes in the wider social context of the 1960s and 1970s were reflected in changes within both professions of psychology and psychiatry and also influenced the relationship between these two professions. Since the 1970s the main influence on clinical psychology and the main determinant of its relationships with other professionals has been the legislation passed by successive Conservative governments. This political context set the agenda for issues of collaboration or competition between professions. It was against this background that counselling was established as a profession within the NHS. This context has determined the development of counselling as well as the employment of counsellors and counselling psychologists and has influenced their relationship with both existing psychological services and other professions. As we shall see in the next chapter, issues concerning the wider social context are mirrored in the frame of reference within which psychology, counselling and psychotherapy define themselves, and in the role they play in contemporary society.

# SIX

# A critique of counselling in psychological services

Clinical psychologists as a professional group undergo a training in which there is considerable emphasis on critical thinking. In the past, part of the clinical psychologist's role could be viewed as that of being a critic within the system. It was a role that, it might be argued, often led to conflict and uncomfortable relationships – for example, conflicts with the psychiatric model generally, as well as with specific issues to do with forms of treatment and choice of treatment settings. In that situation, the conflict and tensions often generated creativity, illustrated for example by the research, writing and development of alternative treatment models by clinical psychologists. All this offered the hope of the possibility of change. There was a place, albeit often an uncomfortable one, for criticism and for conflicts within the NHS. Today we have a situation where criticism or alternative values and viewpoints are seen at best as evidence of a 1960s-type of relapse, which is treated by managerial strategies such as marginalisation or denial; and at worst as evidence of not fitting in with the machismo management ethos, but instead being wilfully insubordinate to the management hierarchy. Criticism can be perceived as a display of absolute disloyalty to the caring, sharing and expensively brochured presentation of the NHS trusts.

Nevertheless criticisms there are, although in this chapter I concentrate more upon the criticisms as they reflect upon the delivery of counselling and therapy by the psychological services. The evidence suggests, as I shall show, that psychologists have to put their own house in order. However, psychologists are themselves part of a wider NHS structure, with its attendant values and methods of treatment influencing what they can or cannot deliver, and it would not be true to the critique required of this concluding chapter if I did not draw equal attention to the total picture.

## CURRENT EMPLOYMENT PRACTICES WITHIN THE NHS

As I outlined in Chapter Five, the employment practice encouraged in society generally also affects the employment practices within the NHS. We are told that the concept of 'continuous employment in a particular work setting or a job for life' is now a thing of the past; and what is relevant is that particular skills are specified in order to carry out a particular task or project. It might be argued that 'employment' itself as an outmoded term, with its implications of continuous work and its related benefits, not necessarily related to the accomplishment of a given task or project which is implied by the term 'job'. There is a trend within the new NHS trusts to embrace this tag of 'the person with the right skills for the particular job', preferably on short-term contracts, at the expense of the employment of professionals, especially those on long-term contracts. This procedure is not only less expensive, it also makes people more expendable and therefore insecure about their jobs. Although this may make for a cost-effective and compliant workforce, it is frequently at the expense of the wider perspective and depth of knowledge inherent in much professional training. By limiting job specifications to operational task definitions, and rendering the less tangible aspects of professional knowledge and clinical practice of little or no importance, it has become increasingly possible for NHS trusts to employ people with the discrete qualifications that meet the job specifications.

Thus much of the work previously carried out by nurses has been replaced by the employment of low-paid workers, often with little or minimal training. Such health workers in the mental health field are found to be doing work previously carried out by psychiatric nurses, whether in hospital wards, day hospitals or in the community. They are called by various terms such as 'care assistant', 'community care assistant', etc. They often work directly with patients, more often than not under supervision of a highly variable quality. An increasing observation in both general and psychiatric wards and units is that it is difficult to find the presence of any trained staff. The care of patients is left to what Tony Prior (personal communication 1994) calls a 'mums' army'.

Another increasing trend is the requirement that mental health workers should be flexible and thus able to respond to the particular job that is required at the particular time. This may have some advantages in doing away with some of the job demarcation disputes of some professional practices and provide a more flexible workforce, but it also has disadvantages, such as creating role confusion in who does what, with whom and in which setting, and can also at times have the implication that everybody can do anything and no particular training or expertise is necessary.

Regarding psychological services, some would point to the possibility that the work of clinical psychologists might also have been farmed off for cheaper labour. For example, as we have earlier explored, lay counsellors are employed in many clinical psychology departments and working in many contexts such as general practice. As I have discussed earlier in this book, however competent and experienced counsellors are, they do not have the breadth of training that the clinical or counselling psychologist has, although lay counsellors are of course cheaper.

However, counselling and psychological services exist within a context and that context is embedded within the wider socio-political system of contemporary Britain. Accounts of the wider sociological perspective of 'postmodern' culture, politics and economics and its effects on everyday life may be found in works such as David Harvey's *The Condition of Postmodernity* (1990) and David Smail's *The Origin of Unhappiness* (1993).

Smail outlines how our world is structured by powers at varying degrees of distance from us. Those closest to us, which he terms 'proximal powers', the ones which preoccupy us most, are the most amenable to our personal intervention and the ones focused on by psychology. Those furthest from us, which Smail terms 'distal powers' and the ones focused on by sociology and politics, exert the strongest influence on our lives. People tend to define their reality and attribute the 'cause' of how they feel to the proximal experience of events or the actions of people close to them, which are in fact determined by distal influences well out of their sight. Most of us do not even know the origin of decisions which may be shaping our lives, or if any such decision has been made though proximal events such as parental divorce or loss of job, which may be experienced as events of disastrous and fearful consequences. However, to give an adequate explanation of individual experience it is necessary to take account of the distal powers that operate. It is not that proximal powers do not have the more immediate, and potentially devastating, effect on the individual but that the operation of those powers depends in turn on more distal influences. The influence of political decisions on our lives, the effects of unemployment, social deprivation are widely accepted as causes of emotional distress. The more distal the powers the more universal their influence within a given society and the more likely we are to overlook them. Smail describes how people view their immediate or proximal struggles with the world as being due to their own inadequacy, although the cause lies in more distal influences. These distal influences of power include the effects of the previous government's policies of economic liberalism, the resulting attempts to dismantle the welfare state and the restructuring of Britain according to a philosophy of self-reliance and the pursuit of personal interest. Economic policy in Britain, based on the 'ideal type' free market economic model of the US, over the 18 years of the Conservative government has resulted in a business culture based on the dictates of the free market economy. However, such policies were not just applied in Britain, for similar policies were carried out in other parts of the world. The Conservative government was merely representative of a culture which was prevalent in the Western world. As such it could be seen as the manager or enabler of powers which had dominated in the US for some time. Huge companies, which cross national boundaries, dependent for their survival on ever-increasing expansion, operate in the global market while their effects are eventually controlled and directed by producers, consumers and managers located in those parts of the world best designed for their function. Processes of production and the kinds of alienation and exploitation they involve, which concerned sociologists and political economists up to the first half of this century, have been exported to parts of the world where labour is cheap, conditions of production are less scrupulously controlled and consumers less protected.

With the economic restructuring of British industry such as the dismantling of traditional heavy industries where the labour force was unionised to a concentration on service industries, the patterns of work changed drastically in Britain, as in the emphasis on a 'flexible workforce', meaning contract and part-time work. Many people were likely not to be working at all, some became part of an 'underclass' existing outside the formal economic structure and those in work suffered job insecurity.

A business society built on the dictates of economic rationality affected every aspect of British life. For individuals and families to grab what they could for themselves was accepted no longer as selfishness or greed but as the sensible thing to do. An ideological framework existed in which life was structured by a need for money and consumer goods, with the most important function for the population being to consume. During the 1980s almost every form of activity was appropriated by business or sponsored by business.

The free market economy meant that the economy as a whole had to be far more responsive to the imperatives of big business, money had to be transferred quickly and easily, and obstacles had to be removed in the way of rationalisation of working practices. To expand the scope and influence of the market meant the removal of as much as possible of the pre-existing social institutions and ideology identifiable as incompatible with these aims. The business economy recruited those already in business and others were retrained to become business people. In the business society ideology infiltrated language into every aspect of culture. The language of accountancy replaced any other consideration. As David Smail states:

> To replace with the values of the market, within the space of a decade, the ideology of a social system which at least purported to be based on the values of truth, justice and equality traceable back to the Enlightenment was no mean achievement.
>
> (Smail 1993: 99)

Smail outlines how this was achieved by three means. First the application of raw power – coercive and economic – at the distal region of the political system. This may be seen in the actions of the previous government breaking of the unions following the miners' opposition to mine closures, the 'rationalisation' of industry and the engineering of mass unemployment, the dismantling of the welfare state and deregulation of systems which offered either economic, professional or intellectual protection of any kind. Such measures created conditions of job insecurity which induced cooperation in realising the aims of the business world.

Second, Smail describes the construction of an articulate intellectual rationale which put into place a new pragmatism. Part of the achievement of the business economy was to discredit the value of intellectual criticism and indeed intellectual activity itself. The dilution of the concept of truth and the redefinition of knowledge as a ready-made commodity in which people may be trained threatened to make higher learning a mere extension of technical instruction, removing from it the possibility of criticising the business culture. Universities were affected as much as any other institution; they were no longer the refuge of disinterested seekers of truth or somewhere to go in search of resistance to business values, but instead they, like a host of other academic institutions, became preoccupied with income generation, setting up an ever-increasing number of 'quick learn', 'quick qualification' courses which neglected the traditional academic values of patience, reflection and diligent hard work necessary for any true acquisition of knowledge. Many of these new courses offered counselling training of variable quality. Business needs to be 'economical' with truth if it is to avoid limits on its expansion, i.e. it needs to invent new needs continuously. Also it can substitute training for the pursuit of knowledge since its aim is to maintain a technology of management by managers who do not reflect upon their role. Fashion is more valued than history, for it fits in with continuous production to fit 'new' demands for its products.

Although much of the new ideology was conveyed through superficial rhetoric, it was successful in rendering the workforce receptive through sheer vulnerability to the new business ideology. The managerial mediocrity imposed its language of 'performance indicators', 'quality control', etc. on people who had all their lives spoken a far more ethical language. Many people were left without a language in which they could articulate and understand their experience and often struggled to force the unarticulated complexity of their experience into the language imposed by the business world. Language was altered so that people's role, whether they were travelling by train or attending a hospital appointment, was that of a client or customer of business.

The third means was the putting into place of mediators or people whose task it was to transmit the influence of the distal powers to the population generally. Such an enterprise as the transmission of a business culture needs the cooperation of people in a project they believe in. Once someone is convinced that his or her 'motives' are for the best, he or she may happily be recruited to the task in hand. Some of these people already formed part of the business world; others were products of an expanded tertiary education system who were not quite members of established professions and not quite possessing the qualifications for entry but close enough to believe that given the opportunity they could do the job. The managers' role in putting into place the disciplinary and instructional apparatus of the business society was crucial to its success. Traditional methods of assessing vocational ability and professional competence, traditional institutional practices of hiring and firing, accepted even if unwritten rules concerning the rights and duties of employers and employed were suddenly replaced by new definitions of competence, formal systems of appraisal, restrictions on information and communication and authoritarian lines of accountability. These 'new' systems of discipline, backed by the real threat of unemployment, were usually introduced as the effects of reorganisation and change.

Change itself was emphasised as being a positive force and those who were deemed to fear change were seen as lacking in some way. This ideology extended, across the entire working world, forms of uncertainty and insecurity which had previously been the lot only of an exploited industrial workforce. Almost no place of work escaped the upheavals of reorganisation – large public institutions in health and education, public and private companies of every size and form, seemed overrun by management consultants advising on change and trainers instructing in its accomplishment. The managerial group having a 'time out' weekend at an expensive hotel could be NHS administrators or the board of a large conglomerate. Everyone who wasn't made redundant underwent a change of role or change of rank; everyone was taught the new language of efficiency and effectiveness, quality control, appraisal and time management. University lecturers, teachers, clinical psychologists and social workers alike smartened up their appearance. Doctors found themselves studying business systems and learning to audit accounts rather than reading case histories. To those who enjoyed these new activities their participation may have seemed like an act of personal choice. But to many it was experienced as a nightmare in which they were forced to compromise or abandon their ethical values, feeling painfully out of tune with themselves. Yet others found themselves unable to cope and looked for help. There were many casualties of the business culture. Many competent and successful professional and technical employees of both public and private concerns who had formerly occupied positions of respect and influence were marginalised by a mediocracy which first usurped their managerial function and then maintained its position by importing at great expense hired consultants or 'experts' to perform the very same technical/professional functions, but on its own terms. The newly exploited class turned to long clinical psychology waiting lists.

As Smail describes, the rule of the mediocracy had begun. The composition of the 'mediocracy' closely reflected the principal concerns of the culture. Works such as Alasdair MacIntyre's *After Virtue* (1985) and David Smail's *The Origin of Unhappiness* (1993) highlight the role of managers and therapists, and the part they play in maintaining the ethos of individualism, in a social world which has abandoned virtue. Management on the one hand and therapy and counselling on the other are amongst the most prominent components of modern mediocracies. They point out that people such as managers and therapists stand between the individuals and the world in accordance with the aims of a business culture, which are, principally, to establish the ideology of the culture and to extend the market. The main coup of the business society was the redefinition of reality itself. The 'real' world was now defined as that of individualism with a corresponding contempt for socialism of any kind. It was a real world of economic rationality and competition on the one hand and of market diversification on the other. Economic exploitation, the transfer of public assets into private control and the running down of public services were disguised by the promotion of the myths of greater opportunity and freedom of choice. Following the pattern in the US, bookshops filled with books on how to find instant happiness. Apparently, with a bit of know-how we could change our lives and find happiness – be it through developing the right 'skills and strategies' to find the right partner, following the guidance of astrology to change our fate or finding the right sort of spiritual enlightenment. David Smail points out that anybody, however well intentioned, who could make money out of an expanding market in promises and illusory appearances did so. Prominent among the purveyors of dreams and illusions were the therapists and counsellors.

## THE EXPANSION OF COUNSELLING AND PSYCHOTHERAPY

As I discussed at the beginning of this book, psychotherapy and counselling became one of the growth industries of the 1980s and continue to expand. Regarding psychology, business is booming as never before. Chapter One documented how, apart from psychoanalysis which formed the exclusive practice of a tightly regulated, largely medical club 50 years ago, there was little psychological involvement in the treatment of 'mental disorder'. The field which, until the advent of the two world wars, had been considered more or less the sole province of medical psychiatry, is today open to almost anyone. Not so long ago, people struggling with emotional pain and distress had little choice but to submit to medical treatments, which they were not permitted to question but which as often as not left them drugged or electrically shocked into compliance with what they took to be the laws of science. Psychiatry is still influential in the field of emotional distress, and seeks to define what may and may not count as mental illness and what are its appropriate treatments. However, psychology is now a growth industry whose principal products – counselling, psychotherapy, psychometric testing, etc. – are familiar aspects of our society, not just in the clinical field but in many aspects of our daily lives, such as psychometric testing at job interviews, programmes of stress management at work and manuals for relationship counselling at home.

Apart from the psychodynamic therapies deriving from the psychoanalytic school, there are many other kinds of therapy from which to choose – behavioural approaches, cognitive approaches, client-centred transactional analysis, Gestalt therapy and counselling – which are flourishing in a rapidly deregulated market. Likewise, psychotherapists and counsellors are proliferating.

However, although there is little doubt that therapists and counsellors believe that their profession is solely concerned with the humane relief of suffering, according to Smail (1993) they are an example of the way in which our motives can be pure while we are engaged in the pursuit of enterprises of which we are completely unaware. He points to well-meaning but naive beliefs of therapists concerning the significance of their role – a role which Smail describes as basically one of profit at the distress of others. He describes their part in appropriating and marketing aspects of care and concern which should be part of the everyday life of any humane society. There may well be an enduring social necessity for the kind of dispassionate confessional role formerly the province of priests and, later, analysts. However, as Smail points out, with psychotherapy this role becomes specifically commercialised as is seen for example in the opening up of new markets during the 1980s. As we saw in Chapter One, during this time there was a huge expansion of the therapy and counselling industry in Britain. The deregulation of the health care market allowed professional groups, voluntary workers and the wide-ranging brand-name school of psychotherapy and counselling to gain access to 'treatment' which had previously been the preserve of medicine or of one of the traditional NHS professionals. As part of this process the market was extended in several new directions and counselling suddenly became the answer to all sorts of problems which previously people had had to cope with as best they could. Furthermore, the market was extended by the development of new fields of therapeutic concern such as 'disaster counselling' and the development of new concepts such as 'post-traumatic stress disorder'. Undoubtedly there is a need for aid and comfort but it is questionable how this may best be achieved. The culture of business swept aside the traditional forms of comfort and coping by, for example, family and friends, and put forward the professional network of counselling as the most appropriate response to distress.

Therapists and counsellors disputed each others' qualifications to attend the scene and offer advice, while commercial groups rapidly formed to lay claim to special expertise. A whole new body of research and literature developed in the field, and treatment programmes were devised and offered to anyone who could be seen as a victim. Smail reflects that few stopped to consider that by their very activity – standing between individuals and the world to mediate their pain and grief – they were claiming for business a previously non-commercial social function and offering a service the effectiveness of which was not particularly convincing. Just as with professional grief counselling, it is not that the advice is wrong or misguided (much of it is common sense), but it breaks down appropriate social conduct and replaces it with commercially available professional knowledge. Once the need for counselling has been created, the demand for it soon increases as people lose confidence in their ability to handle distress as part of a traditional social process.

Another reason for the expansion of counselling in the 1980s was because of the increase in the possibilities for mediating relationships. As Smail describes, relationships had to bear a heavier strain as they became the main source of warmth and intimacy in a world more competitive than it had been for decades. It was not surprising to find a growing number of professional advisers counselling those who found the strain too great. This also reinforced the view that the business of relationships was really a matter for the professionals. This was also seen in the relations between parents and children as child sex abuse was 'discovered' and extensive professional networks of surveillance, protection and corrections were set up, together with the provision of programmes and packages of 'parenting skills'.

The concern of what Smail terms as a mediocratic caste of therapists and counsellors was not only with the expanding market for the mediation of experience and relationships, it also provided shock absorption for a society in which emotional and psychological as well as physical damage was a necessary part of its economic and ideological policies. For many people suffering from the effects of unemployment, ceaseless change, diminished status and insecurity in the workplace, strained domestic relationships at home, and greater isolation in an increasingly mobile society, the only recourse was 'counselling'. Counsellors performed the ideological function of representing as proximal causes of distress, causes which were in fact distal, and then offered comfort and advice to those who felt themselves to be falling short of the norm in aspects such as 'coping skills', or in the 'management of stress'. What were essentially consequences of distal economic influences were represented proximally as personal failings, which could be remedied by counselling.

However, there is no evidence that the wider availability of psychological theories and techniques is leading to a decrease in psychological distress, and the growth of such approaches is not founded on any scientifically established evidence of their validity and effectiveness. Nor is there any indication that this could lead to people being able to understand themselves any better. Smail suggests that the growth of counselling and psychotherapy indicates not so much a breakthrough in enlightened understanding of distress as the success of a commercial enterprise. Psychology as applied to emotional distress is less a unified discipline than a collection of competing factions, each trying to demarcate its own domain, patent its own procedures and prevent intruders from entering the territory. This pattern was set by psychoanalysis which developed from an exclusive club into a business which seeks to restrict its membership. This runs counter to academic tradition and marks therapeutic psychology out from nearly all other forms of scientific pursuit in a way which must cast doubt on any claim to science practitioners make. Psychoanalysis became the first in a line of brand-name therapies, all of which to a greater or lesser extent took exclusivity as a criterion of their validity. All emphasise the distinctiveness of their beliefs and procedures, institute training courses with restricted entry, and accredit recognised practitioners; they all but register their trademarks. In many cases the theory and practice of brand-name therapies are far from being the patiently accumulated knowledge of an academic community, but represent the hastily elaborated ideas of some more or less charismatic figure who developed his or her personal therapeutic style into a pseudo-technical blueprint for all who join the club to follow.

What are being offered in the psychotherapeutic marketplace are not so much substantiated theories of psychological damage or demonstrably effective cures of emotional pain and confusion, but a range of approaches from the biological to the spiritual and even more esoteric. In view of the absence of clear and convincing evidence for the efficacy of any approach to psychological treatment, it seems to Smail that the explanation is that psychology in this area flourishes because we want it to be effective and because it is impossible to demonstrate that it is not effective. First, even though there exists a very wide range of theoretical ideas and practical procedures (many of them markedly incompatible with each other), there are nevertheless some general features common to almost all approaches to therapy and counselling. The most obvious is that the explanation and the treatment of psychological distress are negotiated through the social transactions of two people – the patient and therapist. Smail argues that it is the comfort derived from association with 'experts' perceived as powerful which sustains the practice of 'therapy from the point of view of the 'patient' or 'client'. Therapists and counsellors conceive of therapeutic theory and practice not only because of helpfulness but also out of self-interest. Therapists and counsellors need to make a living in the same way as everyone else, and cannot be expected to be attracted to interpretations of their work which call its validity into question in any fundamental way. Truth cannot be totally detached from interest. Psychotherapists cannot be blamed for believing that the help they offer is effective in the way they commonly conceive it to be, i.e. more than just comfort, but at the same time their claims may be objectively valid. The person in pain must have someone to turn to and this is likely to be filled by a therapist or counsellor whose sincere belief in therapeutic efficacy is coupled with his or her own personal need to survive in the world.

A second factor which Smail claims contributes to the expansion of counselling and psychotherapy is the general lack of evidence for their efficacy and the fact that it is impossible to demonstrate that they are not efficacious. Discussions based on the results of outcome research in psychological therapies are never resolved. This is often taken as an indication of the complexity of the issues, or the lack of an adequate methodology such as adequately sophisticated statistical methods. However, Smail points out that the real problem is that they cannot be resolved. For the problem is not a technical one of how to cure an illness or adjust an abnormality but rather the problem is how to live a life, which is not a closed question with a simple answer.

However, a major difficulty is that the psychology professions have developed a set of conceptions and practices which provide people with more or less plausible perspectives on their painful experiences. This provides intellectual and professional legitimacy for the view that emotional distress and confusion are in essence personal matters of individual development and relationships. Such an approach only serves to limit our understanding of the nature of distress in that there is little consideration of what gives rise to the kinds of distress that lead people to consult experts, or of what might be expected to reduce distress. As such we are left with a wide range of competing psychotherapeutic approaches with little consensus as to the nature of distress.

The third factor responsible for the growth of therapy is societal influence – the interest of a social system in an established view of and approach to psychological pain which it conceptualises as a problem that is caused by and can be cured within the immediate sphere of people's personal lives. Thus, emotional pains are interpreted as individual psychopathology. A society which even inadvertently creates distress in its members is likely to develop an institutional system for distracting attention from the more unfortunate consequences of its organisation and absorbing their worst effects. The level of critical analyis is thus located on the individual rather than on the nature of society.

## PSYCHOTHERAPY, COUNSELLING AND THE ABUSE OF POWER

If those who are employed within the NHS and in psychological services suffer from new employment practices, this as I have discussed is equally true of their patients or clients, and in this social situation an important question that must be asked is whether counselling is socially beneficial? Counselling may be manifestly undermining or latently so, especially in its emphasis on personal responsibility, and in its pressures on the individual to fit in with an inequitable social system.

Traditional and current counselling theories (see Dryden 1990) have not paid much attention to a psychosocial understanding of individuals. Neither have standard works on counselling theory generally dealt with issues such as covert and overt forms of oppression in therapy. However, critiques which indicate the limits of psychotherapy (see, for example, Showalter 1987; Smail 1987, 1993; Masson 1990, 1991; Heath 1992) highlight a major concern regarding the abuse of power in psychotherapy and counselling. Masson, for example, challenges many of the foundations of current psychiatric and psychotherapeutic enterprises and highlights issues revolving around the inappropriate power of psychiatry and psychotherapy, which he views as inherently abusive activities. In his book *Against Therapy* (1990), Masson criticises psychiatry, psychotherapy and counselling as activities which are inherently oppressive or abusive. According to Masson, even when therapy is a voluntary activity 'there is an emotional and mental coercion that is rarely examined by members of the professions. When therapy is not voluntary, the opportunities for oppression become even greater' (p. 287).

Psychotherapeutic abuse has been viewed as emanating from two main sources. The first source lies in the direct or manifest abuse of clients, such as in sexual or financial abuse. The second source lies in the more hidden or manifest aspects of psychotherapy. According to this view, it is the inherently abusive nature of psychotherapy and counselling activities which oppresses and disempowers people. The second source is derived from the hierarchical social structure and consequent disparity in power in society. This leads to issues concerned with the individualisation of distress and, to issues revolving around social inequality, which for example are reflected in the inequality of access to and delivery of psychotherapy services.

One source of therapeutic abuse is seen in the intrinsic imbalance of power between therapist and client, which not only disempowers clients but which is the fundamental source of therapeutic abuse of clients. For example, Masson states: 'The therapeutic relationship always involves an imbalance of power. Only one person is thought to be an "expert" in human relations and in feelings. Only one person is thought to be "in trouble"' (1990, p. 290). Similarly, Dorothy Rowe, in her foreword to Masson's book (1990, p. 16) states, 'In the final analysis, power is the right to have your definition of reality prevail over all other people's definition of reality.'

The type of therapy or counselling selected by clients defines reality within the frame of reference of that particular theoretical approach. The tendency of some approaches, to assert the validity and exclusiveness of a particular therapeutic theory, is disturbing as they present their version of reality as being akin to some kind of 'true' reality or ultimate truth, which is then used as a framework for defining the client's reality. However, there is a growing number of schools of psychotherapy with their corresponding views on the reality and human experience (Karasau 1986 reported 400 different schools). Further, as Dorothy Rowe states, 'It is a good rule of thumb that if many treatments are in use for the same disease it is because there is no real treatment known for that disease' (1991, p. 370).

Other indirect forms of abuse include the abuse of having your truth disbelieved and of being negatively labelled. Accounts of experiences of therapy (see, for example, Li and Greenewich 1991; Ward 1991) illustrate this. For example, Ward gives an account of an oppressive experience of therapy in which her experiences and understandings were reinterpreted and devalued. From such accounts, therapy may be viewed as an abuse of power, and interpretation as an act of aggression. Further examples of indirect abuse on the part of the therapist include the abuse of clients whose pain and distress support a reasonably secure, well-paid and prestigious job for the therapist. This in turn supports the established order, and some psychotherapists and other mental health workers are fearful of challenging the power of medical psychiatry, tending to assume that it is the individual who needs to change and not the social order.

Writers such as Masson (1990, 1991), Heath (1992) and Smail (1993) point out the inappropriateness of some therapies and treatments, given for conditions of which we do not know the fundamental causes, but which may turn out to be psychosocial in origin. They draw attention to the inappropriate and inadequate view of the nature of the self which ignores, as I will discuss later in this chapter, political, economic and social sources of pain and distress and which avoids any real criticism of a social order based on inequality of wealth, opportunity and choice. They challenge the view which focuses simplistically on individuals and families as the target of intervention. In particular Masson criticises Freud for his inherently individualistic view in ignoring external sources of distress, stating:

> Freud is not offering to help a person by altering the external circumstances, but only by getting that person to reconsider his or her life . . . Freud is asking us to shift the direction of our attention, from the external to the internal.
>
> Freud was perpetuating a tradition that did not begin with him. Its basic characteristics were that it was male-oriented, ethnocentric, sexist, and rigidly hierarchical.
>
> It is clear too that had Freud stuck with his first discoveries, in which sexual trauma played such a major role, psychoanalysis would never have become the accepted and popular theory that it is today, because its criticism of existing society would have been too profound, the implications too disquieting. By blaming the victim, Freud was able to unburden society of any need for reform or deep reflection.
>
> (Masson 1991, p. 208)

According to writers such as Heath, Masson and Smail, the imbalance of power in the therapeutic relationship arises from a misunderstanding of the causes and sources of distress and reflects the imbalance of power in society generally. As Smail comments, 'Our society is constructed as a hierarchy of exploitation based on power' (1987, p. 69).

Heath (1992) also points out that society creates conditions to which people react in different ways, such as with anger, frustration, anxiety, low self-esteem, depression, identity crises and various other manifestations of distress. Often people are then labelled as mentally ill or encouraged to seek counselling.

Society, having created conditions which give rise to distress, then has to control the manifestations of these oppressive experiences. It does this by such means as the medicalisation and treatment of symptoms, by giving negative labels to sufferers or by blaming and treating the victims. In support of his view, he cites the disproportionate number of women and people from ethnic minorities who are seen to be in need of treatment and who are defined as 'mentally ill'. In this way, psychiatry and psychotherapy can be viewed as agents of social control. As Heath states, 'They do this by individualizing problems and by putting the emphasis on the individual to improve. Put succinctly: psychiatry and psychotherapy perpetuate social oppression by abuse of power' (1992, p. 33).

Heath points out that this form of oppression is rarely intentional, or carried out through malevolent motives: 'I do not need to be malevolent in order to oppress people. I can oppress people with the best of intentions out of ignorance and I may perpetuate my ignorance to protect my power' (1992, p. 33). Further, Smail also points out that as a generalisation, the more specialist or individually focused the form of knowledge – medical, psychoanalytic and other tightly defined therapies – the higher the prestige it is accorded, from the group itself and from society. The more that professions identify with their client or user groups and seek to understand their social, political and economic experiences, the lower the prestige it is accorded by society. The former compared with the latter do not threaten the existing oppressive system.

David Smail emphasises the limitations of psychotherapy as an answer to emotional distress and questions psychology itself as an undertaking of any real relevance to issues which seem essentially political in nature. He is not rejecting psychotherapy and counselling out of hand, but stressing that we need to be mindful of their intellectual blinkers as well as critical of the grandiosity of their claims. What is and is not possible to achieve in struggling with adversity – the difficulties and distress of people who are not especially privileged and well resourced – throws into sharp relief the poverty of conceptions such as 'insight' and 'responsibility'. An aspect of their role from which nearly all counsellors are able to dissociate is that of increasing the likelihood of the social ills whose effects they are there to mitigate. They do offer comfort to those in distress, but also, through an ideology of personal change which suggests that people have a choice over their predicaments, they make the occurrence of such predicaments more likely. Just as the 'redundancy counsellor' legitimises putting people out of work, so 'disaster counselling' makes possible the 'acceptable' limits of expenditure on safety.

## THE RELATIONSHIP BETWEEN THE INDIVIDUAL AND THE SOCIAL CONTEXT

In a fundamental way it may be said that there is no such thing as the individual. In discussing the process of socialisation, psychoanalysts, psycholinguists and social philosophers, albeit with different emphases, point out how the individual's sense of self is primarily the result of a pattern of relationships which he or she has experienced with various other persons, and how the attitudes and characteristics of significant others are somehow internalised and structured as part of the self.

Significant contributions in our understanding of the social context in the development of the individual are based on the work of social philosophers, notably George Herbert Mead. Mead (1934) described two main stages in the process of the full development of the self. The first stage in the development of the individual self is constituted by the organisation of the particular attitudes of other individuals towards him- or herself and towards one another in the specific social acts in which the individual participates with them. However, at the second stage, in the full development of the self, the self is constituted not only by an organisation of these particular individual attitudes, but also by the individual making, as part of him- or herself, the social attitudes towards him or her of the 'generalised other' or the social group as a whole to which he or she belongs. These social or group attitudes are as important as the attitudes of particular individuals in the development of the self.

A major criticism that may be made of counselling or psychotherapy generally is that it is inherently too individualistic from its theoretical conceptualisations to its practice. Even though many of the theoretical conceptualisations acknowledge the significance of social influences in the developmental process, scant attention is given to the continuing social influences of the wider social context.

The social aspects of development were not completely ignored by the psychoanalytical school, as may be seen in Freud's emphasis on how the unique attributes of each person's ego and superego structures are determined to a great extent by the sorts of objects such as parental models, that he had 'introjected' and how many parental values and prohibitions which were incorporated became forces that guided behaviour. D.W. Winnicott (1958) stressed that there was no such thing as an individual infant – only an infant in relation to its mother. From a psychoanalytical perspective a sense of a separate identity is formed through a process of separation from the mother. However, it is in the course of an evolving relationship with the mother that the child identifies with and internalises values and standards which contribute to the determination of the view of him- or herself. The outcome of this double trend of differentiation and assimilation is the achievement of a sense of separate identity. Separation is never absolute in the sense that part of the mother and later significant others become assimilated into the child. Various terms used in the psychoanalytical literature – such as internalisation, introjection, identification, projection, transference, etc., imply that the self involves the 'taking in' of attitudes, feelings, values and other aspects that initially derive from the other.

Generally, however, it may be said that psychological approaches have mainly confined themselves to considering the influences on human development of our immediate relations with each other, such as with 'significant others' or the immediate family, and this has led to serious limitations on the explanatory power of the theories it has produced. A few approaches, interestingly psychoanalytically based, have paid more attention to societal influences, as seen for example in the work of Alfred Adler (1925), Karen Horney (1939), Erich Fromm (1941) and H.S. Sullivan (1953), who consider the influences that the wider society has on individual development and experience. However, for a more detailed analysis of how the individual and the social are inextricably bound, we have to generally step outside the field of psychotherapy and counselling and look to the theoretical analyses of psycholinguists. Theorists who may be described as psycholinguists or social philosophers such as Bakhtin (1981), Voloshinov (1976), Bakhtin and Medvedev (1985) and Vygotsky (1939) all point to the social construction of experience. Writing from within the Soviet Union, Bakhtin, Voloshinov and Medvedev collaborated with many of their ideas in the 1920s, and wrote their main works in the 1930s; these writers give historically and socially grounded accounts of language.

Indeed the work of Bakhtin (1895–1975) was profoundly affected by the social context of his times. One of Bakhtin's basic tenets was that communicative acts only have meaning in particular social situations or contexts. Nothing demonstrates this principle more clearly than the fate of Bakhtin's own utterances, many of which could have no force in his own lifetime because they could not be published in the Soviet Union between 1929 and the 1960s, and when they were published and translated in the West in 1968 it was within the context of specific situations with different expectations and agendas.

These theorists all formulated their work at the same time as Freud but wrote, although with different emphases, within the context of Marxism. Voloshinov and Medvedev wrote in avowedly Marxist ways, although Bakhtin's relationship with Marxism is more controversial. They stress the social context of experience and view language as a social phenomenon. Since language is inescapably social and occurs between people, the values of the social milieu reach to the core of the individual experience or the psyche, making what is 'other' or 'external' to them 'internal'. Voloshinov and Medvedev's account of language concerns the literary and psychological life in what they respectively called the 'ideological environment' and the 'social milieu'. Both writers describe how what we take as the given reality of any individual psychological phenomenon turns out to be complex refractions of realities that are in fact social and thus value laden and may be contested. For Voloshinov the centrality of the sociality of language leads to what he terms the 'multiaccentuality of the sign', the idea for example that signs such as words bear different inflections, emphases and therefore meanings in different contexts. Meanings emerge in society and society is not a homogenous mass but is itself divided by such factors as social class. Similarly, one of Mikhail Bakhtin's main principles is that communicative acts only have meaning, and only take on their specific force, in particular situations or contexts. The utterances of spoken language are formed in a social context and are carriers of social meaning. He does not suggest that we cancel out that which historically separates us but rather that we should understand that other's historical specificity as fully as possible.

The Bakhtin circle contributed to the debate of the new psychology of Freud with a book by Voloshinov, *Freudianism: A Marxist Critique* (1927/1976) which was translated and published in the West in 1976. Voloshinov begins his critique by seeing Freud as a representative of a wider intellectual trend which seeks to explain and ground human behaviour in fundamentally biological rather than social and historical terms. Voloshinov replaced the Freudian concept of the unconscious with the multiplicity and contradictions of internalised social language. Working in effect from Freud's starting point of the patient's language and the talking cure, Voloshinov sees the contents of the psyche as being made up of inner speech. Since language is inescapably social and occurs between people, the valuations of the social milieu reach to the core of the psyche. What in Freud's terms remains a distinction within the individual becomes, according to this perspective, a version of the conflicts of the social milieu. The conflicts and tensions of psychic life are not disputed by Voloshinov but they are recast as versions of the conflicts of the social milieu. His work concentrates on the relationship of the social milieu to the psyche, which results in the content of the psyche being fundamentally ideological.

David Smail also reaches this conclusion in his view that a person's 'state of mind' is thus explainable in principle through an understanding of the influences operating in the environmental space in which he or she is located. Similarly, Vygotsky's (1896–1934) *Thought and Language* (1962) is concerned with the activity at the boundaries between people and their environment – with the activities involved in them making what is 'other' or 'external' to them 'internal'. He proposes a social developmental psychology in which he views man's socially organised experiences as determining the structure of human conscious activity. For Vygotsky, the organising principles of thought and feeling rest in the structure of the shared language through which we express those thoughts and feelings.

David Smail, writing from a socio-psychological perspective, points out that as social beings we live according to shared rules of meaning. Language is an example of one such set of rules. Language forms an intensely personal and fundamentally important part of 'me' – it's not 'inside' me but exists in the social space I share with others. Nearly all the rules and concepts which give shape and meaning to our experience – many of them constructed linguistically – are not our personal inventions but are acquired in the process of development. Such rules and concepts Smail terms 'forms', and it is these that give form to our experience. For example, one's view of oneself as male or female is important to our emotional well-being; Smail points out that this view is inseparable from the forms of masculinity and femininity, which are culturally established independently of us as individuals. How far I am considered feminine depends on a form of femininity which is outside me. Hence, any concept such as 'self' is socially determined.

Our personal assimilation to and adaptation of these meaning systems is what is meant by our 'psychology'. This psychology, all those linguistic and nonlinguistic systems for making sense of the world – thought, memory, dreams, perceptions, feelings, etc. – does not exist independently of the environment of which they are partly constituted. Part of what an individual consists of is in fact non-individual, such as the social conventions, practices, meanings and institutions we all share.

All the verbal psychotherapies, by definition, are dependent on language and also on the discourse that occurs between people. There are crucial implications of the social context of language to be considered in the theory and practice of psychotherapy and counselling. Because a phenomenon is not verbally named by a society does not mean that it does or does not exist. Cultural or social muteness is reflected in individual understanding so that the individual may also be rendered mute. For example, doubtless the phenomenon of childhood sexual abuse has always existed. However, it is only in the last decade or so that its prevalence has been generally articulated and acknowledged. Once acknowledged, the survivors of such abuse came forward in significant numbers to request psychotherapy and counselling. Sexual abuse is now given prominence, as a major cause of distress, in the field of psychotherapy and counselling. The same applies to many phenomena, such as that labelled shell shock in World War I or more recent labellings of distress such as post-traumatic stress. Conversely, because a phenomenon is given a verbal label does not mean that it exists. For example, writers such as Szasz (1972) and Marshall (1996) explore many of the myths behind our understandings of such constructs as psychosis, schizophrenia and mental illness. Any understanding of such manifestations of psychological distress must take into account not just the social context in which they occur but the social context which gives the distress a verbal construction or label and thus a social reality. David Smail shows how the social and individual are inextricably linked and emphasises that to ignore this essential fact is a serious error in both the theory and practice of counselling and psychotherapy. This error is also reflected in our conceptualisations of science and research in psychotherapy and psychology generally. The current scientific paradigm individualises science and ignores the fundamentally interactive nature of experience in its quest for 'objectivity'. Bakhtin emphasises the essentially social and interactive aspects of any human science. In his essay 'Towards a methodology for the human sciences' (1986) he draws a fundamental distinction between the 'exact' and the human sciences. Where the exact sciences are what Bakhtin terms 'monologic' because they are concerned with the objects of knowledge, the human sciences are necessarily 'dialogic' because they are concerned with other subjects.

## INDIVIDUALISATION OF DISTRESS

In books such as *Illusion and Reality* (1984), *Taking Care* (1987), *The Origin of Unhappiness* (1993) and *How to Survive without Psychotherapy* (1996), David Smail documents how psychotherapy, psychology and psychiatry have helped shape a culture of individualism where it has become almost impossible for people to differentiate inside from outside and to attribute the pain they often feel about themselves to its appropriate source. He points out the error of viewing the causes and cures of individual experience and distress as being purely an individual matter, as aspects of our so-called 'individuality' are a feature of a world we have in common. Smail states, 'The explanation of our conduct is . . . not to be sought in a psychological analysis of individuals, but in a socio-economic, historical analysis of relations between people, and of the ways these have shaped the world we have to live in' (1987, p. 70).

Smail argues that the notion that there is something wrong with the person in distress that has to be put right is central to the medical and psychological disciplines which have grown up over the past 150 years. Distress is viewed as pathology or abnormality, and as located in the single individual either biologically inside the body or psychologically in some kind of nonmaterial interior space. A great deal of effort has gone into identifying, categorising, isolating and treating these physical and mental faults – they are the basis of entire professions. Yet the evidence that despair, confusion, misery and madness can really usefully be seen as varieties of pathology is slender and even then rests on the ideological interpretation of otherwise ambiguous research findings rather than on any intellectually compelling demonstration of its validity. For example, medically trained psychiatrists are likely to assert that 'schizophrenia' is indisputably a form of 'mental illness', while many non-medically trained psychologists will point to the lack of any consistent evidence for this view. This is seen for example in such analyses as Mary Boyle, *Schizophrenia: A scientific delusion?* (1990) and *Schizophrenia: The fallacy of diagnosis* (1996), and Richard Marshall (1995), *Schizophrenia: A constructive analogy or a convenient construct?*

Outlining the ways in which the operation of social power comes to be reflected in individual experience, in particular the experience of distress, David Smail points out that orthodox psychiatry and psychology have ignored wider social elements for the cause of unhappiness and have displayed little interest in pursuing their origins other than with matters revolving around the immediate context of personal experience, so that the link between the wider social influence and immediate personal experience is left obscure. He points out that the usual interpretation of emotional distress which is typically labelled as 'neurosis' or 'mental illness' is that it originates from within the individual. Frequently some sort of therapeutic process that 'treats' people is considered to be the most appropriate solution for such distress. According to Smail, instead of looking inward to detect within ourselves the products of 'psycho-pathology' we need to look out into the world to identify the sources of our pain and unhappiness. Instead of viewing our suffering as being due to some failure in our personal development and under-standing and labelling distress in such terms as 'symptoms', 'illness', 'unconscious complexes', 'faulty cognitions' and as other failures of development, we need to clarify what is wrong with a social world which gives rise to such forms of suffering. 'That is not to say that we are not psychologically and emotionally damaged by our experi-ence of life, but that neither the causes nor "cures" of such damage can usefully be treated as "internal" matters' (Smail 1993: 2).

When the deprivation or exploitation has occurred so far back that its origin is beyond the easy reach of memory or lies in that prelinguistic period of life in which memory cannot properly be said to be operating (and where events get remembered only as unde-cipherable metaphors or inexplicable 'feelings'), their manifestation in the present will be often, perhaps irresolvably, baffling. However, as Smail points out the nature of the ideologically distorted inward projection of an outer deprivation is very obvious. He gives the example of how we usually view as eccentric the need of the rich for privacy, seen in such ways as in their desire to live in secluded areas. However, the discomfort caused by lack of privacy, for example on many council estates, is not diagnosed as a 'lack of privacy' to be 'cured' through the provision of an adequately constructed and tended physical environment, but is projected inwards as 'ago-raphobia' and 'treated' with drugs and psychotherapy.

Smail points out that the more essential task of a psychology which sets out to expose the myth of 'inferiority' is to point out that our strengths are not more to be held to our credit than our weak-nesses are to our discredit. Whatever may make an individual admir-able or effective as a human being does not arise from some interior moral superiority, but from the good fortune of having acquired through proximal influence abilities and characteristics which become part of the individual's moral or psychological structures. That we almost always experience and talk about as being 'inside' us those aspects of our selfhood whose source is actually 'outside' leads to confusion in our concept of self. This is because we either take upon ourselves or apportion to others blame for faults or shortcomings which in fact lie outside us in the world we share, and in our ideas about how to change ourselves which can only be set right by attending to that world.

According to Smail, the error of psychology has been to consider individual meaning-systems as belonging to and in the control of people of whom they form a part. The assumption is made that things like beliefs and attitudes, as well as the nonverbal meaning-systems like dream and metaphor which order our experience, are located inside a person, also that they are, in a way which is almost always never clarified, subject to the operation of his or her will. Thus, if the person sees fit, perhaps through some process like gaining insight, he or she can decide to alter beliefs or attitudes which have now come to be seen as inappropriate or inconvenient. However, Smail argues that our psychology is not ours to manipulate at will. The explanation of individual experience and conduct is to be sought in a complex set of social interactions in which powerful distal events are transformed into the proximal relations which make up the context of the individual's personal life. What makes a difference to the way we are, what changes us or permits us to change, is not the voluntary manipulation of inner resources but the influence of or access to outer resources and powers. This does not mean that we as individuals do not possess personal resources, but rather that what we experience as 'inner resources' are usually outer resources acquired over time.

Political movements are less likely to make the error of individualisation. For example, feminism recognises that for women to gain a more equitable share of social power requires a change in the socially determined rules and concepts, which David Smail terms 'forms', such as those relating to masculinity and femininity in our culture. Feminism does not take as its basic premise that each individual woman needs to change herself. Psychological approaches to personal distress, on the other hand, are likely to fail to recognise that distress is often the pain of an individual who finds that he or she is unable to meet the requirements of 'form'. The problem lies in change in the outside world, not in some kind of personal inadequacy. Problems often arise when we cannot fulfil the demands of cultural forms. For example, we cannot change homo- to heterosexuality. While psychologists no longer expect their clients to be able to alter their sexual preferences at will, they still often assume that people do have access 'within' them to forms of behaviour which are more 'adjusted' than those they are currently displaying and all that is needed is some kind of individualistic enterprise often framed in terms such as 'moral effort', 'cognitive understanding or restructuring' or 'emotional insight'. It is often the absence of form in our continuously changing mobile society which leads to distress. For example, there are few forms to guide our relationships with each other following the break-up of relationships and reconstituting of families, which would serve as some sort of guide, however imperfect, to those involved. To acquire new 'forms' when old ones have disappeared or disintegrated may or may not be possible. Where an individual's experience cannot receive its meaning from an appropriate public form, Smail points out that the result is likely to be experienced as either poetry or pain – the first a struggle to create form; the second the expression or sensation of its lack. There are forms of pain itself and those most usually invoked are blame and guilt. 'People who find themselves isolated with feelings, impulses, ideas on thoughts which find no ready echo in formal, public concepts or meanings are likely to succumb to a guilty sense of failure. They are also likely to find a psychiatric/ therapeutic industry only too ready to produce a formal diagnosis for their difficulty' (Smail 1993, p. 89). Failures of form may come about through a failure of proximal powers to mediate them (for example, parents not communicating some essential form of feeling may result in hate, then experienced as terrifying mystery, about which the only communicable feeling is guilt), or through the cultural absence or disintegration of forms capable of giving sense to individual experience. Our experience is unintelligible if we are not taught a language with which to describe it. Manifestations of 'psychopathology' are often puzzling to us because for one reason or another there are no adequate 'forms' through which they can be rendered socially intelligible. 'Madness' is not the person's loss of contact with 'reality' but rather reality's failure to make contact with and to explicate the personal experience of the sufferer.

One implication of this is that the 'symptoms' of 'pathology' or variations in the expressions of human distress are not constant and will fluctuate according to what is happening in the social environment. When we express the pain caused us it's not because there is anything 'wrong' with our essential make-up but because there are or have been things in our environment which would be better not there. Numerous community studies point out that the prevalence of psychological distress is as great as 18 per cent to 20 per cent of the population. Given these figures, as the work of the American community psychologist George Albee (1996) emphasises, one has to question the appropriateness of psychotherapy generally. He emphasises that it is both practically and unethically unreasonable to suggest that the distress of such a high proportion of the population should be addressed by such means as counselling or psychotherapy alone.

Although psychotherapy and counselling can be an enriching and rewarding experience for many of us, providing us with insights into ourselves and our experience and at least offering some possibility of change, we nevertheless need to be aware of the limitations of counselling, set as it is in a particular social, political and economic context. No form of therapy can pretend to be a cure-all for distress. Neither is it appropriate to view therapy as a highly skilled activity which fails only because the therapist or the patient is lacking in some way. Sometimes we are presented with clear cases of clients whose social or economic circumstances are such that no amount of therapy, nor any model of therapy, can change those circumstances. We are in danger of side-stepping or ignoring these factors, present in some form in the experience of all our clients.

Research findings based mainly upon epidemiological data indicate that social class and poverty influence physical and mental health. Further, being female, being black or being elderly are also linked with economic and social class status. A careful consideration of the nature of the distress our clients present would locate a fundamental economic causality. For many of us, psychologists and counsellors, this is a difficult issue to confront honestly, as it often threatens our personal agenda concerning the efficacy of therapy. It also conflicts with the institutional and professional cultures of our working environment, and the present political, moral and intellectual climate. We work in situations where the ethos is to take the patient's presenting problems and help make them at least more bearable. The institutions we work in encourage a throughput of 'cured' patients, carefully monitored, evaluated and hopefully reasonably satisfied with the service they receive. Our political climate emphasises individual responsibility and even at times denies the existence of society at all. When she was the Conservative Party's leader, Baroness Thatcher claimed that there was no such thing as society, only individuals. This political ethos is reflected not only in legislation, affecting almost all aspects of our lives and in government policies directing our public institutions, but it also creates a moral climate which emphasises individual effort and responsibility. Our intellectual world has also undergone a transformation. Whereas until at least the last decade, serious intellectual discourse on the human predicament would consider basic economic resources as a causative factor, it is now intellectually unfashionable to raise the issue. A form of cultural and public autism has afflicted many of the erstwhile adherents of these views.

A common theme in the literature and one emphasised by writers such as Karl Marx and R.D. Laing, who analyse the human condition from different perspectives, is that one of the main determinants of emotional well-being is the ability to exercise control in one's life, to be acting as an individual rather than to be acted upon. An appropriate assessment of patients should at the very least consider the resources available to them (such as their economic situation, emotional and social supports), and the constraints that limit their lives (such as the lack of positive resources and institutional constraints). The effects of these constraints are seen in all aspects of life and in all relationships, from personal relationships to our relationships to societal structures such as school, family and public institutions.

Janet Bostock (1994) points out that extreme patriarchal behaviour is upheld by societal influences (for example, by the media) and that it is destructive to working-class women and to children and to men themselves. Furthermore, unequal social structures are often organised on the basis of class position, gender, race, and age and may promote extreme, patriarchal patterns of behaviour in the private realm of the family. In this way destructive forces can spiral into cycles of powerlessness, bullying and intimidation, leading to more powerlessness and to social alienation.

There are features of the therapeutic situation which may be at variance with people's cultural experience and expectations. For example, Barry Richards (1995) and Eric Bromley (1994) describe the cultural gap which may hinder communication between middle-class therapists and working-class clients. Bromley (1994) compares individual to political liberation, in that both aim to demystify and liberate people from oppression. However, he describes how many people are denied access to analytical tools to understand and act upon and thus be in a position to change their situation.

Richards demonstrates empirically how the purpose of therapy may be apparent to the therapist but not be clear to the client. Discussing the 'discourse of personal reflection' of the therapeutic encounter, Richards points out that therapeutic engagement is dependent on the client possessing a certain amount of what Bourdieu terms 'cultural capital'. Furthermore, the establishment and maintenance of the therapeutic alliance is difficult if the client has internalised culturally derived experiences such as those of inferiority, exclusion and incompetence. Psychotherapy may mitigate the painful psychological consequences of alienation and marginalisation, but as Richards (1995) points out, therapists need to be open and flexible in identifying the aims of therapy and how it is conducted. Davies (1995) also emphasises this issue and how we need to question the appropriateness of therapeutic interventions. For example, we can help a client explore feelings, or offer relaxation training to try to alleviate signs and symptoms of distress. However, this is of limited relevance without an understanding of how such symptoms are a reflection of the client's actual circumstances, which may be based in the past and/or in the present.

I have already observed that many of the issues to do with social inequality revolve around those of economic poverty. The corrosive power of economic poverty in its destructive influence upon our relationships with ourselves and with others is perhaps most vividly illustrated in the works of an author like Emile Zola, the nineteenth-century French novelist. In *Germinal*, a novel in the series *Les Rougon-Macquart*, Zola articulates the desperate misery of poverty, with its social and psychological consequences. These same themes are present in contemporary society, where over the last few years an increasing number of our clients have become unemployed, or are threatened by the prospect of unemployment, while others are in low-paid jobs resulting in similar economic conditions and leading to comparable social and psychological effects. Government policies regarding health issues were outlined in a White Paper, *The Health of the Nation* (1993). These policies included the reduction of suicide rates as well as the reduction of physical problems. However, as Whitehead (1987) discussed in *The Health Divide*, a high percentage of all these problems are associated with unemployment. There are not only economic costs associated with unemployment, but also social and psychological costs of poor physical and mental health. This puts even more pressure upon the NHS, which is rarely acknowledged, as well as on welfare systems generally, which are already severely strained.

Studies, for example Burchell (1994) and Lampard (1994), indicate that the 'flexible' labour market encouraged by the Conservative government in the 1980s and 1990s created a new form of job insecurity of which unemployment is the most extreme form. The close relationship between job security and psychological well-being is demonstrated in the study by Burchell, who categorised a sample according to whether they were in secure jobs or in insecure jobs. The findings of this study indicated a close link between psychological well-being and perceived job security. Men in low-paid, insecure jobs exhibited about the same level of distress as those out of work completely.

Research findings on the effects of unemployment on mental health consistently demonstrate the same conclusions. As Fryer (1993) notes, research carried out in Britain in the 1930s came to the same conclusions as contemporary research, where surveys consistently indicate that groups of unemployed people have poorer mental health than groups of comparable employed people. A series of studies carried out in the 1970s and 1980s in Britain on the mental health effects of unemployment (Warr, Jackson and Banks 1988) indicate that the psychological effects of unemployment include low self-esteem, dissatisfaction with one's present life, hopelessness regarding the future, low self-confidence, social isolation, anxiety, depression, disturbed sleep, increase in alcohol use and abuse, and an increased risk of suicide, as well as impaired physical health. Research findings such as those of Burchell (1994) and Lampard (1994) indicate that psychological and physical stresses are a result of being made unemployed, rather than predisposing factors towards unemployment.

Unemployment may have direct consequences such as the loss of a means of earning a living. However, there are also indirect consequences for those who are in employment, such as providing a way of organising their time, providing a status and identity, contributing to feelings of a sense of purpose, and facilitating the means of establishing social contacts. The effects of unemployment are so often psychologically corrosive because of the loss of these indirect consequences, which function as psychological and social supports. The whole nature of unemployment revolves around themes of deprivation and loss. The financial effects of unemployment can be disastrous or relative, and include the removal of choices and loss of the means of giving quality to life, which can result in feelings of hopelessness. As a paper by Nottingham NHS psychologists (1993) points out, vulnerability to ill health often coincides with the threat of redundancy rather than with the exact time that redundancy actually begins.

It is not just the individual who is affected by unemployment, but partners and other family members also. The study by Lampard (1994) demonstrated that unemployment directly increases the risk of marriage break-up, with the chances of marriage coming to an end in the year following unemployment 70 per cent higher than for those remaining in work. The effects of unemployment may include a change of roles within the family, for example the wife for the first time taking on the main bread-winning role. The unemployed husband may feel resentment, guilt, anger or depression as he may resent his perceived loss of status, and may feel resentful at undertaking any domestic responsibilities, which he may view as belonging to the female role and as signifying a further diminishing of his masculine role. The outcome of this may be a hostile home environment with negative consequences for all the family members.

There are numerous ways in which social factors are played out in the lives of our clients, who come to us in the hope that we may alleviate some of their personal pain. The following cases illustrate some of the themes which occur in psychotherapy, and the way in which psychologists need to be aware of much more than the individual's internalised psychological issues.

The first case is that of a 35-year-old woman, whom I shall call Carol. She was referred to the clinical psychology department by her GP, who in his referral letter described her as suffering from anxiety and depression and insomnia. She had been prescribed benzodiazepines for both day- and night-time use for the past nine months. Her GP was reluctant to continue prescribing and was seeking an alternative form of help for her. When I first met Carol, she appeared tired and anxious. She described her difficulties as beginning 18 months previously, when her husband lost his job in a local factory which was cutting down its labour force. Carol had retained her part-time job as a cleaner in another local factory. She and her husband Joe had four children of 13, 11, 9 and 7 years of age; Joe also had a 15-year-old son by a previous marriage who was living with Joe's ex-wife. Since Joe had lost his job, the family had suffered financial difficulties, made worse by having to try to meet repayments on credit facilities arranged when Joe was in work. The result was escalating debt.

A few years ago they had bought their house from the local council and had subsequently spent considerable sums in home improvement and refurbishment. After losing his job, Joe had at first felt confident about finding another, but all his efforts were unsuccessful, leading to continual feelings of rejection and disappointment. He had now given up trying to find work in what was an area of high unemployment. He had gradually become more and more depressed, and began drinking more than usual in order to alleviate his feelings of hopelessness. He withdrew from social contacts, feeling ashamed at being out of work, and spent most of his days indoors drinking alone. By the time Carol arrived home in the afternoon, Joe would be drunk and the house a mess. Joe would then become physically and verbally abusive, blaming Carol for not taking proper care of the home and family. He refused to carry out what he viewed as female domestic tasks. The arguments between them often included the children, and one was being referred to an educational psychologist for behavioural problems at school, which added to Carol's worries.

The family's financial problems were increasing and after a few sessions Carol anxiously revealed that a few weeks prior to our first appointment, she had taken on extra part-time work as a cleaner on a night-time shift. She described how the family needed the extra money to meet escalating debts, as well as to meet daily living requirements, made more burdensome by her husband's drinking expenses. The whole situation was made worse by the letter Joe had recently received from the Child Support Agency regarding his eldest child, with whom he had lost contact after an acrimonious divorce from his first wife and had presumed would never hear of again. This had made Joe more anxious and angry and he tried to avoid dealing with this additional worry by blotting out his feelings through drinking even more. Carol was further concerned that her children should be well provided for and not be seen to be materially worse off than their peers. She was paid in cash for her extra work and was not declaring it to the Inland Revenue. This made her feel guilty and ashamed, as she described how she had never previously done anything illegal in her life. She was anxious about being found out and the consequences that would follow if she was. The additional work added to Carol's strain and exhaustion and also made life even more difficult at home. Joe was ambivalent about the extra income as it fuelled his feelings of resentment regarding his loss of role.

The actual causes of manifestations of distress from panic attacks, depression to full-blown madness often lie in more social explanations. The cases I have described show that whatever the causes for distress, whether they are located in poverty and degradation or in the experience of abandonment and isolation in an alien society, people are often unable to articulate the nature of their unhappiness as they are engulfed in an ideological mystification which prevents them from criticising the grounds of their pain. Carol's situation illustrates a number of themes revolving around issues of social inequality, such as gender roles, social class and economic deprivation. Even though it was Carol who was referred for treatment, it can be seen that the whole family was experiencing difficulties. Her unemployed husband became depressed and abused alcohol to try to cope with his worries. He felt a loss of social status and role both in the world at large as well as within the home. His unemployment placed the whole family under severe financial and emotional strain. His wife became anxious and exhausted, which was made worse by her additional efforts to cope with the situation. Joe's sense of powerlessness resulted from what he perceived as the loss of his male role in society, both in the world of work and at home. His reaction to this was to exercise oppressive power within the family in his expression of hopelessness, anger and frustration. His abusive reaction to other family members left them feeling powerless in turn.

This case illustrates how many issues to do with social inequality are crucial in understanding the nature and cause of distress, even though the referral to the therapist may just request the alleviation of the signs and symptoms of distress. It also illustrates how full-time paid employment is highly valued in our society, and the loss of this has direct and indirect social and psychological consequences affecting a wider reference group than just the individual concerned. In discussing the context of counselling and psychotherapy, many questions are raised regarding the meaning of work in our society. There are also gender issues regarding what are viewed as appropriate male and female roles. For example, what is defined as appropriate for women is more frequently of poor financial and social status, and domestic tasks within the home are not even defined as work.

## SOCIAL INEQUALITY IN PSYCHOTHERAPY

There is no psychotherapeutic approach which addresses the way class position is reflected in the self-consciousness of the individual. Psychotherapists may encourage people to esteem or value themselves more highly. However, therapy prefers to overlook difficulties which cannot be dealt with within the confines of the therapeutic relationship. Class is a social phenomenon and not one over which individuals can be expected to exercise a great deal of control. Social class assigns people to power relationships of inferiority and superiority. We are often unaware of the difficulty one person may have in understanding or communicating with another when there is a significant power differential between them. C. Wright Mills shows how in the US the workings of class are even less recognised but yet more powerful.

Clinical psychologists are frequently referred clients whose problems are directly if not indirectly associated with issues of social inequality. Psychologists do not work in a vacuum but are located in a wider political-economic system in which resources are unequally distributed and the social structure is hierarchically organised. Therapy cannot cure the cause of the distress when it is the result of social inequality. Rather, the cure for social inequality is social equality. We can take the view that therapy can ameliorate distress associated with or made worse by social inequality. We can also argue that psychological interventions may make the experience less destructive to the psychological and physical well-being of the individuals concerned. For example, there are wide individual differences in how people cope with distress: some of the ways people cope are less destructive than others. Thus clients need to be offered a range of therapeutic interventions, from counselling and support, stress management, the encouragement of positive problem-solving and coping strategies, to the facilitation of social networks, etc.

However, we are in danger of individualising psychological distress; and, in offering different forms of therapy, of adding further validation to the view that it is our clients who are 'sick' or not coping in different ways. Our role here may be viewed as an effective 'elastoplast', covering up the effects of social and economic inequalities, which are then perceived as being the individual client's problems labelled as 'symptoms' or 'illness'. We can also be in danger of ignoring certain central issues such as the appropriateness of the referral and the appropriateness of our perceived task. The greatest danger is that we can ignore what is often at the basis of our clients' presenting problems, which is the economic and social organisation of our society. Bostock (1994) emphasises the need for the development of socio-psychological ideas which search for meaningful accounts of subjective experiences in a material, social and political context. The philosophy of individual determinism that is pervasive in our culture and is reflected in the field of psychotherapy generally needs to be challenged. Much of the theory and practice of the psychological therapies are based on the assumption that social organisation is functional rather than being inherently destructive for many people. Bostock advocates that psychologists in their work should aim to clarify how the unequal distribution of power and resources translates into individual strengths, needs and limitations.

### Access to counselling

Common to all counselling situations are questions of who is able to access such services and the treatment such people receive. People experiencing the effects of social inequality, for example, because of their race, gender, sexual orientation or social economic status are particularly vulnerable to distress, and are more likely to receive unhelpful responses from services (see, for example, Fernando 1988). This includes practitioners abusing power within the 'helping' relationship and the limitations of the mechanisms to address these issues. There is also differential access to psychotherapy because of societal prejudice and stereotyping (Bromley 1994; Pilgrim 1994). Clients and practitioners also have different expectations of counselling (Richards 1994). Psychiatric treatment generally is experienced as undermining, yet few alternatives are available. The overall picture is that people who are poor, black or elderly are less likely to receive counselling or psychotherapy.

The psychological services are in an almost unique position amongst counselling and psychotherapy services: they are open to, and indeed required as part of a National Health Service to be available for, the whole population. Unlike many counselling services they are not circumscribed as being solely for students, or for couples in relationships, or for people with particular problems, or open only to those who can afford private therapy. Therefore in the delivery of counselling and the talking therapies in the psychological services, a major concern is the issue of equality of access. This is particularly important given the potentially abusive nature of the alternatives to counselling or psychotherapy, such as ECT and pharmacology. Of course, although psychological approaches should be equally available to all sections of the population, they are not necessarily useful. For example, a 'psychotherapy or counselling culture' is potentially as oppressive as a psychiatric model if it encourages beliefs that distress is solely individually determined and essentially an issue of personal responsibility, ignoring environmental and social realities with their consequent pressures. There are potential difficulties involved not just with physical treatments but also with psychological interventions as illustrated by issues concerning covert and overt abuse in psychotherapy. The literature on sexual and emotional abuse in psychotherapy suggests that psychotherapy is not always benign.

There is, however, differential access to different types of mental health treatment. Studies have been carried out that demonstrate that NHS patients receive more biological than psychological treatments, that patients are denied a range of treatments to choose from, and that psychotherapists, like biological psychiatrists, often deny patients access to information about their treatment. A survey carried out by MIND, 'People First' (Rogers et al. 1992), demonstrates three main aspects of service delivery that long-term psychiatric patients receive. First, NHS patients receive more biological than psychological treatments, with over 98 per cent of NHS patients receiving drug treatments and only 60 per cent receiving any psychological intervention. Second, patients are denied a range of treatments to choose from. Third, psychotherapists as well as biological psychiatrists often deny patients access to information about both the rationale and possible dangers of their treatment. Working with both adult acute patients and those with long-term difficulties, a common theme is that the majority request some form of counselling. Although this is frequently available to those with less severe mental health problems, rarely is it offered to those with long-term problems. In my experience psychological approaches with people with long-term difficulties, whether in an individual counselling session or in group work, provide a rewarding and worthwhile experience.

One issue for people who have been prescribed drugs for their mental health problems is that the effects and side-effects of the medication are frequently unpleasant. Often the rationale or the physical and psychological effects of these drugs are not explained, leaving the client even more confused, anxious and isolated. For the individual client the worrying issues may range from concerns about weight gain to concerns that they no longer feel anything, and that their feelings are numbed to such an extent that they feel they are no longer really living. Another common theme brought up by clients, especially those with long-term problems, is that the rationale of their treatment is not explained or made explicit at the beginning of the therapeutic relationship.

A paper by Pilgrim (1994) outlines some of the reasons for the pattern of mental health treatment that long-term psychiatric patients receive. As I have shown in Chapter One, some of the reasons for this are historical. Psychiatry took very little interest in psychological forms of treatment until the First World War when the eugenic/bio-determinist model conflicted with a model of treatment then viewed as more appropriate for shell shock victims. Even though psychiatry has expanded to encompass a wider frame of reference than the purely biological, the medical model has nevertheless still influenced the development and practice of psychological as well as biological therapies this century. Furthermore, the most influential psychological approach until recently has been that of psychoanalysis which, as Pilgrim (1994) points out, actively denies patients informed choice in order to engender transference. Indeed the need to know is often viewed as a transference problem rather than as a civil right. Choice for clients is further restricted by assumptions made by therapists that psychotic patients or those with long-term difficulties, especially those of lower socio-economic status, are unsuitable for verbal therapy, even though there is reasonable empirical evidence to refute this assumption. Their social and economic poverty is often the result of the difficulties they have experienced which makes it difficult, for example, to obtain or maintain full-time paid employment.

Furthermore, because of the nature of their problems such clients are often viewed as difficult to work with. Pilgrim comments that such clients are given a limited choice of treatments, because of the collusive division of labour between biological hospital doctors and out-patient psychotherapists, who for personal financial reasons evade contact with unrewarding patients. However, even within the NHS such clients are often evaded by mental health professionals who do offer psychological therapies, because of the pressures to keep waiting lists down. This leads to the favouring of shorter therapies, a model of treatment which is often not appropriate for clients with long-term difficulties. There is also the implicit view that these are generally unrewarding clients to work with. They are viewed as unrewarding because, for example, they 'refuse' to 'get better' in the prescribed length of time before they can be duly discharged off a therapist's caseload. Within the sessions themselves, the therapists may experience particular difficulties, for example, it may be more difficult to share such a client's perception of the world and to empathise with their inner world. The therapist often has to pay more acute attention to therapeutic issues such as establishing trust, establishing and maintaining a therapeutic alliance as well as having to be acutely sensitive to internal and external boundary issues. The psychologist, we have to remember, is working in a context where past experience of hospitals and of medical or paramedical intervention may have created real barriers to trust, and where there has been no previous experience of anything equating to a therapeutic alliance where the client is invited to be a co-worker in the treatment.

### Social inequality in access to mental health care; cultural expectations

Another difficulty for the therapist arises from the differing expectation of therapy between therapist and client, affecting not only the model of therapy which may be appropriate for the client, but also the conventional structuring of sessions with regard to place and time. The models and style of therapy offered to people with long-term difficulties are often inappropriate, when the treatment should be shaped to the needs of the clients. However, a frequent finding is that when long-term users are asked what form of treatment they would like, one of the most cited therapies is counselling. An equally frequent finding is that most, even after many years of out-patient, in-patient and day-patient services, state that they have never had or have had very little counselling.

Discussing the issue of social inequality and access to the psychiatric services generally, Bromley cites Freud's (1905) remark: 'those

patients who do not possess a reasonable degree of education
. . . should be refused' (Bromley 1994: 1). This view was so prevalent that David (1938) criticised the fact that few working-class people
were accepted for psychotherapy. The historical context in which
psychotherapy developed has been outlined in Chapter One, and to
this we must add that psychotherapy failed to establish a secure
place in the welfare state system in the post-war years. Even though
the therapeutic social movements of the 1970s had their advocates
in Britain, these largely originated in the USA and served to maintain the links between psychotherapy and the intellectual strata of
the British middle class.

Richards (1995) points out that the class structure and class
cultures of Britain have changed significantly even over the last
decade. He gives as one instance of this the increasingly diverse
membership of professions such as social work, applied psychology
and counselling, which are central to the definition and delivery of
therapeutic services. However, Richards emphasises that the social
impact of the psychotherapies remains shaped and restricted by
social class in the sense of differences in cultural and material worlds.
Restrictions due to social inequality operate at many levels. Psychotherapeutic help is unavailable to many, due both to referral patterns
and to the unequal distribution of specialised resources.

At another level access to psychotherapy involves the ability
to make optimal use of what psychotherapeutic help is available. Richards describes, as we have seen, how being a 'successful' patient requires a certain amount of 'cultural capital', which
includes a readiness to enter the discourse of personal reflection.
What may be perceived as unwillingness to engage in this discourse,
and has traditionally been termed 'resistance', is sometimes difficult
to distinguish from a lack of a shared or cultural understanding
of the psychotherapeutic process. Richards gives examples from a
study of mental health services in East London, based on interviews
with service users and practitioners, and illustrating the disparity
that can often exist between the professionals' understanding of
psychotherapeutic work and the ways such interventions are experienced by clients. While psychotherapeutic interventions may not
be the most appropriate service for some clients, much work needs
to be done to render psychotherapy a more appropriate vehicle in
attracting and engaging many people whose understanding of it
cannot be necessarily assumed or taken as given.

One of the first empirical studies which demonstrated the discriminatory nature of the psychiatric services was carried out by
Hollingshead and Redlich (1958). In this study it was shown that

lower-class patients were more likely to receive ECT, tranquillisers or confinement, and much less likely to receive psychotherapy than those of higher social status. The findings of this study were confirmed by a study in the same region by Mollica and Milic (1986), who found that the effect of social class on psychiatric care was smaller than in the findings of 1958, but nevertheless still present.

Bromley (1994) reviews the literature on the relationship between social class and psychotherapy, and points to some general conclusions. First, lower-class patients are less likely to be chosen for psychotherapy. This is demonstrated in studies based on surveys (e.g. Sutton and Kessler 1986) and on actual practice (e.g. Culberg and Stefanson 1983). Second, regarding the question of whether lower-class patients want psychotherapy, the evidence is equivocal. Some studies – for example, Overall and Aronson (1968), Balch and Miller (1974), and Brill and Storrow (1960) – suggest that working-class patients tend to adopt a more passive role in their treatment, demand more direction and support from the mental health system and tend to view their difficulties in physical rather than psychological terms. They lack an understanding of psychotherapy and express little need for it. Other studies – such as Fitzgibbons (1972), Lorion (1974) and Frank (1978) – show that lower-class patients do express a desire for psychotherapy. Third, there is the question of whether lower-class patients derive less benefit from psychotherapy compared to non-working-class patients. Again the evidence is equivocal. In a survey of the literature, Jones (1974) found that nine studies showed that lower-class patients were more likely to be early drop-outs against two studies which failed to confirm this trend. Other studies such as Pettit et al. (1974) and Wold and Steger (1976) fail to find evidence that lower-class patients had a higher drop-out rate from therapy, while a study by Gottschalk (1967) suggests that low social class predicted a *better* prognosis in psychotherapy.

Another question addressed by Bromley is why there are social class differences in psychotherapy variables. One suggestion offered to explain the alleged difficulty of psychotherapy with working-class patients has to do with the social distance between patient and therapist (see, for example, Haase 1964; Harrison et al. 1970). In the study by Harrison et al. carried out in a child psychiatric setting, a relationship was found between the social class of origin of the psychiatrist, the social class of the patient and the diagnosis and recommendation for treatment. Working-class children were less likely to be recommended for psychotherapy, but were 11 times more likely to be given a chronic brain syndrome diagnosis if the psychiatrist came from an upper-class than if the psychiatrist came from a lower-class backgound. In addition to the social distance theory, other explanations consider that difficulties in psychotherapy are mediated by the language attributes of working-class patients (e.g. Bernstein 1964), or by other psychological mediating variables. Bromley (1994) discusses the work of Bernstein, who applies concepts of restricted and elaborated code to the practice of psychotherapy. However, Bromley points out the empirical and theoretical weakness of Bernstein's theories citing, for example, the work of William Labov, who showed that given the right context deprived working-class children could speak in an elaborate, logically sophisticated way. Bromley further points out that verbal elaboration can itself be a defence against psychotherapy, in, for example, rationalisation and distancing from feelings. As Bromley states: 'It seems fallacious to equate emotional articulateness which probably is necessary for psychotherapy, with elaborated code, which almost certainly is not' (1994: 4).

Bromley also draws attention to the fact that there have been only a small nature of studies published since the early 1980s exploring the relationship between social class and psychotherapy. He suggests that this might be a reflection of a change in political attitudes to social class both nationally and internationally. Instead Bromley points out that the concept of class as part of the political debate has been largely replaced by discussions on the politics of gender or ethnicity. This brings up the question of whether counselling is a social good, for a criticism that can be made of counselling and psychotherapy generally is that it is inherently individualistic and acts as a force to encourage individuals to fit into inequitable social and political systems.

### Discrimination in mental health care provision

The discrimination and prejudice found in the larger society are reflected in society's institutions, such as the criminal, legal and psychiatric systems. Many studies which document racial discrimination in the mental health service have been carried out. The findings of a survey carried out by MIND (Rogers and Faulkner 1987) indicate that black people are more likely to be removed to a place of safety by the police under Section 136 of the Mental Health Act (1983), and are more likely to be detained under Sections 2, 3 and 4 of the Mental Health Act (see also Cope 1989). Black people are more often diagnosed as suffering from schizophrenia or other forms of psychotic illness (McGovern and Cope

1991) and they are also more likely to receive higher doses of medication or receive medication in the form of depot injections (Chen *et al.* 1991). The overall picture is one of social inequality, where black people are less likely than white people to receive alternative treatment approaches to traditional psychiatric treatment, such as are offered in psychotherapy or counselling.

Many studies have been carried out purporting to show diagnostic differences between racial groups. However, as Fernando (1988) points out, the Western diagnostic research criteria used by conventional psychiatric research fail to consider the cultural differences in the ethnic groups being studied. Factors such as cultural, social and economic influences have to be taken into account, which they rarely are, if research into the mental health of ethnic minorities is to have any validity.

The proportion of clinical psychologists from ethnic minority backgrounds is small (see, for example, Gurani and Sayal 1987; Bender and Richardson 1990). This raises issues about discrepancies between the cultures of service providers and their clients. It also suggests that educational and career opportunities may be less available to certain groups than to others. The low number of clinical psychologists from ethnic minority groups could be explained by several factors. For example, it could be that there are very few applications from ethnic minority candidates; or that applications from these groups are of lower quality; or that they are treated unfavourably; or students from these groups may be less likely to complete their course; or be less likely to practise after having qualified. The BPS does not as yet have an overall strategy for monitoring selection, progress and outcome, although systems may be developed under the BPS's equal opportunities initiatives, and the National Clinical Training Group. Although comprehensive data is not available for applicants to the older courses in psychology, figures are available for recent applicants to the erstwhile polytechnic courses.

There are few ethnic minority students in clinical psychology training, which Boyle *et al.* (1993) suggest may be related to the selection procedures applied within the selection process. The criteria for selecting clinical psychology students are not made explicit. Boyle *et al.*'s (1993) paper on selection for clinical psychology courses compared applicants from ethnic minority and majority groups to the University of East London training course in clinical psychology in 1991, at each stage of the selection process. The findings suggest that candidates from ethnic minority groups were not treated unfairly in the selection process, at least in the sense that those independently rated as possessing certain positive attributes were as likely to proceed to the next selection phase as their ethnic majority counterparts. Rating criteria included such items as: a well-structured application form, prior experience as a psychology assistant, knowledge of current professional and health-related issues, exceptional clinical references, and the class of degree already obtained. Other criteria, although not explicitly stated but used in the selection procedure, were a degree from a UK or Irish university, *not* a polytechnic, and a typed application form.

Boyle *et al.* conclude that overall the applications received from ethnic minority candidates may be of slightly lower quality than those from majority groups, at least in terms of the criteria used in this selection process. The general finding is that the ethnic minority applicants as a group were somewhat less knowledgeable of and integrated into the profession, less likely to have secured employment as a psychology assistant, and thus less likely to be conversant with current issues or to have exceptional clinical references. This group is also less likely to type application forms, and more likely to apply before obtaining a degree. Thus they may be less realistic about the amount of competition for places and about the need for high-quality presentation. This study also goes some way towards answering the question of whether the low number of clinical psychologists from ethnic minority groups is at least partly due to their low numbers on undergraduate courses.

Some caution needs to be taken in interpreting the results, due to the lack of comprehensive data: for example, the data on applicants to former polytechnic courses almost certainly over-estimates the proportion of ethnic minority students who successfully apply to all undergraduate courses in psychology. Despite this, the general finding of the study suggests that the proportion of applicants to clinical psychology courses who are from ethnic minority groups is not less than would be expected from their presentation on undergraduate courses. This study throws up questions such as the nature of the selection criteria themselves, and whether at least some of them may not disadvantage certain groups of applicants.

Another issue concerns the criteria of 'relevant experience'. Although minority group applicants tended not to have gained the experience of being employed as a psychology assistant and consequently not to have gained knowledge of the profession or obtained strong references, the definition of what constitutes 'relevant experience' may itself be too narrow and needs to be expanded to include, for example, fluency in ethnic minority languages or work experiences with ethnic minority groups.

There are a wide range of people who come under the headings of 'black' or 'ethnic minority' according to race, religion, language and culture from, for example, Asian gay men to Muslim women or Afro-Caribbean men. The differences between such groups in many ways are far greater than their similarities. To view all these groups under one unitary heading is based on misleading assumptions and preconceptions, and is likely to lead to misleading and inappropriate conclusions. The one issue that such groups have in common is that they are members of a minority group, differing in certain aspects from the majority culture. However, an examination of this statement soon highlights that it is not the numerical issue which is salient, but rather that they are members of groups who do not hold power in our culture. They are further disempowered by the different institutions in our society, including health systems, which have been developed and are largely organised to meet the needs and requirements of those groups which reflect the power structure of society in general.

Pillay (1993) reports on a workshop on race and culture which explored issues of equality and power in psychology. The theme of 'visible minorities' – that is, visibility by colour or blackness and other possible physiognomic characteristics that define people of African and Asian origin – was elaborated from the fact that they are a numerical minority. This issue arose largely from the Runnymede Trust's (1992) report on the public's perception of visible minority people in Britain. The 1991 Census identified 2.54 million black people in Britain, or 4.8 per cent of the total population. Pillay (1993) notes that a National Opinion Poll carried out in 1991 indicated that almost a third of all white people think that ethnic minorities constitute over ten million of the population, that is, four times the actual number. Only 10 per cent of the population surveyed made an accurate estimate. This misperception is partly explained by the physical concentration of visible minority people in some inner city areas and in some of the electoral constituencies in the country. There are 51 constituencies out of the 615 where minority group people are 15 per cent or more of the constituency population (they range from 15–46 per cent), according to estimates based on the 1981 Census data.

Racially motivated attacks are increasing, according to figures of incidents reported to the police in England and Wales, rising from 4,383 attacks in 1988 to 7,800 attacks in 1991. A Carlton TV 'Fact Sheet on Race Attacks' (January 1993) summarises a 1981 Home Office report showing that Asians were 50 times and Afro-Caribbeans 36 times more likely than whites to be victims of racially motivated attacks. In the year ending June 1992 Metropolitan Police statistics show that the victims of racially violent attacks were: Asian 53 per cent; Afro-Caribbean 22 per cent; Jewish 5 per cent. Pillay (1993) notes that is not surprising that, in a survey of ethnic group health needs in an outer London suburban borough, Asians identified their primary need as security.

The workshop reported by Pillay highlighted many important issues for clinical psychologists. For example, it may well be that greater knowledge of racism and racist-inspired violence and rejection would be more useful in understanding psychological processes than assumed culturally based psychosis in Afro-Caribbeans and somatisation in Asians. The workshop concluded that race and culture in a multi-ethnic society should receive greater consideration in psychology, both at the level of training and continuing professional development.

### Cultural determinants of symptoms of distress

Certain syndromes and forms of distress are differentially manifested by groups in society. One such example is HIV/Aids. Mann stated:

> AIDS exploits societal weaknesses. It proceeds along the major fault lines of society, inequity and discrimination. Belonging to a marginalized or stigmatized group creates an increased risk of HIV infection and increases the risk of receiving inadequate care and support . . . To be effective against AIDS society must attack discrimination, stigmatization of people with AIDS, the low status of women, and unequal access to care.
>
> (Mann, quoted in Tanne 1992: 6847)

Clarke and Brindley (1993) point out that black women are highly represented in the population of people with HIV in London. Although there is little research exploring the experiences and needs of this group, it is likely that they experience numerous stressors and that they will be psychologically vulnerable. Clarke and Brindley discuss the role of the clinical psychologist in working with other health professionals in developing accessible and appropriate psychological services. They point out that psychologists have taken an important lead in developing the services on offer to people with HIV and AIDS. Providing emotional and psychological support for black women with HIV needs to be considered within the context of the multiple problems faced by black people living in Britain. Rates of poverty and unemployment are higher. They live in the worst housing, and their uptake of benefits is lower. The context of their socio-economic situation means that coping with health concerns is often given less priority than other concerns. Clarke and Brindley point out that racism can not only lead to harassment and violence, but also to discrimination from social, welfare and health services. For some black people, language and communication difficulties can impede or prevent even simple tasks being accomplished.

Black women's needs are often even further marginalised because the needs of women generally have not always been taken into consideration in planning. Although comprehensive data is not available, Clarke and Brindley note that most black women presenting with HIV/AIDS in London are from Africa, and the duration of their residence ranges from a few months to many years. While some have permanent residence, others are students or refugees, with all the attendant multiple practical, social and psychological problems associated with being a refugee. As well as the often devastatingly traumatic situations from which they have fled, refugees often have to cope with multiple losses of people and places, ongoing uncertainty, anxieties about the future and feelings such as guilt regarding the plight of friends and relatives. On arrival in Britain the process of seeking asylum is itself extremely stressful, from facing often unwelcoming immigration officials to the seemingly interminable delays in establishing their refugee status. All this time they are living with an often constant fear of deportation. In becoming refugees, people have also lost any position and status that they may have had in their country of origin, which compounds still further the feelings of low self-respect and self-esteem. They frequently live in isolated accommodation and have limited financial resources.

A common observation is that refugees are anxious not to upset authorities in any way and that they tend to avoid statutory services for fear that their immigration status may be questioned. Added to this is the issue of whether health authorities are prepared to treat immigrants of questionable legal status. A diagnosis of HIV is itself a traumatic event, bringing with it fear of death as well as anxieties about stigmatisation and rejection. This is further compounded by problems such as those outlined in the paragraph above.

Clarke and Brindley outline some of the complex therapeutic issues which arise for black women with AIDS. They may experience isolation from family and friends, whether or not they reveal that they have AIDS. If they tell others they may be stigmatised and rejected, but if they do not tell others they will feel even more isolated from those people who are important in their lives. The implications of this diagnosis for both themselves and their families and for any decisions a woman may make are issues which could be explored in therapy. Other issues include their often realistic fears that they will be blamed for contracting the virus even though their partner may have partners outside their relationship. They frequently have concerns relating to children and HIV. Some women first learn of their own diagnosis through their child's illness. Because of the prospect of their own or their partner's death before that of their children, they have to face issues concerning the children's need for fostering or adoption. The stresses for the whole family where one member or more is HIV-positive are enormous.

In discussing the whole range of losses experienced by women with HIV, Clarke and Brindley state: 'They represent losses of almost incalculable magnitude; loss of health, self-respect, social support, and, for some, of hope' (1993: 7). Their view is that psychological services need to be developed as part of the total provision of care and provided in such a way that they are seen as acceptable and accessible to such women. For example, psychologists can be involved in training health workers to encourage dialogue and joint communication, especially relevant to those who, in order to obtain any care, assume a culturally based attitude of submissiveness that implies agreeing to anything. Training in assessment is also important, since an individual rather than an ethnocentric approach is appropriate when assessing black people's needs. It is important to avoid stereotyping and to focus on the experiences which have influenced each person's life. Making assumptions about clients' need based on their ethnic origin ignores the differences between and diversity of black cultural groups. In order to provide a better multi-cultural service, a comprehensive assessment of the individual's social and economic situation is needed together with an assessment of the individual's history, culture, religion and particular needs. Cultural issues may have important implications regarding support, especially with regard to illness, death and bereavement.

User involvement is a crucial factor in planning services which are appropriate to black women's needs. Clarke and Brindley (1993) describe such a service, made up of health workers and users, who aim at monitoring and working for improvements in services for women with HIV and AIDS using certain central London hospitals. Such services have tried to develop practices which might make them more accessible to women, including a more amenable appointment system and a flexible service with a range of health and welfare workers available. For many people psychological therapy may not be a priority. Nevertheless, many people who have overwhelming material and practical needs often also need emotional support. Psychological therapies can provide a means to an understanding and working through of some of the multiple losses and stresses for clients such as those with a diagnosis of HIV/AIDS.

## *Issues of social inequality*

Issues of social inequality are embedded in the wider cultural and historical context of society and are manifested at an individual and an institutional level. These themes of social inequality are reflected in our mental health services. As 'normality' is typically defined in relation to male, white, English behaviour it is not altogether surprising that mental health services fail to match the needs of many individuals in our society.

The sociology of knowledge highlights how cultural factors are embedded in and shape what we think we 'know'. Both the process and content of our knowledge are culturally determined. What we assume to be 'facts' are determined by our cultural and historical perspectives. These processes are reflected, for example, in what is defined as science and in our professional institutions. In turn this gives legitimacy to certain forms and content of 'knowledge'. A paper by Sayal (1989) on black women and mental health illustrates some of the issues. There are often sweeping generalisations made about black people, such as that 'passive' Asian women are subjected to oppressive practices within the family; or that the Afro-Caribbean woman is strong and dominant. Sayal points to the colonial legacy of black people's respective differences being played off against each other, with one community held up as a negative reference point for another.

Stereotypes which are accepted as 'facts' are frequently used by mental health workers. For example, by accepting pathologising notions about 'black families' we collude with the pseudo-science that gives legitimacy to popular racism, since we make presumptions about homogeneity which we do not make about white families. This process is seen at the level of professional 'science', for example, in concepts such as 'ethnicity' and 'transcultural psychiatry'. An examination of the studies conducted in this area suggests that most of the studies which purport to be on black family life are actually concerned with poverty. Sayal points out that the poor are frequently identified as '"culturally deprived" . . . so that poverty is discussed as if it is a personal trait rather than a social condition, and deviations from ethnocentric norms are viewed as deprivation' (1989: 4). A consequence of this is that a high proportion of black children are in care because black women are viewed as unfit for mothering, and until recently as unfit for fostering and adoption.

It is not only health care that is racist and sexist but also psychiatric care. Historically there has been a tendency to view black people as physically and mentally 'ill'. Physically, black skin was held to be a form of leprosy. Mentally, runaway slaves were often diagnosed as suffering from 'drapetomania', an incurable urge to run away. Although in Britain black people make up less than 5 per cent of the population, 25 per cent of patients on psychiatric wards are black (Black Health Workers and Patient Group 1983). Racism is currently reflected in psychiatry in the formulation of black-specific mental illnesses, such as 'West Indian psychosis'. Black people receive more physical treatments, including ECT and injected drugs at high doses. Black people are also less likely to see consultants or highly qualified staff (Littlewood and Lipsedge 1983). The psychiatric theories which claimed that black genes were causal factors in mental illness have now been replaced by theories which view black culture as a causal factor in mental illness.

Sayal (1989) discusses the increased use of psychiatry as a method of control and punishment of black people and the increasing use of psychiatric expertise in prisons and courtrooms. There are double the number of Section 136s (compulsory admission) for black in comparison with white people, and patients can be deported if they have no right of abode and are receiving in-patient treatment. Black women are over-represented in the prison population and 70 per cent of them are diagnosed as having some sort of mental disorder.

Sayal points out that for those black women who are offered therapy or counselling, the wider social and political context is often ignored and the techniques and goals chosen are often inappropriate. 'Distress is seen as being located within the individual, never without, and so the impact of racism and poverty on black women is ignored. The pathologisation of women continues as black women clients are deceived into believing that there is something wrong with them' (1989: 4). Theories which label the effects of prejudice as being due to some individual determinant or 'sick personality' oppress and pathologise even further. Thus psychoanalytic explanations have never addressed racism directly; for example, black riots have been interpreted as violent outbreaks of infantile father hatred.

Class inequality in socio-economic terms is reflected in unequal levels of health. Socio-economic factors lead to high levels of stress for many black women. Their unemployment rate is three times the national average and probably higher, since the figures do not include married or co-habiting women. As has already been pointed out in this chapter, lack of income is a major source of stress. It limits choice in a range of activities which affect our daily lives and future plans, including clothing, recreation, diet, transport, housing and education. Sayal comments: 'I am sure that arduous and exhausting work, if you can get it, at unsocial hours, uncongenial housing and racist attacks must have a cumulative effect. Expressions of frustration and anger may then be assumed to be symptoms of mental illness' (1989: 5). However, despite these factors, the impact of racism on black people's lives is not viewed as a central factor, but rather as subordinate to what are assumed to be universal dynamic forces. Although there have been attempts by women psychotherapists to bring anti-racist perspectives into their work, this framework nevertheless often reflects the ideological biases of society. The result is that black women are still not the subjects of their own understanding of the world, but rather are considered as they relate to whites in a social system designed by whites.

Sayal (1989) emphasises the dangers of individualising distress and locating pathology within the individual rather than considering the wider socio-political system. She states:

> As a clinician, I think it is crucial to relate personal misery to its environment, history and political context. If you rob a person of their history, you rob them of their sense of self. Therapy with black women should not pathologize and punish rage so that it is internalized into self-hatred and depression. Instead, an awareness of oppression can become a major force creating the anger that focuses the energy needed for the fight.
>
> (1989: 6)

She continues by discussing how psychotherapy can be a useful means of enabling people to identify their distress by moving the discourse from the personal to the political. Mental health and economic and political self-determination are inseparable. It may well be that collective movement to gain power through political action, as Sayal suggests, may protect and save black women's mental health far more than any therapy.

She points out that white women therapists are often regarded with suspicion and resentment by black women clients, and that many black women like to share their feelings with other black women. However, due to selective non-entry and non-employment of black clinical psychologists and psychotherapists in the NHS, black women do not have such a choice. As such service provision is biased in favour of one section of the community, Sayal stresses the importance of more black women mental health workers.

On a more optimistic note, reports on race, culture and ethnicity teaching on clinical psychology training courses in this country indicate that there is more interest and concern about the process and content of this area (see, for example, Davenhill *et al.* 1989 and Nadirshaw 1983). As a result of the survey by Patel *et al.* 1994, a training working party was formed within the Clinical Psychology Race and Culture Special Interest Group (CPRC SIG) to develop a model academic and practice curriculum, flexible enough to allow for changing needs in training and to accommodate current research.

## GENDER AND MENTAL HEALTH

There is a substantial literature on the topic of 'women and mental health' (e.g. Baker Miller 1971; Chesler 1972; Chamberlain 1988; Dutton-Douglas and Walker 1988; Ussher 1991, 1994; Ussher and Nicolson 1992).

Reviews of research carried out in this area point to consistent statistical findings (see reviews by Ussher 1991; Williams *et al.* 1993). A frequently quoted fact is that more women than men suffer from depression or anxiety. Research findings indicate that approximately four times as many women than men present to their GP with psychological problems. This ratio is similarly reflected in GP referrals to clinical psychologists. Studies suggest the 30–40 per cent of women in particular demographic groups are depressed at any one time. There are also gender imbalances in the treatment of women who are more likely to be prescribed psychotropic drugs than men (Ashton 1991) and to receive ECT (Frank 1990). Women generally are less likely than men to be referred on to a specialist mental health worker following a psychological assessment by their GP (Brown *et al.* 1988b), while the mental health needs of women from ethnic minorities (CRE 1992), lesbian women (Rothblum 1990) or older women (Bruce *et al.* 1991) are frequently dismissed or ignored. In a summary of the main findings in this area, Williams *et al.* (1993) point out that such studies may be categorised into five main areas: the mental health consequences of women's everyday life; black and ethnic minority women; older women; lesbian women; and the topic of abuse and mental health.

First, studies demonstrate the psychological costs for women of daily life in a society structured by gender. Marriage is more likely to be beneficial to the psychological well-being of men, and detrimental to the psychological well-being of women (McRae and Brody 1989). Childbirth is associated with depression for a significant number of women, with estimates varying between 10 and 30 per cent (Nicolson 1989). Caring for children and dependent relatives carries high mental health costs when linked with isolation, low social value and a lack of resources (Brown and Harris 1978; Smith 1991). The links between poverty and psychological distress and disturbance are well documented (Bruce *et al.* 1991). However, poverty and levels of economic deprivation are much higher amongst women than men, with poverty among women being correlated with being a single parent (National Council for One-Parent Families 1987); being divorced (Day and Bahr 1986); being old (Bruce *et al.* 1991); being black or a member of an ethnic minority group (EOC 1992). Domestic violence occurs in an estimated one in every four households in this country, and is inflicted mainly on partners (Smith 1989). The links between battering and long-term mental health problems are well established (Rosewater 1985). Being female is itself a risk factor. Women's feelings, thoughts and behaviours are more likely to be defined as mad than are men's (Broverman *et al.* 1970; Ussher 1991).

A second group of studies involves black and ethnic minority women suggesting that the often hidden causes of mental health difficulties are not being acknowledged within mental health services. Racism, poverty and isolation shape the lives and experiences of black and ethnic minority women who use mental health services (e.g. Jervis 1986; Holland 1992). Black women are more likely to receive physical treatments or drugs or ECT than counselling (MIND 1992b). There is little provision of black and ethnic minority counsellors (Webb-Johnson and Nadirshaw 1993). Further, racism also affects black and ethnic minority women who provide mental health services (Sayal-Bennett 1991).

The group of studies concerning older women indicates that over 60 per cent of women in Britain over the age of 65 years live below the official poverty line (Titley *et al.* 1992). This group are the least likely (because of gender and age) to be offered counselling and therapy for mental health difficulties (Wallen *et al.* 1987). Psychotropic drugs are prescribed more often to older women than to any other age or gender group (Catalan *et al.* 1988). This is also the group most at risk from side-effects of medication (Grohmann *et al.* 1989; Woerner *et al.* 1991).

A fourth area of study concerns lesbian women, pointing out that lesbian women service users and workers are invisible within most mental health services; and that these services typically assume heterosexuality, which intensifies the stress of homophobia for both service workers and users (Martin and Lyon 1984). Mental health services often minimise major life events experienced by lesbian women, and assumptions are often made that it is their sexual orientation and lifestyle which are the cause of their mental health difficulties (Perkins 1991).

There are two major explanations put forward for the gender imbalance in mental health. These are, first, the vulnerability model, which argues that women's experiences and their role within patriarchal society predisposes them to depression. The second major explanation is the labelling model, which avers that women are more likely to be labelled as 'mad'. Ussher argues that there is evidence for both models. For example, behaviour that is viewed as 'acceptable' in men, such as assertion or aggression, is often labelled as a sign of pathology when women exhibit the same behaviour. In addition to this, there are many aspects of women's lives that act as risk factors for depression, for example, economic vulnerability, lack of power or control, and physical and sexual abuse (Ussher 1991).

In addition to the studies which document the psychological costs of women's 'normal' lives, there is now a significant body of literature which documents the effects of sexual and physical abuse of women. These socially unacceptable although not unusual means by which men in our society use their power have major implications for the mental health of women. In their review of the research in this area, Williams *et al.* (1993) conclude that at least 50 per cent of women who use community- and hospital-based mental health services have been sexually or physically abused as children and as adults (e.g. Carmen *et al.* 1984; Beck and Van 1987; Bryer *et al.* 1987). There is also evidence that sexual and physical abuse are central to much that is diagnosed as severe mental illness (e.g. Herman *et al.* 1984), and that abuse is strongly linked with high service use (e.g. Walker and James 1992). Williams and Watson (1994) stress that given the high incidence and the mental health implications of abuse, neglecting to enquire about a history of abuse is clearly malpractice. Contact with unhelpful service providers is likely to replicate and perpetuate women's previous experiences of their abuse not having been recognised and accepted by others. This in turn may lead to the maintenance of substance abuse, psychotic symptoms or self-harm, and high use of mental health services.

Given the mental health implications, Williams and Watson (1994) stress the importance in their training of clinical psychologists gaining knowledge of the dynamics of power relations, and the uses and abuses of power in a wide range of contexts, in order to intervene effectively in providing or finding appropriate help for women. These contexts need to include the training itself, and also the settings and relationships that provide services. Physical, emotional and sexual abuse takes place in these contexts. Recently, clinical psychologists have taken more responsibility in this area. For example, clinical psychologists have made a significant contribution to the 1994 public inquiry at Ashworth Hospital, which was concerned with the management and treatment of patients. The BPS has publicly committed itself to addressing the problem of therapist abuse (Mihill 1993); and guidelines have been developed to help prevent supervisors and trainers misusing their power in relation to trainees.

It is important to recognise that in Great Britain and elsewhere there have been sustained attempts to develop practice that acknowledges rather than denies the impact of social inequalities on women's mental health. These have typically been developed in contexts without male management, supervision and theorising. In Britain these include Shanti (see Williams *et al.* 1993), Threshold (Davis 1993), the White City Project (Holland 1992), Newpin (Newpin 1992), POPAN (Edwards and Fasal 1992). There are also numerous examples of good practice to be found in self-help groups, mutual aid groups, help lines and the Women's Aid Movement (see GPMH 1993). Some of the practice developed in the context of such women-centred projects has influenced theories of therapy practice and processes which empower women (e.g. Dutton-Douglas and Walker 1988; Watson and Williams 1992).

Although over the past few decades many would point to the increased awareness of and consequent changes in the role of women in our society, these changes may be more apparent than real. Our society's view of women or the cultural stereotype contains the same elements that are used to describe neuroses. In other words, in our society to be a woman is to be neurotic. Women are defined in relation to men. Thus they are defined in terms of either what they lack or what they have more of compared to men. Then those attributes are deemed inferior. Feminist writers highlight how historically patriarchal power is reflected in the categorisation and control of women, for example, from episodes of witch hunts to the nineteenth-century mass outbreaks of hysteria; likewise, in the contemporary situation many women are diagnosed by the dominant medical model as suffering from mental illness. Sexism follows the same process as racism, in that women's distress and discontent are medicalised and institutionalised. Thus, it may be argued that the appropriate solution to this situation is feminism rather than therapy.

A major influence on the feminist view of the nature of distress in women was the anti-psychiatry movement of the 1960s. This highlighted the coercive nature of psychiatry, with its adherence to medical models in providing explanations for human distress, and it acknowledged the importance of socio-political factors in mental health problems. Writers such as Thomas Szasz (1971), who highlight how illness is not located within the individual, but rather within the system, view psychiatric classification systems and their attendant labels as just another way of imposing control, even though the ostensible aim is not to imprison but to cure. The concept of madness or mental illness may be viewed as a social construction and a means of defining as deviant that behaviour which society finds unacceptable. From this perspective, psychologists, psychiatrists and all those engaged in therapy may be viewed as agents of social control attempting to 'cure' people in order that they should conform to social norms.

Feminists, writing specifically on the experience of women, point out that it is often those who are classified as 'mentally ill' who are the ones who have rejected the traditional, passive feminine role, as femininity has been shown to be synonymous with ill health (Broverman *et al.* 1970). The use of concepts of mental illness, and the individualisation of distress either through medical or psychological models, further oppresses women, by defining behaviour which may be a normal reaction to domination as pathological. This process itself further emphasises women's inequality and powerlessness. From a feminist perspective, women's distress may be viewed not as a problem located in women as individual persons, but rather as a reflection of their experience in a masculine-dominated society. Jane Ussher (1994) shows how many feminist writers (e.g. Daly 1979; Fulani 1987) redefine 'mental illness' as a socially constructed phenomenon, and view the use of professional medical or psychological help to address these issues as inappropriate. Mary Daly (1979: 276) argues:

> Therapists create a market for their 'healing'. A woman seduced into treatment is 'inspired' with dis-ease she had never before suspected . . . The multiplicity of therapies feeds into this disease, for they constitute an arsenal for the manufacture of many forms of semantic bullets used to bombard the minds of women struggling to survive in the therapeutically polluted environment.

If problems are located within the system rather than located within the individual woman then the appropriate means of change is through the socio-political system. This raises the question of the role of therapists or clinical psychologists, because according to this view their role, if any, could well be that of perpetuators of women's oppression. Such awareness brings with it enormous difficulties for clinicians working with distressed women, if they can allow themselves not to separate their knowledge of critical theory from their clinical practice. Even though an analysis of the wider socio-political context may well indicate that referral to mental health professionals is an inappropriate solution to the problem and may be viewed as a further act of oppression, many women have no one else to whom they can turn.

Ussher observes how sociological critique and theoretical analysis that dismiss individualised treatments and theories do not provide any immediate help for these women in the short term, even if they manage to change services and systems in the long term. Indeed many of these theories have been used as a justification for the abolition or removal of services by those who in any other context would be utterly opposed to sociological analysis or feminist perspectives. Radical critiques have served both the far right and the left, both of whom advocate the dismantling of mental health systems, for different reasons and with different, alternative solutions. The unhappiness and distress of many women may well not be an 'illness', but renaming it as oppression does not alleviate the pain for the individual client.

However, the question remains whether women should unquestioningly accept psychological intervention as it is constructed at present. A problem highlighted by Ussher (1994) is that gender issues are often not acknowledged and that a critical analysis of practice is the exception rather than the rule. A woman referred for therapy will be offered behaviour therapy, cognitive therapy or psychodynamic therapy, often without any choice and without discussion of the approach offered. All these psychotherapies may be viewed as sharing at least one common feature, that of viewing the woman as patient and the therapist as the powerful healer. The presenting 'symptom' or 'problem' is conceptualised differently within each theoretical framework, but each ignores the political context of the client's life, and therefore of the distress. It is questioned whether these different frameworks accurately help clients to understand their unhappiness, or merely reify the notion of illness. Further, the scientist–practitioner model within mainstream therapy and especially in clinical psychology (Ussher 1992) emphasises an objective, scientific analysis and the treatment of problems, and ignores issues of gender and politics. Clinical psychologists are acting in a political way by adhering to 'objective' positivistic methodologies.

Psychology is not and cannot be value-free, yet too frequently the discourse on the socio-political context within which psychotherapy and clinical psychology operate is itself marginalised, and not seen as really relevant to the mainstream process of therapy. The current climate will probably make this situation worse. Many political and economic factors facing therapists and psychologists in different contexts make the marginalisation of feminism and gender issues more likely. These factors include moves towards private practice, and the pressure on accountability of time and salaries, which are all potentially detrimental to the quality of services offered to women. Theoretical critiques by feminists and socio-political critiques do not offer much help to individual women in distress.

Psychologists must acknowledge that what they do has political implications and direct impact on policy, however much we might like to see ourselves as rational scientists set apart from such issues. There is now a vast amount of literature indicating that the values and politics of the individual researcher or practitioner directly affect research and practice. There is clearly a need for continuing debate and reflection on both theory and practice.

As with problems of race and ethnicity, the picture is not all negative. Gender issues are becoming less marginalised and positive working practices are developing in many areas of the country. In some ways the most important developments in providing mental health services for women have been outside the statutory services, in areas such as women's aid, women's refuges, self-help groups, crisis lines and intervention services. These services are all run by women for women, with no assumptions of illness or failure implicit in the relationships between service users and providers. Such a group is the Women's Mental Health Forum, a community group for women users and ex-users of mental health services described by Williams and Watson (1994). They describe a mixed-race group of 15 women ranging in age from the mid-20s to the mid-60s, most of whom seem poor. When asked about what brings them to the mental health services, they describe sexual abuse, violence, emotional abuse and neglect experienced as children and as adults. They talk about poverty, loss, no feeling of being loved or valued, of feeling responsible and blamed, and powerless for what has happened in their families. Several women also recount traumatic experiences around childbirth. When discussing their experiences of mental health services the themes are of widespread dissatisfaction. They are not listened to; therapists are incompetent and sometimes damaging; they tell of inappropriate treatments, including those provided by rehabilitation and day services, the enormous amounts of psychotropic drugs they had taken, their courses of ECT, multiple admissions to psychiatric hospitals, their children taken into care, and sexual and physical abuse in services. This particular group gave their local mental health service purchasers and providers some feedback about their experiences with recommendations for services to meet their needs.

Such groups illustrate the ways that women together can empower and enable each other. In a number of the neighbourhood projects already mentioned clinical psychologists have played a key role, e.g. the White City project (Holland 1992), the Newpin project (Newpin 1992) and the Shanti project (Mills 1992). Furthermore, a number of policy documents on the subject of women's mental health have been published (e.g. MIND 1992b; Williams *et al.* 1993) which integrate critical theory and research with the practical needs of women in distress.

### *The links between social inequalities and psychological distress*

It is important that mental health professionals develop an awareness of the ways in which multiple discrimination and disadvantage exact costs on mental health. It is also important to be aware that the findings indicate that multiple discrimination and disadvantage decrease the likelihood that the needs of people will be met by mental health services as they are presently organised.

Social inequalities are often a major cause of the despair, distress and confusion that is termed 'mental illness' or 'mental disorder'. The training of mental health professionals, including clinical psychologists, often ignores the link between social inequalities and psychological distress. This is evident in surveys and studies of clinical psychology training in Britain (e.g. Williams and Watson 1991; Alladin 1992; Ussher and Nicolson 1992), and elsewhere (e.g. Bekker 1991; Brown 1991). It is not therefore surprising that qualified practitioners find it difficult to consider the effects of structural inequalities on the lives of clients, on their own behaviour and on the services and organisations in which they work. Some writers (e.g. Penfold and Walker 1984; Showalter 1987) argue that when mental health professionals ignore the links between social inequalities and psychological distress they serve the interest of privileged social groups rather than the interests of clients. This creates an unhappy dilemma for clinical psychologists who have often entered the profession in order to help others not to support unjust social division.

## A CONSTRUCTIVE WAY FORWARD?

We have seen in this chapter how there is different access to therapy amongst groups in our society. These include women, people from ethnic minorities, people of lower socio-economic status and those viewed as being from different cultural backgrounds from mainstream society. There have been suggestions of promoting a better therapeutic outcome for this large group of people, for example by offering more appropriate forms of help. Some research suggests that self-help groups are more effective, and that it is more helpful when helpers share the same cultural and social background as their clients (see, for example, Sayal 1989).

A way forward often advocated by writers working with these different groups is the development of a therapy that acknowledges the significance of social issues. However, such writers usually restrict their observations within the frame of reference of a particular group. For example, Ussher (1991) and Watson and Williams (1992) put forward positive suggestions for a more appropriate therapy for women and illustrate how therapy can work explicitly to empower women. Ussher also advocates training in feminist theory and therapy for all therapists and clinical psychologists, so that feminist therapy does not develop as a marginalised speciality. However, as Masson (1989) points out, feminist therapy is still therapy, with all the problems the concept entails, so therapy cannot be the only solution to the causes of women's distress.

We could go on *ad infinitum* to develop more appropriate psychotherapies to include people with emotional and physical disabilities of various forms, older people, etc., and subdivide any of these categories. Indeed there is differential access to therapy by any group disempowered or marginalised by what is taken to be mainstream society. The problem is that most of us are marginalised in some way or another. The issue is not one concerned with minority groups as such. For example, there is a differential demand for and access by women for psychotherapy and counselling, yet they are not a numerical minority in our society and neither do white middle-class males make up the majority numerically in our society. It would be an error to locate the source of power as residing in white middle-class males as such. Rather, the issue revolves around the nature and unequal distribution of power in our society and, as David Smail illustrates, the sources of power are more distal.

David Smail points out that before we can even contemplate what an appropriate solution might be, we need to explore the ideology which surrounds the whole question of emotional distress. We know, reflect upon and judge our world through personal experience. The importance of social power in the shaping of ourselves and our lives, and in particular our distress, is seen by considering how its influence comes to be lived out in our personal experience. Fundamental though such experience is to our understanding of ourselves, it's not the whole story. Our personal view is not wide enough to take account of all the factors which contribute to a given state of affairs. For a more complete and accurate understanding we need to consider arguments and evidence which may not be immediately apparent to us personally. This is what is meant in part by being 'scientific': the ways in which personal distress is generated in a world over which we as individuals have very little control.

A more constructive approach to people's distress would, rather than focus on what is 'wrong' with them, seek to help people examine how much of their own self-attribution of personal weaknesses or deficits is actually the result of an external deprivation or exploitation. Smail also suggests that a more benign approach might also remove the stigma of abnormality from people so that they could live their lives as themselves and understand their own experiences as valid. The validity of people's experience – the judgemental clinical eye of psychology psychiatry and psychotherapy – needs to be replaced by an appreciation of the resourceful and often courageous ways in which people come to deal with their fate. Writers such as Smail (1987) and Heath (1992) point to ways forward in therapy. This would involve a greater awareness on the part of therapists and counsellors, such as in the recognition of the limitations of current knowledge and the danger of the dogmatic commitment to any particular theory or therapy of the individual's sense of self. A more equitable therapeutic endeavour would also include an awareness of the pervasive effects of the inequality of power in society manifested in the often debilitating effects on the individual's sense of self, in institutions and in interpersonal relationships including therapeutic relationships. Further, more attention needs to be given to the pervasive influence of the inequality of power reflected for example in issues revolving around class, race and gender and the ways in which these experiences of oppression become internalised as distress, confusion, self-doubt and anger. Serious consideration rather than just lip service to these issues should be given in the training of counselling and psychotherapy so as to avoid the traditional individualism of therapy.

Smail advocates 'the cultivation of a society which takes care of its members. To achieve this we have to recognise the importance of the conditions in which we live and the way we conduct ourselves towards each other' (1987, p. 91).

Present-day Britain is characterised by an increasing individualisation of society, under the world economic power of Americanisation. Even though the term 'community' is back in fashion, it is debatable whether the term has any real meaning other than as some economy-saving rhetoric. The comfort of friends, the communal sharing of grief, are partitioned off and commercialised and the traditional forms of comfort and support are in danger of being ignored. This is so even for those of us who are relatively fortunate in our personal experiences and are able to draw on personal and economic resources and have a social community within which we can share our suffering. For those of us without this good luck at any point in our lives the result can be disastrous. If we articulate the inevitable adversities or reversals of fortune which will affect each and every one of us at some time or other in the course of our lives, often the immediate reaction of people is to advise us to seek the 'professional' or 'expert' help of a counsellor or psychotherapist. The psychologising of interpersonal relations and the development of a counselling culture which suggests that the answer to our distress rests somewhere within us, and the refusal to acknowledge the realities of power, is reflected back to us as our society becomes increasingly Americanised, individualised and psychologised. As Smail comments, 'What we need is not an unlimited supply of psychological therapy so much as the rehabilitation of politics: the realization, that is, that power can be used for good as well as for ill, and should be' (1993, p. 55).

I began this book by exploring the factors influencing the formation and development of psychology services in Britain. These factors were embedded in the social context of the time and were reflected in the cultural and academic influences which shaped the form and content of clinical psychology. This context also led to the acknowledgement of the verbal psychotherapies in mental health. It was the wider contemporary context which defined the psychological professions of which clinical and counselling psychology form a part. For historical reasons the formation and development of clinical psychology in this country was based on the scientist–practitioner model which emphasised research and 'objectivity' at the expense of subjectivity and personal reflection. The scientist–practitioner model was advocated in the training of clinical psychologists and viewed as a core element of their role in practice. Changes in the social context during the late 1960s were reflected in changes in the form and content of clinical psychology. There was a greater emphasis on eclecticism on training courses and an increasing interest in and acknowledgement of psychotherapy in clinical practice. This led to tensions with the traditional view of science as propounded by the scientific–practitioner model. In Chapter Three, I outlined some of the limitations of the traditional view of science with its emphasis on 'objectivity'. The evolution of theories and concepts in the physical sciences has led to the challenging of traditional notions of science. Concepts revolving around subjectivity and the subjective methodology have been reintegrated into science. It was the limited view of 'objectivity' inherent in the scientific–practitioner model which delineated the frame of reference for clinical psychology and led to the view that issues of reflexivity and personal therapy were unnecessary in both the training and practice of clinical psychologists. Counselling does not inherit the same historical or professional legacy as clinical psychology. Counselling, from its formation and development, has traditionally concerned itself with reflexivity, at least in so far as it regards personal therapy as a central aspect of training and personal reflection as part of clinical practice. The necessity for personal development remains a crucial difference in the criteria for training in clinical and counselling psychology. However, regarding psychotherapy and counselling research there is as yet little evidence that such research has challenged the traditional scientific paradigm and brought reflexivity and subjectivity in any serious way into its research concerns and methodology.

The development of the relationship of counselling within psychological services continues to reflect the social context of our times. Chapter Five explores how factors in the social context have determined the form and nature of professional relationships both within professions and between different mental health professions. In particular, the political context of the last two decades has resulted in government policies which have determined employment practices and the organisation of services providing mental health care. One effect has been the expansion of counselling services generally and counsellors are now employed within the NHS together with the traditional NHS professions which provided counselling. Nationally there has not been a consistent approach to the employment of counsellors either from within existing psychology services or other services within the NHS. The structure and organisation of counselling services within the NHS is an evolving one.

When considering counselling within the context of psychological services it is necessary to address the criticisms that have been made of psychological approaches generally to different forms of distress that people experience in our society. For example, criticisms have been made concerning the manifest and latent abuse of power in therapy and concerning the fact that social inequalities are reflected in differential access to psychological services. However, a major concern is that psychological approaches have been too individualistic, ignoring the inextricable relationship between the individual and society. Conceptually, psychological approaches have narrowly defined the nature of the individual, ignoring the fundamental social nature of the development of the self and the social context that gives rise to meaning. This has led to psychological approaches individualising distress, locating its causes as being within the individual rather than locating the causes in the social context. This has been true of the psychological approaches generally whether they are called psychotherapy, counselling, clinical psychology or counselling psychology. Counselling has developed as a profession more recently than clinical psychology and other psychology professions. It does not have the historical legacy which has determined the structure and content of the other psychological services. However, it remains to be seen whether counselling as a profession will develop, in any meaningful sense, differently from the other psychological services.

# Bibliography

Adler, A. (1925) *The Practice and Theory of Individual Psychology*. New York: Harper.

Albee, G. (1996) Searching for the magic marker, paper presented at the J. Richard Marshall Memorial Conference of the Psychotherapy Section of the British Psychological Society. Nottingham, 27 April.

Alladin, W.J. (1992) Clinical psychology provision. Models, policies and prospects, in W.I.U. Ahmad (ed.) *The Politics of 'Race' and Health*. Bradford: University of Bradford.

Allen, C. (1985) 'Training for what? Clinical psychologists' perceptions of their roles', unpublished MSc dissertation. University of Newcastle upon Tyne, Department of Psychiatry.

Allport, G.W. (1962) Psychological models for guidance. *Harvard Educational Review*, 32: 373–81.

Ashton, H. (1991) Psychotropic drug prescribing for women. *British Journal of Psychiatry*, 158: 30–5.

Askoy, A. and Robins, K. (1992) Exterminating angels. Morality, violence, and technology in the Gulf War, in H. Mowlana, G. Gerbner and H.I. Schiller (eds) *Triumph of the Image*. New York: Westview Press.

Bacon, H. (1992) Supervision in clinical training. The integrative model, or muddling through. *Clinical Psychology Forum*, 45: 24–8.

Baker Miller, J.B. (1971) Psychological consequences of sexual inequality. *American Journal of Orthopsychiatry*, 41: 767–75.

Bakhtin, M.M. (1981) *The Dialogic Imagination: Four essays*. Texas: University of Texas Press.

Bakhtin, M.M. (1986) Towards a methodology for the human sciences, in V.W. McGee (trans.) *Speech Genres and Other Late Essays* (pp. 159–72). Texas: University of Texas Press.

Bakhtin, M.M. and Medvedev, P.N. (1985) *The Formal Method in Literary Scholarship: A critical introduction to sociological poetics*. Harvard: Harvard University Press.

Balch, P. and Miller, K. (1974) Social class and the community mental health center. *American Journal of Community Psychology*, 2: 243–53.

Bannister, D. (1960) Conceptual structure in thought disordered schizophrenics. *Journal of Mental Science*, 106: 1230–49.

Bannister, D. (1965) The rationale and clinical relevance of repertory grid technique. *British Journal of Psychiatry*, 11: 977–82.

Bannister, D. (1966) A new theory of personality, in B. Foss (ed.) *New Horizons in Psychology*. Harmondsworth: Penguin.

Bannister, D. and Fransella, F. (1965) A repertory grid test of schizophrenic thought disorder. *British Journal of Social and Clinical Psychology*, 2: 95–102.

Bannister, D. and Mair, J.M. (1970) *The Evaluation of Personal Constructs*. London: Academic Press.

Bannister, D. and Salmon, P. (1966) Schizophrenic thought disorder: Specific or diffuse? *British Journal of Medical Psychology*, 39: 215–19.

Barker, P. (1991) *Regeneration*. London: Penguin.

Barlow, D. (1981) On the relation of clinical research to clinical practice. Current issues, new directions. *Journal of Consulting and Clinical Psychology*, 49: 147–55.

Barlow, D., Hayes, S. and Nelson, R. (1984) *The Scientist–Practitioner*. New York: Pergamon.

Barrom, C.P., Shadish, W.R. and Montgomery, L.M. (1988) PhD's, PsyD's and real-world constraints on scholarly activity. Another look at the Boulder Model. *Professional Psychology: Research and Practice*, 19: 93–101.

Baruch, G. and Treacher, A. (1978) *Psychiatry Observed*. London: Routledge & Kegan Paul.

Beck, J.C. and Van, D.K.B. (1987) Reports of childhood incest and current behavior of chronically hospitalized psychotic women. *American Journal of Psychiatry*, 144(11): 1474–6.

Bekker, M.H.J. (1991) Sex inequality in the training of Dutch clinical psychologists. *Feminism and Psychology*, 1: 96–100.

Bender, M.P. and Richardson, A. (1990) The ethnic composition of Clinical Psychology in Great Britain. *The Psychologist*, 3: 250–2.

Berger, M., Coles, C., Kirk, J., Marzillier, J., Lavender, A., Morley, S., Revell, J. and Watts, F. (1988) The assessment of clinical psychologists in training: A discussion document. *Clinical Psychology Forum*, 15: 3–14.

Bernstein, B. (1964) Social class, speech systems and psychotherapy. *British Journal of Sociology*, 15: 54–64.

Black Health Workers and Patients Group (1983) Psychiatry and the corporate states. *Race and Class*, 25: 49–63.

Bostock, J. (1994) Social class, unemployment and psychotherapy. Discussant's presentation. British Psychological Society Conference, Psychotherapy Section Symposium (March 1994). *Psychotherapy Section Newsletter*, 16: 39–42.

Boyle, M. (1990) *Schizophrenia: A scientific delusion?* London: Routledge.

Boyle, M. (1996) Schizophrenia: The fallacy of diagnosis. *Changes*, 14: 43–9.

Boyle, M., Baker, M., Bennett, E. and Charman, T. (1993) Selection for clinical psychology courses. A comparison of applicants from ethnic minority and majority groups to the University of East London. *Clinical Psychology Forum*, 56: 9–13.

Bozarth, J. (1990) The essence of client-centred therapy, in G. Lietaer, J. Rombauts and R. Van Balen (eds) *Client-Centred and Experiential Psychotherapy in the Nineties*. Leuven: Leuven University Press.

British Association for Counselling (1991) *Information Sheet*. Rugby: British Association for Counselling.

British Association for Counselling (1992) *Invitation to Membership*. Rugby: British Association for Counselling.

British Psychological Society (1934) *Report of the BPS Professional Standards Committee*. Leicester: British Psychological Society.

British Psychological Society (1979) *Working Party on the Psychological Therapies*. Leicester: British Psychological Society, Division of Clinical Psychology.

British Psychological Society (1982) Training in clinical psychology. A statement of policy. *Bulletin of the British Psychological Society*, 35: 153–5.

British Psychological Society (1988) The Future of the Psychological Sciences: Horizons and Opportunities for British Psychology. Leicester: British Psychological Society.

British Psychological Society (1990) Psychological Therapy Services: The Need for Organizational Change. Policy Statement. Leicester: British Psychological Society.

British Psychological Society (1991a) *Clinical Psychology, Core Purpose and Philosophy*. Leicester: British Psychological Society.

British Psychological Society (1991b) Criteria for the Assessment of Postgraduate Training Courses in Clinical Psychology (CTCP). Leicester: British Psychological Society.

British Psychological Society (1991c) The British Psychological Society, Code of Conduct, Ethical Principles and Guidelines. Leicester: British Psychological Society.

British Psychological Society (1992a) *Guidelines on Clinical Supervision*. Leicester: British Psychological Society.

British Psychological Society (1992b) *Criteria for the Assessment of Courses*. Leicester: British Psychological Society.

British Psychological Society (1992c) *Opportunities and Careers for Psychologists*. Leicester: British Psychological Society.

British Psychological Society (1993) *Codes of Conduct, Ethical Principles and Guidelines*. Leicester: British Psychological Society.

British Psychological Society (1994a) Regulations and Syllabus for the Diploma in Clinical Psychology. Leicester: British Psychological Society.

British Psychological Society (1994b) Core Purpose and Philosophy of the Profession. Division of Clinical Psychology. Leicester: British Psychological Society.

British Psychological Society (1994c) Regulations for the Diploma in Counselling Psychology. Leicester: British Psychological Society.

British Psychological Society (1994d) Directory of Chartered Psychologists. Leicester: British Psychological Society.

British Psychological Society (1995a) *Guidelines for the Professional Practice of Counselling Psychology*. Leicester: British Psychological Society.

British Psychological Society (1995b) Criteria for the Accreditation of Post-graduate Training Courses in Clinical Psychology. British Psychological Society, Membership and Qualifications Board, Committee on Training in Clinical Psychology. Leicester: British Psychological Society.

British Psychological Society (1996) *Regulations and Syllabus for the Diploma in Counselling Psychology*. Leicester: British Psychological Society.

Bromley, E. (1983) Social class issues in psychotherapy, in D. Pilgrim (ed.) *Psychology and Psychotherapy: Current trends and issues*. London: Routledge & Kegan Paul.

Bromley, E. (1994) Social class and psychotherapy revisited, paper presented at the British Psychological Society Annual Conference, Psychotherapy Symposium, Brighton, March.

Brill, N.Q. and Storrow, H.A. (1960) Social class and psychiatric treatment. *Journal of Clinical Psychology*, 20: 513–15.

Broverman, K., Broverman, D., Clarkson, F., Rosencrantz, P. and Vogel, S. (1970) Sex role stereotyping and clinical judgement of mental health. *Journal of Consulting and Clinical Psychology*, 34: 1–7.

Brown, G.W. and Harris, T. (1978) *Social Origins of Depression*. London: Tavistock.

Brown, L.S. (1991) Plus ça change . . . or, who writes the scripts for these guys anyway? *Feminism and Psychology*, 1: 89–92.

Brown, P., Loftus, M. and Hackett, F. (1988a) Clinical psychology in crisis. *The Psychologist*, 1: 393–5.

Brown, R.M., Strathdee, G., Christie, B.J.R. and Robinson, P.H. (1988b) A comparison of referrals to primary care and hospital out-patient clinics. *British Journal of Psychiatry*, 153: 168–73.

Bruce, M.L., Takeuchi, D.T. and Leaf, P.J. (1991) Poverty and psychiatric status. Longitudinal evidence from the New Haven Epidemiologic Catchment Area Study. *Archives of General Psychiatry*, 48(5): 470–4.

Bryer, J.B., Nelson, B.A., Miller, J.B. and Krol, P.A. (1987) Childhood sexual and physical abuse as factors in adult psychiatric illness. *American Journal of Psychiatry*, 144(11): 1426–31.

Burchell, B. (1994) The effects of labour market position, job insecurity, and unemployment on psychological health, in D. Gallie, C. Marsh and C. Vogler (eds) *Social Change and the Experience of Unemployment*. Oxford: Oxford University Press.

Burt, C. (1927) *The Young Delinquent*. London: London University Press.

Burt, C. (1949) Recent discussions of juvenile delinquency. *British Journal of Educational Psychology*, 19: 31–43.

Burton, M.V. and Ramsden, R. (1994) A survey of GP referral patterns to outpatient psychiatry, clinical psychology, community psychiatric nurses, and counsellors. *Clinical Psychology Forum*, 74: 13–17.

Busfield, J. (1985) *Managing Madness*. London: Hutchinson.

Caine, T.M. and Smail, D.J. (1967) Personal relevance and choice of constructs for the repertory grid technique. *British Journal of Psychiatry*, 113: 517–20.

Carchedi, G. (1977) *On the Economic Identification of the New Middle Class*. London: Routledge & Kegan Paul.

Carmen, E.H., Felip Russo, N. and Baker Miller, J. (1984) Inequality and women's mental health. An overview, in P.P. Reiker and E.H. Carmen (eds) *The Gender Gap in Psychotherapy: Social realities and psychological processes.* New York: Plenum.

Catalan, J., Gath, D.H., Bond, A. and Edmonds, G. (1988) General practice patients on long-term psychotropic drugs. A controlled investigation. *British Journal of Psychiatry,* 152: 262–3.

Chamberlain, J. (1988) *On Our Own.* London: MIND.

Chen, E., Harrison, G. and Standen, P. (1991) Management of first episode psychiatric illness in Afro-Caribbean patients. *British Journal of Psychiatry,* 158: 517–22.

Chesler, C. (1972) *Women and Madness.* New York: Doubleday.

Chomsky, N. (1968) *American Power and the New Mandarins.* Harmondsworth: Penguin.

Claridge, G.S. and Brooks, D.N. (1973) A survey of applicants for the Glasgow M.Sc. course in clinical psychology. Some applications for selection and training. *Bulletin of the British Psychological Society,* 26: 123–7.

Clarke, D. and Brindley, H. (1993) Black women and HIV: Developing health services to share the challenge. *Clinical Psychology Forum,* 58: 6–9.

Collins, S. and Murray, A. (1995) A pilot project employing counselling psychologists within an adult mental health clinical psychology service. *Clinical Psychology Forum,* 78: 8–12.

Committee of the Division of Clinical Psychology (1992) The core purpose and philosophy of the profession. *Clinical Psychology Forum,* 42: 34–6.

Committee on Counselor Training, Division of Counseling and Guidance (1952) Recommended standards for training counseling psychologists at the doctorate level. *American Psychologist,* 7: 175–81.

Committee on Definition, Division of Counseling Psychology (1956) Counseling psychology as a specialty. *American Psychologist,* 11: 282–5.

Committee on Training in Clinical Psychology (1947) Recommended graduate training program in clinical psychology. *American Psychologist,* 2: 539–58.

Committee on Training in Clinical Psychology (1982) Criteria for the Assessment of Postgraduate Training Courses in Clinical Psychology. Leicester: Professional Affairs Board of the British Psychological Society.

Committee on Training in Clinical Psychology (1987) Guidelines on Clinical Supervision. Leicester: British Psychological Society.

Committee on Training in Clinical Psychology (1991) Criteria for the Assessment of Postgraduate Training Courses in Clinical Psychology. Leicester: British Psychological Society Membership and Qualifications Board.

Committee on Training in Clinical Psychology (1992) Guidelines on clinical supervision. *Clinical Psychology Forum,* 40: 31–4.

Committee on Training in Clinical Psychology (1995) *Criteria for the Accreditation of Postgraduate Training Courses in Clinical Psychology.* Leicester: Membership and Qualifications Board, Committee on Training in Clinical Psychology, British Psychological Society.

Cooper, D. (1967) *Psychiatry and Anti-Psychiatry.* London: Tavistock.

Cope, A. (1989) The compulsory detention of Afro-Caribbeans under the Mental Health Act. *New Community*, 15: 343–56.

Cormack, M., Nichols, K. and Walsh, S. (1991) Creating a system for professional development and personal support. *Clinical Psychology Forum*, 37: 8–10.

Corsini, R. and Wedding, D. (1989) *Current Psychotherapies*, 4th edn, Ifasca, IL: Peacock.

CRE (1992) Race Relations Code: For the elimination of racial discrimination and the promotion of equal opportunity in the provision of mental health services. London: Commission for Racial Equality.

Crockatt, P. (1976) Reflections on training in clinical psychology. *Bulletin of the British Psychological Society*, 18: 12–17.

Cullberg, J. and Stefansson, C.G. (1983) Social class and psychotherapy. *Acta Psychiatrica Scandinavia*, 68(5): 33–45.

Cushway, D. (1988) Stress in clinical psychology trainees. Unpublished MSc thesis. University of Birmingham.

Cushway, D. (1992) Stress in clinical psychology trainees. *British Journal of Clinical Psychology*, 31(2): 169–81.

Cushway, D., Dent, H., Howells, K. and Offen, L. (1993) Providing personal support at Birmingham. Answering the challenge to training courses. *Clinical Psychology Forum*, 58: 20–3.

Dabbs, A. (1965) Personal reflections on training as a clinical psychologist. *Bulletin of the British Psychological Society*, 18: 17–20.

Dabbs, A. (1972) The changing role of clinical psychologists in the National Health Service. *Bulletin of the British Psychological Society*, 25: 107–9.

Daly, M. (1979) *Gyn/Ecology: The metaethics of radical feminism*. London: Women's Press.

Danzinger, K. (1990) *Constructing the Subject: Historical origins of psychological research*. Cambridge: Cambridge University Press.

Dauncey, K., Giggs, J., Baker, K. and Harrison, G. (1993) Schizophrenia in Nottingham: Lifelong residential mobility of a cohort. *British Journal of Psychiatry*, 163: 613–19.

Davenhill, R., Hunt, H., Pillay, H.M., Harris, A. and Klein, Y. (1989) Training and selection issues in clinical psychology for black and minority ethnic groups from an equal opportunities perspective. *Clinical Psychology Forum*, 21: 34–7.

David, K. (1938) Mental hygiene and the class structure. *Psychiatry*, 1: 55–65.

Davies, D.R. (1995) Themes in psychotherapy with the unemployed. *British Psychological Society Psychotherapy Section Newsletter*, 17: 36–46.

Davis, S. (1993) *Threshold – a local initiative for women and mental health*. London: Springer.

Day, R.D. and Bahr, S.J. (1986) Income changes following divorce and remarriage. *Journal of Divorce*, 9(3): 75–88.

Dent, H. and Milne, D. (1987) Clinical supervision. A survey of selection and training. *Clinical Psychology Forum*, 13: 22–7.

Department of Health (1989) *Working for Patients*. London: HMSO.

Department of Health and Social Security (1977) The Role of Psychologists in the Health Service (The Trethowan Report). London: HMSO.

Desai, M. (1967) The concept of clinical psychology. *Bulletin of the British Psychological Society*, 20: 29–39.

Dicks, H.V. (1970) *Fifty Years of the Tavistock*. London: Routledge & Kegan Paul.

Digby, A. (1985) Moral treatment at the retreat, 1796–1846, in W.F. Bynum, R. Porter and M. Shepherd (eds) *The Anatomy of Madness*, Vol. 2. London: Tavistock.

Dryden, W. (ed.) (1990) *Individual Therapy: A handbook*. Milton Keynes: Open University Press.

Dryden, W. and Norcross, J.C. (1990) *Eclecticism and Integration in Counselling and Psychotherapy*. Loughton, Essex: Gale Centre Publications.

Dutton-Douglas, M.A. and Walker, L.E.A. (1988) *Feminist Psychotherapies: Integration of therapeutic and feminist systems*. Norwood, NJ: Ablex Publishing.

East, P. (1995) *Counselling in Medical Settings*. Buckingham: Open University Press.

Eayrs, C., Appleton, P. and Lewis, K. (1992) Personal development counselling for clinical psychology trainees. A pilot scheme in the North Wales In-Service Training Course, *Clinical Psychology Forum*, 40: 11–14.

Eckstein, R. and Wallerstein, R. (1972) *The Teaching and Learning of Psychotherapy*. New York: International Universities Press.

Edwards, G. (1985) Helping and hindering. *Changes*, 4: 20–3.

Edwards, M. and Fasal, J. (1992) Keeping an intimate relationship professional. *OPEN MIND*, 57: 10–11.

Einstein, I. and Infield, L. (1971) *The Evolution of Physics*. Cambridge: Cambridge University Press.

Elliott, R. (1979) How clients perceive helper behaviours. *Journal of Counselling Psychology*, 30: 285–94.

EOC (1992) *Some Facts about Women, 1992*. Manchester: Equal Opportunities Commission.

Eysenck, H.J. (1949) Training in clinical psychology. An English point of view. *American Psychologist*, 4: 173–6.

Eysenck, H.J. (1950) Function and training of the clinical psychologist. *Journal of Mental Science*, 96: 710–25.

Eysenck, H.J. (1952) The effects of psychotherapy. An evaluation. *Journal of Consulting and Clinical Psychology*, 16: 319–24.

Eysenck, H.J. (1953) *Uses and Abuses of Psychology*. Harmondsworth: Penguin.

Eysenck, H.J. (1958) The psychiatric treatment of neurosis, paper presented to the Royal Medico-Psychological Association, London.

Eysenck, H.J. (1960a) *Behaviour Therapy and the Neuroses*. London: Pergamon.

Eysenck, H.J. (1960b) *Handbook of Abnormal Psychology*. London: Pitman.

Eysenck, H.J. (1971) Behavior therapy as a scientific discipline. *Journal of Consulting and Clinical Psychology*, 36: 314–19.

Eysenck, H.J. (1975) *The Future of Psychiatry*. London: Methuen.

Eysenck, H.J. (1990) Maverick psychologist, in E. Walker (ed.) *A History of Clinical Psychology – An Autobiography*. New York: Harper & Row.

Eysenck, H.J. and Rachman, S. (1965) *Causes and Cures of the Neuroses*. London: Routledge & Kegan Paul.

Fernando, S. (1988) *Race and Culture in Psychiatry*. London: Croom Helm.

256      Counselling in psychological services

Fiedler, K. (1991) Heuristics and biases in theory formation. *Theory and Psychology*, 1(4): 407–30.

Fitzgibbons, D.J. (1972) Social class differences in patients' perceived treatment needs. *Psychological Reports*, 31: 987–97.

Foulkes, S.H. and Anthony, E.J. (1957) *Group Psychotherapy: The psychoanalytical approach*. Harmondsworth: Penguin.

Frank, A. (1978) Are there social class differences in patients' treatment conceptions? *Archives of General Psychiatry*, 35: 61–9.

Frank, J.D. (1957) Why patients leave psychotherapy. *Archives of General Neurology and Psychiatry*, 77: 283–99.

Frank, L.R. (1990) Electroshock. Death, brain damage, memory loss and brainwashing. *Journal of Mind and Behaviour*, 11: 489–512.

Fransella, F. (1977) The self and the stereotype, in D. Bannister (ed.) *New Perspectives in Personal Construct Theory*. London: Academic Press.

Freud, S. (1905) On psychotherapy, in *Standard Edition of the Complete Psychological Works of Sigmund Freud*, Vol. 7. London: Hogarth Press, 1953.

Freud, S. (1937) Analysis terminable and interminable, in E. Jones (ed.) *Collected Papers*, Vol. V. (pp. 316–57). London: Hogarth Press, 1950.

Fromm, E. (1941) *Escape from Freedom*. New York: Holt, Rinehart and Winston.

Frosh, S. and Levinson, F. (1990) Identifying clinical skill components of training in clinical psychology. *Clinical Psychology Forum*, 25: 20–3.

Fryer, D. (1993) 'Unemployment and mental health', paper prepared for the British Psychological Society media briefing, 'The Psychological Effects of Unemployment', London, 26 January.

Fulani, L. (1987) *The Psychopathology of Everyday Racism and Sexism*. New York: Harrington Press.

Galton, F. (1869) *Hereditary Genius*. London: Macmillan.

Garfield, S. and Kurtz, R. (1976) Clinical psychologists in the 1970s. *American Psychologist*, 31: 1–9.

Georgiades, N.J. and Phillimore, L. (1975) The myth of the hero innovator and alternative strategies for organisational change, in C.C. Kiernan and F.D. Woodford (eds) *Behaviour Modification with the Severely Retarded*. Amsterdam: Associated Scientific Publishers.

Gibson, H.B. (1981) *H.J. Eysenck*. London: Croom Helm.

Godsi, E. (1995) Life as trauma. *Changes*, 13: 261–9.

Goin, M.K. (1965) Therapy congruent with class-linked expectations. *Archives of General Psychiatry*, 13: 133–7.

Goldie, N. (1974) Clinical psychology. Statutory lackey or unwilling and informal handmaiden of psychiatry?, paper presented at the British Medical Sociological Conference, University of York.

Goldie, N. (1975) Eclecticism as the dominant ideology, and its contribution towards the maintenance of the status quo in British psychiatry, paper presented at the British Sociological Society conference, University of Bath.

Goldie, N. (1977) The division of labour among mental health professionals – a negotiated or an imposed order?, in M. Stacey and M. Reid (eds) *Health and the Division of Labour*. London: Croom Helm.

Gore, V. (1994) 'Counselling and Primary Care: Promoting Good Practice', a conference held on 10 December 1993 at the King's Fund Centre. *Clinical Psychology Forum*, 72: 32–3.

Gorsuch, N. (1994) Going by the way of ignorance. Reflections on the first six months of training. *Clinical Psychology Forum*, 63: 10–12.

Gottschalk, L.A. (1967) Prediction and evaluation of outcome in an emergency brief psychotherapy clinic. *Journal of Nervous and Mental Disease*, 144: 77–96.

GPMH (1993) *Women's Project Working Papers*. London: Good Practices in Mental Health.

Green, D. (1995) Carry on learning. *Clinical Psychology Forum*, 76: 37–40.

Greenberg, R.P. and Staller, J.S. (1981) Personal therapy for therapists. *American Journal of Psychiatry*, 138: 1467–71.

Griffiths, V. and Cormack, M. (1993) General practitioners and mental health services. A survey. *Clinical Psychology Forum*, 56: 19–22.

Grohmann, R., Schmidt, L.G., Spiess, K.C. and Ruther, E. (1989) Agranulocytosis and significant leucopenia with neuroleptic drugs. Results from the AMUP program. *Psychopharmacology*, 99 (Suppl.): 109–12.

Gurani, P.D. and Sayal, A. (1987) Ethnic minorities and Clinical Psychology. Some further comments. *Clinical Psychology Forum*, 7: 20–3.

Haase, W. (1964) The role of socio-economic class in examiner bias, in J. Riessman (ed.) *Mental Health of the Poor*. New York: Free Press.

Hall, J.N. and Baker, R. (1983) *Rehabilitation Evaluation*. Glasgow: Vine.

Harrison, G. (1990) Searching for the causes of schizophrenia: The role of migrant studies. *Schizophrenia Bulletin*, 16: 663–71.

Harrison, G., Holton, A., Neilson, D., Owens, D., Boot, D. and Cooper, J. (1989) Severe mental disorder in Afro-Caribbean patients. Some social, demographic and service factors. *Psychological Medicine*, 19: 683–96.

Harrison, S. (1970) Social status and child psychiatric practices. The influence of the clinician's socio-economic origin. *American Journal of Psychiatry*, 127: 652–8.

Hart, L. (1972) *History of the First World War*. London: Pan Books.

Harvey, D. (1990) *The Condition of Postmodernity*. Oxford: Blackwells.

Hawkins, P. and Shohet, R. (1989) *Supervision in the Helping Professions*. Milton Keynes: Open University Press.

Hayes, N. (1992) Continuing professional development: Keeping up to date. *The Psychologist*, 5(11): 507–9.

Head, D. and Harmon, G. (1990) Psychologists and research. Do we practise what we preach? *Clinical Psychology Forum*, 25: 15–16.

*The Health of the Nation* (1993) London: HMSO.

Hearnshaw, L.S. (1964) *A Short History of British Psychology*. London: Methuen.

Hearnshaw, L.S. (1987) *The Shaping of Modern Psychology*. London: Routledge & Kegan Paul.

Heath, G. (1992) Is there therapy after Masson? *Clinical Psychology Forum*, 45: 32–6.

Heidegger, M. (1966) *Discourse on Thinking*. New York: Harper & Row.

Herman, J.L., Perry, J.C. and van der Kolk, B.A. (1989) Childhood trauma in borderline personality disorder. *American Journal of Psychiatry*, 146(4): 490–5.

Hirons, A. and Velleman, R. (1993) Factors which might contribute to effective supervision. *Clinical Psychology Forum*, 57: 11–13.

Holland, R. (1978) *Self and Social Context*. London: Macmillan.

Holland, S. (1992) From social abuse to social action. A neighbourhood psychotherapy and social action project for women, in J.M. Ussher and P. Nicholson (eds) *Gender Issues in Clinical Psychology*. London: Routledge.

Hollingshead, A.B. and Redlich, F.C. (1958) *Social Class and Mental Illness*. New York: John Wiley.

Holloway, E. and Wampold, B. (1983) Patterns of verbal behaviour and judgements of satisfaction in the supervision interview. *Journal of Counselling Psychology*, 30: 227–34.

Horney, K. (1939) *New Ways in Psychoanalysis*. New York: Norton.

Houston, J., Revell, J. and Woolett, S. (1989) The need for a basic grade training programme. Results of a survey of basic grade psychologists in S.W. Thames Region. *Clinical Psychology Forum*, 19: 29–32.

Husserl, E. (1970) *The Crisis of European Sciences and Transcendental Phenomenology*, trans. D. Carr. Evanston, IL: Northwestern University Press.

Ingleby, D. (ed.) (1980) *Critical Psychiatry*. Harmondsworth: Penguin.

Ivey, A.E. (1979) Counseling psychology – the most broadly-based applied psychology specialty. *The Counseling Psychologist*, 8: 3–6.

Jervis, M. (1986) Female, Asian and isolated. *OPEN MIND*, 20: 10–12.

Jones, E. (1974) Social class and psychotherapy. *Psychiatry*, 37: 307–20.

Jones, M. (1952) *Social Psychiatry*. London: Tavistock.

Jung, C. (1978) *Collected Works*, Vol. 9 (Bollingen Series XX). London: Routledge & Kegan Paul.

Jung, C. and Pauli, W. (1955) *The Interpretation of Nature and the Psyche* (Bollingen Series LI). Princeton, NJ: Princeton University Press.

Kadushin, A. (1968) Games people play in supervision. *Social Work*, 13: 23–32.

Karasu, T.B. (1986) The specificity versus non-specific dilemma: Toward identifying therapeutic change agents. *American Journal of Psychiatry*, 183: 687–95.

Keegan, J. (1978) *The Face of Battle*. Harmondsworth: Penguin.

Kelly, G. (1955) *The Psychology of Personal Constructs*. New York: Norton.

Kennard, B., Stewart, S. and Gluck, M. (1987) The supervision relationship. Variables contributing to positive versus negative experiences. *Professional Psychology: Research and Practice*, 18: 172–5.

Kierkegaard, S. (1941) *Concluding Unscientific Postscript*, trans. D.F. Swenson and W. Lowrie. Princeton, NJ: Princeton University Press.

Kirschenbaum, H. (1979) *On Becoming Carl Rogers*. New York: Delacorte Press.

Koch, S. (1974) Psychology as a science, in S. Brown (ed.) *Philosophy of Psychology*. London: Macmillan.

Kottler, J. (1986) *On Being a Therapist*. San Francisco: Jossey-Bass.

Kuhn, T.S. (1962) *The Structure of Scientific Revolutions*. Chicago: University of Chicago Press.

Laing, R.D. (1960) *The Divided Self*. London: Tavistock.

Laing, R.D. (1968) *The Politics of Experience and the Bird of Paradise*. Harmondsworth: Penguin.

Laing, R.D. and Esterson, A. (1964) *Sanity, Madness and the Family*. London: Tavistock.

Laing, R.D., Phillipson, H. and Lee, A.R. (1966) *Interpersonal Perception*. London: Tavistock.

Lampard, R. (1994) An examination of the relationship between marital disillusion and unemployment, in D. Gallie, C. Marsh and C. Vogler (eds) *Social Change and the Experience of Unemployment*. Oxford: Oxford University Press.

Li, C.K. and Greenewich, J.P. (1991) A view from within: Reflections on psychotherapy. *Changes*, 9: 201–13.

Littlewood, R. and Lipsedge, M. (1983) *Aliens and Alienists*. Harmondsworth: Pelican.

Loganbill, C., Hardy, E. and Delworth, U. (1982) Supervision. A conceptual model. *The Counselling Psychologist*, 10: 3–42.

Lorion, R.P. (1974) Social class, treatment attitudes and expectations. *Journal of Consulting and Clinical Psychology*, 42: 920.

MacIntyre, A. (1985) *After Virtue*. London: Duckworth.

Mair, J.M.M. (1970) Psychologists are human too, in D. Bannister (ed.) *Perspectives in Personal Construct Theory*. London: Academic Press.

Malan, D. (1979) *Individual Psychotherapy and the Science of Psychodynamics*. Cambridge: Butterworths.

Manpower Planning Advisory Group/Management Advisory Service (1990) *Clinical psychology project*. London: Department of Health.

Marcuse H. (1964) *One Dimensional Man*. London/New York: Routledge & Kegan Paul.

Marcuse, H. (1966) *One-Dimensional Man: Studies in the ideology of advanced industrial society*. Boston, MA: Beacon Press.

Marks, D.F. (1994) Psychology's role in *The Health of the Nation*. *The Psychologist*, 7: 3.

Marshall, J.R. (1990) The genetics of schizophrenia. Axiom or hypothesis?, in R. Bentall (ed.) *Reconstructing Schizophrenia*. London: Routledge.

Marshall, J.R. (1992) *Schizophrenia:* A constructive analogy or a convenient construct? Paper presented at the International Psychotherapy Conference, 'Psychosis – Understanding and Treatment', University of Essex, 18–20 September.

Marshall, J.R. (1994) Is biological determinism heritable? *Clinical Psychology Forum*, 67: 3.

Marshall, J.R. (1995) Schizophrenia: A constructive analogy or a convenient construct?, in J. Ellwood (ed.) *Psychosis: Understanding and Treatment*. London: Jessica Kingsley.

Marshall, J.R. (1996) Science, 'schizophrenia' and genetics. The creation of myths. *Clinical Psychology Forum*, 95: 5–13.

Martin, D. and Lyon, P. (1984) Lesbian women and mental health policy, in L.E. Walker (ed.) *Women and Mental Health Policy*. London: Sage.

Martin, P.R. (1987) 'The scientist–practitioner model and clinical psychology. Time for change?', paper presented to the BPS Annual Conference, Brighton, March.

Masson, J. (1990) *Against Therapy*. London: Fontana.

Masson, J. (1991) *Final Analysis*. London: HarperCollins.

Maxwell, R.J. (1984) Quality assessment in health. *British Medical Journal*, 288: 1470–2.

McGovern, D. and Cope, R. (1991) Second generation Afro-Caribbeans and young whites with a first admission diagnosis of schizophrenia. *Social Psychiatry and Psychiatric Epidemiology*, 26: 95–9.

McRae, J.A. and Brody, C.J. (1989) The differential importance of marital experience for the well-being of women and men. A research note. *Social Science Research*, 18(3): 237–48.

Mead, G.H. (1934) *Mind, Self and Society from the Standpoint of a Social Behaviourist*. Chicago: University of Chicago Press.

Meikle, J. (1989) Reality, reflexivity and the NHS. *Clinical Psychology Forum*, 20: 32–4.

Mihill, C. (1993) Plea to eject psychologist sex abusers. *Guardian*, 5 April.

Miller, P. and Rose, N. (eds) (1986) *The Power of Psychiatry*. Cambridge: Polity Press.

Miller, P. and Rose, N. (1988) The Tavistock programme. The government of subjectivity and social life. *Sociology*, 22(2): 171–92.

Miller, R. (1994) Clinical psychology and counselling in primary care. Opening the stable door. *Clinical Psychology Forum*, 65: 11–14.

Mills, M. (1992) *SHANTI: A consumer-based approach to planning mental health services for women*. London: Women's Counselling Services.

Milne, D. (1983) Some paradoxes and findings in the training of clinical psychologists. *Bulletin of the British Psychological Society*, 36: 281–2.

Milne, D. (1989) Personal issues in clinical supervision. *The Irish Journal of Psychology*, 10(3): 353–67.

Milne, D. (1991) Why supervise? A survey of costs and benefits. *Clinical Psychology Forum*, 32: 27–9.

Milne, D. (1993) Personal support for psychologists. Too little, too soon? *Clinical Psychology Forum*, 58: 24–6.

Milne, D. (1994) A 'quality supervision' refresher workshop. *Clinical Psychology Forum*, 74: 18–20.

Milne, D.L. and Britton, P.G. (1994) A workshop on skilled supervision. *Clinical Psychology Forum*, 67: 4–6.

Milne, D., Britton, P. and Wilkinson, I. (1990) The scientist–practitioner in practice. *Clinical Psychology Forum*, 30: 22–30.

MIND (1992a) *The Hidden Majority*. London: MIND Publications.

MIND (1992b) *Stress on Women: Policy paper on women and mental health*. London: MIND Publications.

Moldowsky, A. (1980) Psychoanalytic psychotherapy supervision, in A.K. Hess (ed.) *Psychotherapy Supervision: Theory, research and practice*. New York: Wiley.

Mollica, R.F. and Millic, M. (1986) Social class and psychiatric practice. A revision of the Hollingshead and Redlich model. *American Journal of Psychiatry*, 143(1): 12–17.

Mollon, P. (1989) Narcissus, Oedipus and the psychologist's fraudulent identity. *Clinical Psychology Forum*, 23: 7–11.

Mollon, P. (1991) Anxiety, supervision and a space for thinking. Some narcissistic perils for clinical psychologists in learning psychotherapy. *British Journal of Medical Psychology*, 62: 113–22.

Morgan, S. (1993) Trainees in therapy. Why not? *Clinical Psychology Forum*, 59: 32–3.

Morris, B.S. (1949) Officer selection in the British army. *Occupational Psychology*, 23: 219–34.

Nadirshaw, Z. (1993) Issues of race in clinical psychology training: Reports from two workshop groups. *Clinical Psychology Forum*, 61: 27–8.

National Council for One-Parent Families (1987) *Information Sheet*. London: National Council for One-Parent Families.

Nelson-Jones, R. (1982) *The Theory and Practice of Counselling Psychology*. London: Cassell Educational.

Newpin (1992) *Annual Report, 1992*. London: National Newpin.

Nguyen, T.D., Atkinson, C.C. and Stegner, B.L. (1983) Assessment of patient satisfaction. *Evaluation and Programme Planning*, 6: 299–314.

Nichols, K. (1988) Practising what we preach. *The Psychologist*, February: 50–1.

Nichols, K., Cormack, M. and Walsh, S. (1992) Preventive personal support. A challenge to the training courses. *Clinical Psychology Forum*, 45: 29–31.

Nicolson, P. (1989) Counselling women with post-natal depression. Implications from recent qualitative research. *Counselling Psychology Quarterly*, 2(2): 123–32.

Nicolson, P. (1992) Gender issues in the organization of clinical psychology, in J.M. Ussher and P. Nicolson (eds) *Gender Issues in Clinical Psychology*. London: Routledge.

Nitsun, M., Wood, H. and Bolton, W. (1989) The organization of psychotherapy services. A clinical psychology perspective. *Clinical Psychology Forum*, 23: 32–7.

Norcross, J. and Prochaska, J. (1982) A national survey of clinical psychologists. Characteristics and activities. *The Clinical Psychologist*, 35: 1–8.

Norcross, J.C., Brust, A.M. and Dryden, W. (1992a) British clinical psychologists: I. A national survey of the BPS Clinical Division. *Clinical Psychology Forum*, 40: 19–24.

Norcross J.C., Brust, A.M. and Dryden W. (1992b) British clinical psychologists: II. Survey findings and American comparisons. *Clinical Psychology Forum*, 40: 24–8.

Norcross, J.C., Dryden, W. and DeMichele, J.T. (1992c) British clinical psychologists and personal therapy: III. What's good for the goose? *Clinical Psychology Forum*, 44: 29–33.

Norcross, J.C., Prochaska, J.O. and Gallagher, K.M. (1989) Clinical psychologists in the 1980s: 1. Demographics, affiliations, and satisfactions. *The Clinical Psychologist*, 42: 138–47.

Nottingham NHS Psychologists (1988) Unpublished circulated document.

Nottingham NHS Psychologists (1993) Large scale unemployment. A clinical psychological perspective, paper prepared for the British Psychological Society Media Briefing, 'The Psychological Effects of Unemployment', London, 26 January.

Noyes, E., Franklin, B. and Val Baker, J. (1989) Letter. *The Psychologist*, 2(5): 214.

Oppenheimer, M. (1975) The proletarianisation of the professional. *Sociological Review Monograph*, 20.

O'Sullivan, K. and Dryden, W. (1990) A survey of clinical psychologists in the S.E. Thames Health Region. Activities, role and theoretical orientation. *Clinical Psychology Forum*, 29: 21–6.

Overall, B. and Aronson, H. (1968) Expectations of psychotherapy in patients of lower socio-economic class. *American Journal of Orthopsychiatry*, 124: 88–93.

Owens, D., Harrison, G. and Boot, D. (1991) Ethnic factors in voluntary and compulsory admissions. *Psychological Medicine*, 21: 185–96.

Patterson, C.H. (1974) *Relationship Counseling and Psychotherapy*. New York: Harper & Row.

Peebles, M.J. (1980) Personal therapy and the ability to display empathy, warmth and genuineness in psychotherapy. *Psychotherapy: Theory, Research and Practice*, 17: 252–62.

Penfold, P.S. and Walker, G.A. (1984) *Women and the Psychiatric Paradox*. Milton Keynes: Open University Press.

Penzer, W. (1984) The psychopathology of the psychotherapist. *Psychotherapy in Private Practice*, 2: 51–9.

Perkins, R. (1991) Therapy for lesbians? The case against. *Feminism and Psychology*, 1(3): 325–38.

Petchey, R. (1986) The Griffiths re-organisation of the health service. Fowlerism by stealth? *Critical Social Policy*, 17: 87–101.

Pettit, I.B. (1974) Relationship between values, social class and duration of psychotherapy. *Journal of Consulting and Clinical Psychology*, 42: 482–90.

Pilgrim, D. (1990) 'Clinical psychology in the 1980s. A sociological analysis', unpublished MSc thesis. Polytechnic of the South Bank.

Pilgrim, D. (1994) Some are more equal than others. Paper presented at the British Psychological Society Annual Conference, Psychotherapy Symposium, Brighton, April.

Pilgrim, D. and Treacher, A. (1992) *Clinical Psychology Observed*. London: Tavistock/Routledge.

Pillay, H.M. (1993) The DCP workshop on race and culture issues of equality and power in psychology. *Clinical Psychology Forum*, 61: 24–5.

Poole, R. (1972) *Towards Deep Subjectivity*. London: Allen Lane The Penguin Press.

Powell, G.E. and Adams, M. (1993) Introduction to research on placement. *Clinical Psychology Forum*, 53: 12–16.

Priestley, J.B. (1996) *The Image Men*. London: Mandarin.

Prochaska, J.O. and Norcross, J.C. (1983) Contemporary psychotherapists. A national survey of characteristics, practices, orientations, and attitudes. *Psychotherapy: Theory, Research and Practice*, 20: 161–73.

Rachelson, J. and Clance, P. (1980) Attitudes of psychotherapists toward the 1970 APA standards for psychotherapy training. *Professional Psychology*, 11: 261–7.

Raimy, V.C. (ed.) (1950) *Training in Clinical Psychology*. New York: Prentice-Hall.

Reason, P. and Rowan, J. (eds) (1981) *Human Inquiry: A sourcebook of New Paradigm research*. New York: John Wiley.

Richards, B. (1977) *Newsletter of the Division of Clinical Psychology*, 19: 9–10.

Richards, B. (1983) 'Clinical psychology, the individual and the state', unpublished PhD thesis. Polytechnic of North East London.

Richards, B. (1995) Psychotherapy and the injuries of class. *British Psychological Society Psychotherapy Section Newsletter*, 17: 21–35.

Richards, G. (1993) Reflexivity problems in psychology. Too embarrassing even to talk about? *Clinical Psychology Forum*, 55: 2–8.

Richardson, A. (1992) Training courses and Working Paper 10. *Clinical Psychology Forum*, 41: 32–6.

Ricoeur P. (1967) *Husserl: An Analysis of His Phenomenology*. Evanston: Northwestern University Press.

Rippere, V. and Williams, R. (1985) *Wounded Healers – Mental Health Workers' Experiences of Depression*. Chichester: Wiley.

Rogers, A. and Faulkner, A. (1987) *A Place of Safety*. Rochdale: MIND, RAP Ltd.

Rogers, A., Pilgrim, D. and Lacey, R. (1992) *People First: Users' Views of Psychiatric Services*. London: Macmillan.

Rogers, C.R. (1939) *The Clinical Treatment of the Problem Child*. Boston, MA: Houghton Mifflin.

Rogers, C.R. (1951) *Client-Centered Therapy*. Boston, MA: Houghton Mifflin.

Rogers, C.R. (1957) The necessary and sufficient conditions of therapeutic personality change. *Journal of Consulting Psychology*, 21: 95–104.

Rogers, C.R. (1961) *On Becoming a Person*. Boston, MA: Houghton Mifflin.

Rogers, C.R. (1974) In retrospect. Forty-six years. *American Psychologist*, 29(2): 115–23.

Rogers, C.R. (1985) Toward a more human science of the person. *Journal of Humanistic Psychology*, 25(4): 7–24.

Rosewater, L.B. (1985) Schizophrenic, borderline, or battered?, in L.B. Rosewater and L.E.A. Walker (eds) *Handbook of Feminist Therapy: Women's issues in psychotherapy*. New York: Springer.

264        Counselling in psychological services

Rothblum, E.M. (1990) Depression among lesbians. An invisible and unresearched phenomenon. *Journal of Gay and Lesbian Psychotherapy*, 1: 67–87.

Rowe, D. (1971a) An examination of a psychiatrist's predictions of a patient's constructs. *British Journal of Psychiatry*, 118: 231–44.

Rowe, D. (1971b) Poor prognosis in a case of depression as predicted by the repertory grid. *British Journal of Psychiatry*, 118: 297–300.

Rowe, D. (1991) *Breaking the Bonds*. London: Fontana.

Runnymede Trust (1992) *Politics For All: Equality, culture and the general election 1992*. Briefing paper. London: Runnymede Trust.

Salkovskis, P. (1984) Psychological research by NHS clinical psychologists. An analysis and some suggestions. *Bulletin of the British Psychological Society*, 37: 375–7.

Salmon, P. (1969) Differential conforming as a developmental process. *British Journal of Social and Clinical Psychology*, 8: 22–31.

Sayal, A. (1989) Black women and mental health. *Clinical Psychology Forum*, 22: 3–6.

Sayal-Bennett, A. (1991) Equal opportunities – empty rhetoric? *Feminism and Psychology*, 1(1): 74–7.

Scrivens, E. and Charlton, D. (1985) *The Nature and Size of Clinical Psychology. Bath Social Policy Papers*, 6. University of Bath.

Scull, A. (1977) *Decarceration*. Englewood Cliffs, NJ: Prentice-Hall.

Scull, A. (1979) *Museums of Madness*. London: Allen Lane.

Scull, A. (1984) *Decarceration*, 2nd edn. Englewood Cliffs, NJ: Prentice-Hall.

Sedgwick, P. (1982) *PsychoPolitics*. London: Pluto.

Shapiro, M. (1963) A clinical approach to fundamental research with special reference to study of the single patient, in P. Sainsbury and N. Krietman (eds) *Methods in Psychiatric Research*. London: Oxford University Press.

Sharrock, R. and Hunt, S. (1986) A national survey of trainees' satisfaction with supervision. *Clinical Psychology Forum*, 6: 27–31.

Showalter, E. (1987) *The Female Malady: Women, madness and English culture, 1830–1980*. London: Virago.

Skultans, V. (1979) *English Madness*. London: Routledge & Kegan Paul.

Smail, D. (1973) Clinical psychology and the medical model. *Bulletin of the British Psychological Society*, 26: 211–14.

Smail, D.J. (1970) Neurotic symptoms, personality and personal constructs. *British Journal of Psychiatry*, 117: 645–8.

Smail, D. (1982) Clinical psychology – homogenized and sterilized. *Bulletin of the British Psychological Society*, 35: 345–6.

Smail, D. (1984) *Illusion and Reality: The meaning of anxiety*. London: J.M. Dent and Sons Ltd.

Smail, D. (1987) *Taking Care: An alternative to therapy*. London: J.M. Dent and Sons Ltd.

Smail, D. (1993) *The Origin of Unhappiness: A new understanding of personal distress*. London: HarperCollins.

Smail, D. (1996) *How to Survive without Psychotherapy*. London: Constable.

Smith, H. (1991) Caring for everyone? The implications for women of the changes in community care services. *Feminism and Psychology*, 1(2): 279–92.

Smith, L.J.F. (1989) Domestic Violence: An Overview of the Literature. A Home Office Research and Planning Report. London: HMSO.

Stapp, H. (1972) The Copenhagen Interpretation and the nature of space–time. *American Journal of Physics*, 40: 1098.

Stone, M. (1985) Shellshock and the psychologists, in W.F. Bynum, R. Porter and M. Shepherd (eds) *The Anatomy of Madness*, Vol. 2. London: Tavistock.

Storr, A. (1979) *The Art of Psychotherapy*. London: Secker & Warburg/ Heinemann Medical.

Street, E. (1990) Dimensions of supervision. *Clinical Psychology Forum*, 26: 26–8.

Street, E. (1992) Clinical, health and counselling psychology. *Clinical Psychology Forum*, 47: 34–5.

Sturmey, P. (1991) Paradigms for applicable research in clinical practice. *Clinical Psychology Forum*, 31: 18–19.

Sullivan, H.S. (1953) *The Interpersonal Theory of Psychiatry* (eds H.S. Perry and M.L. Gawel). New York: Norton.

Super, D.E. (1977) The identity crisis of counseling psychologists. *The Counseling Psychologist*, 7: 13–15.

Sutton, R.G. and Kessler, M. (1986) National study of the effect of clients' socioeconomic status on clinical psychologists' professional judgements. *Journal of Consulting and Clinical Psychology*, 54(2): 275–86.

Szasz, T. (1972) *The Myth of Mental Illness*. London: Routledge.

Tanne, J.H. (1992) AIDS epidemic grows but response slows. *British Medical Journal*, 305: 6847.

Tausch, R. (1990) The supplementation of client-centred communication therapy with other validated therapeutic methods. A client-centred necessity, in G. Lietaer, J. Rombauts and R. Van Balen (eds) *Client-Centred and Experiential Psychotherapy in the Nineties*. Leuven: Leuven University Press.

Taylor, A.J.P. (1966) *The First World War*. Harmondsworth: Penguin.

Thorne, B. (1992) *Carl Rogers*. London: Sage Publications.

Titley, M., Watson, G. and Williams, J. (1992) Working with women, including older women, in the mental health services, paper presented to the British Psychological Society London Conference, 15 December.

Trinder, H., Mitchell, S.A. and Todd, L. M.-K. (1994) Valuing patient feedback: 1. Shelton Hospital's acute wards. *Clinical Psychology Forum*, 70: 6–11.

Truax, C. and Carkhuff, R. (1967) *Towards Effective Counselling and Psychotherapy*. Chicago: Aldine.

Turner, I. and Newnes, C. (1993) In-patient views of the service at Shelton psychiatric hospital. *Clinical Psychology Forum*, 56: 23–9.

Turpin, G. (1994) Service evaluation within the NHS. The challenge to applied psychological research. *Clinical Psychology Forum*, 72: 16–19.

Turpin, G., Ashcroft, J. and Holland, E. (1993) A survey of staffing and resources for clinical psychology postgraduate education and training. *Clinical Psychology Forum*, 58: 32–6.

Tyler, L. (1961) *The Work of the Counsellor*, 2nd edn. New York: Appleton-Century-Crofts.

Ussher, J.M. (1991) *Women's Madness: Misogyny or mental illness.* London: Harvester Wheatsheaf.

Ussher, J.M. (1992) Science sexing psychology, in J.M. Ussher and P. Nicolson (eds) *Gender Issues in Clinical Psychology.* London: Routledge.

Ussher, J.M. (1994) Women's conundrum. Feminism or therapy? *Clinical Psychology Forum,* 64: 2–5.

Ussher, J.M. and Nicolson, P. (1992) *Gender Issues in Clinical Psychology.* London: Routledge.

Vitz, P. (1977) *Psychology as Religion: The cult of self-worship.* Grand Rapids, MI: William B. Eerdmans.

Voloshinov, V.N. (1976) *Freudianism: A Marxist critique.* New York: Academic Press. Originally published in 1927.

Vygotsky, L.S. (1962) *Thought and Language.* Cambridge, MA: MIT Press.

Walker, S. and James, H. (1992) Childhood physical and sexual abuse in women. *Psychiatry in Practice,* 11(1): 15–18.

Wallen, J., Pincus, H.A., Goldman, H.H. and Marcus, S.E. (1987) Psychiatric consultations in short-term general hospitals. *Archives of General Psychiatry,* 44(2): 163–8.

Walsh, S. (1990) 'Personal and professional threat. A model of self-care for clinical psychologists', MSc dissertation. University of Exeter.

Walsh, S., Nichols, K. and Cormack, M. (1991) Self-care and clinical psychologists. A threatening obligation? *Clinical Psychology Forum,* 37: 5–7.

Ward, M. (1991) Notes on therapy. *Changes,* 9: 113–18.

Warr, P., Jackson, P. and Banks, M. (1988) Unemployment and mental health. Some British studies. *Journal of Social Issues,* 44(4): 47–68.

Watson, G. and Williams, J. (1992) Feminist practice in therapy, in J. Ussher and P. Nicolson (eds) *Gender Issues in Clinical Psychology.* London: Routledge.

Watts, F.N. (1984) Applicable psychological research in the NHS. *Bulletin of the British Psychological Society,* 37: 41–2.

Webb-Johnson, A. and Nadirshaw, Z. (1993) Good practice in transcultural counselling. An Asian perspective. *British Journal of Guidance and Counselling,* 21(1): 20–9.

Whitehead, A. and Parry, G. (1986) National training needs in clinical psychology. *Clinical Psychology Forum,* 6: 7–11.

Whitehead, M. (1987) *The Health Divide. Inequalities in health in the 1980s.* London: Health Education Council.

Williams, A., Harris, K. and Newnes, C. (1994) The Patients' Council: Shelton Hospital. *Clinical Psychology Forum,* 73: 30–1.

Williams, B. (1996) *Counselling in Criminal Justice.* Buckingham: Open University Press.

Williams, J., Watson, G., Smith, H., Copperman, J. and Wood, D. (1993) *Purchasing Effective Mental Health Service for Women: A framework for action.* Canterbury: University of Kent/MIND Publications.

Williams, J.A. and Watson, G. (1991) Sexual inequality and clinical psychology training in Britain. Survey report. *Feminism and Psychology,* 1(1): 78–88.

Williams, J. and Watson, G. (1994) Mental health services that empower women. The challenge to clinical psychology. *Clinical Psychology Forum*, 64: 6–12.

Winnicott, D.W. (1958) *Collected Papers*. London: Tavistock Publications.

Woerner, M.G., Kane, J.M., Lieberman, J.A. and Alvir, J. (1991) The prevalence of tardive dyskinesia. *Journal of Clinical Psychopharmacology*, 11(1): 34–42.

Wogan, M. and Norcross, J.C. (1985) Dimensions of therapeutic skills and techniques. Empirical identification, therapist correlates, and predictive utility. *Psychotherapy*, 22: 63–74.

Wold, P. and Steger, J. (1976) Social class and group therapy in a working class population. *Community Mental Health*, 12: 335–41.

Worthington, E. and Roehlke, H. (1987) Effective supervision as perceived by beginning counsellors-in-training. *Journal of Counselling Psychology*, 26: 64–73.

Yates, A.J. (1970) *Behavior Therapy*. New York: Wiley.

Zola, E. (1954) *Germinal*. Harmondsworth: Penguin.

Zukav, G. (1979) *The Dancing Wu Li Masters: An overview of the new physics*. London: Random House.

# Index